£14-95

DICTIONARY OF
COMPUTING
&
INFORMATION
TECHNOLOGY

DICTIONARY OF COMPUTING & INFORMATION TECHNOLOGY

A J Meadows, M Gordon,
A Singleton & M Feeney

THIRD EDITION

Kogan Page, London
Nichols Publishing Company, New York

First published in Great Britain in 1982 by
Kogan Page Ltd, 120 Pentonville Road, London N1 9JN
entitled *Dictionary of New Information Technology*.

Reprinted 1982
Second edition 1984
Third edition 1987

British Library Cataloguing in Publication Data
Meadows, A.J.
  Dictionary of computing and information
  technology. – 3rd ed.
  1. Information storage and retrieval
  systems – Dictionaries
  I. Title
  001.5   Z699

ISBN 1 85091 261 0
ISBN 1 85091 262 9 **Pbk**

First published in the United States of America
in 1982 by Nichols Publishing Company,
Post Office Box 96, New York, NY 10024.

Second edition 1984
Third edition 1987

Library of Congress Cataloging in Publication Data
Dictionary of computing and information technology.
Rev.ed. of: Dictionary of computing and new
information technology / A.J. Meadows, M. Gordon,
A. Singleton. 2nd ed. 1984.
  1. Electronic data processing – Dictionaries.
  2. Telecommunication – Dictionaries. 3. Office
  practice – Automation – Dictionaries. I. Meadows,
  A. J. (Arthur Jack)
  Dictionary of computing and information
  technology.
  QA76.15.D52636   1987   004'.03'21   87-5468
  ISBN 0 89397 273 8

Typeset by V & M Graphics Ltd, Aylesbury, Bucks
Printed and bound in Great Britain
by Biddles Ltd, Guildford

628349
⌐
(BC) 16436552

Introduction to Third Edition

The first edition of this dictionary appeared in 1982, and the second in 1984. The fact that another edition is now needed reflects the continuing rapid change of vocabulary in information technology and computing. 'Information technology' itself is a term which has been introduced relatively recently, yet it is already familiarly abbreviated to 'IT'. Though 'IT' may be a new term, some types of information technology – the telephone, for example – have been about for years. What distinguishes new information technology from the older types is the way it combines a variety of communication channels with the information-handling capabilities of computers. New (mainly electronic) methods for dealing with the generation, transmission and reception of information are proliferating rapidly. At the same time, methods of communication which have traditionally progressed separately (for example, telephone and television) are now being drawn together. The rate of development is such that even active participants in the communication system find it hard to keep up with progress outside their own particular sphere. Members of the general public are often, quite naturally, totally confused by what is happening. By way of introduction to this dictionary, it is therefore worthwhile describing briefly some of the techniques that are involved in new information technology. This should also serve to give some indication of the dictionary's intended scope. (Italicized words indicate that the term is discussed, usually at some length, in the body of the dictionary.)

We can start with *computers*, since these represent one of the basic elements of the new technology. Reasonably powerful computers have been decreasing rapidly both in size and cost over the past decade. With the advent of the *microprocessor*, computers have been developed which can sit on a desk top, where they can be used for generating and transmitting information. A typical example of this use is in handling the vast quantities of text generated in the modern world. Specialized computers (called *word processors*) or, more often nowadays, general-purpose *microcomputers* with word-processing software that can automatically produce a range of letters and documents are beginning to revolutionize office work. They are spreading into every field – for example, publishing   that involves the generation and handling of text. The *output* from such computers can be produced as traditional print-on paper; but, since the computer holds the material in electronic form, it can be transmitted with equal ease through other communication channels, eg a telephone *network*, to a distant receiver. A letter can thus by-pass the traditional mail system, to be delivered by *electronic mail*.

This is just one example of information handling with the new technology. Methods both for the *input* of information to, and the output of information from, a system are diversifying at a bewildering speed. Most information is still converted to electronic form via a *keyboard*, as with a typewriter. But it is already possible to talk to a computer, and for some speech to be accepted directly (*voice input*). It is confidently expected that current limitations, eg in the computer's vocabulary, will at least partly disappear by the 1990s.

At the output stage, computerized systems can deal with so much information that new methods must be found for storing it all. The development of various types of storage disc (such as *compact discs* and *optical discs*) should make it possible to store a personal library on a few small discs.

The *data* on such storage discs are typically viewed through ordinary television-style screens. Television systems are already being used as a method of retrieving information via *videotex*. The next step is to employ the system in various other types of transaction. For example, mail order catalogues can be put on television, goods ordered and the money paid from a bank account, all while the viewer is sitting at home.

Just as methods of handling information are becoming more diverse, so, too, are the methods of transmitting it. One of the most spectacular advances in communications during the past two decades has been the growth in the transmission of messages via Earth satellites. *Satellite communication* is now about to make a major impact on the transmission of television programmes, and so on the home viewer. But it is equally significant for the part it can play in the world-wide transmission of very large quantities of data of any kind.

Some of the more complex developments in electronic communication still require large (*mainframe*) computers. For example, translation from one language to another (*computer translation*) is still only moderately advanced, even with powerful machines. Computers that try to duplicate the problem-solving capabilities of human beings (*expert systems*) are likewise at an early (but already useful) stage.

This short account of new information technology is far from comprehensive, but should serve to illustrate its diversity. Almost inevitably, the rapid changes within the field lead to a rapidly changing vocabulary. Confusion results: not only because the new terms may not be easy for all participants to understand, but also because the same term may be used in more than one way. A major purpose of this dictionary is to help dispel such confusion by bringing together and codifying the most important specialized terms currently in use in the various parts of this diverse field.

The diffuseness of the subject matter has made decisions on which items to include and which to exclude particularly difficult. Terms with a restricted application (such as manufacturers' brand names with only limited application) have generally been excluded. Since the emphasis is on information, techniques which are mainly used for entertainment receive less emphasis. For example, 'videotape' is treated for the purposes of this dictionary as less important than 'videodisc', although, since the last edition of this dictionary was produced, new IT uses for videotape have begun to emerge. The main criterion has been that the term should be likely to have a reasonably wide usage for a reasonable period of time.

So far as our intended audience is concerned, it would be true to say that this dictionary is intended for the non-specialist, but it would not be very helpful. Few people would consider the whole of new information technology and computing as their specialism. Rather there are computer specialists whose acquaintance with information terminology may be limited, librarians who may be uncertain of the meanings of some computer-related terms, publishers who may need to learn the jargon of new methods of information handling, and so on. Hence, the contents of this dictionary are aimed not only at non-specialists (that is, at readers with an interest in the field, but with no expertise in any of its branches), but are also designed to aid the various specialist groups whose concerns overlap in the field of new information technology and computing.

Our selection of the words included in this dictionary stems mainly from our own acquisition and vending of periodicals and advertising literature in the field. We hope that, if nothing more, it will help the unfortunate reader through some of the flood of jargon these contain. To give some coherence to the field, a few topics are treated at greater length than the remainder. Such longer entries are intended to act as foci for particular parts of the field: cross-references from and to them allow more specialized entries to be placed in their appropriate context. There have been several hundred additions and alterations to the terms in this new edition of the dictionary. The additions mainly occur amongst the shorter entries: the basic components of information technology and computing discussed in the longer entries have, however, been extensively revised. Nevertheless, it is possible to see some development in the vocabulary. A few previously minor items, such as compact discs, have become more important; whilst the growth in standardization of hardware and software is reflected in the increasing number of terms referring to standards and *protocols*. *Computer graphics* and *expert systems* have also contributed a number of significant new terms.

A few words should be said in conclusion about the use of this dictionary. An italicized word in any entry means that there is a cross-reference to that word: it can therefore be looked up if you feel unsure as to its meaning. Some words, eg 'computer', have entries in the dictionary, but occur so frequently that they are only italicized in special circumstances. Many words can occur in different forms, eg as a noun or a verb. Only one form is normally given in this dictionary, so it is advisable to check under different headings. Several terms have variant meanings: these are distinguished in their respective entries by separate numbers. If there is likely to be any ambiguity of meaning, cross references include the relevant entry number. As a general rule, acronyms have been printed in block capitals.

The three original authors have all moved to new positions since the first edition appeared. We are joined in this edition by a new author, Mary Feeney. We are grateful to Richard Heeks for his advice and help in preparing this edition.

Jack Meadows, *University of Loughborough*

A

A and I Abstracting and indexing.

AB Automated bibliography.

ABC 1. American Broadcasting Corporation. 2. Australian Broadcasting Corporation.

ABCA American Business Communication Association.

abend An abnormal end to a computer task because of an error, or an intervention by the operator.

ABES Association for Broadcast Engineering Standards, US.

ABI/INFORM Abstracted Business Information/Information Needs. A *bibliographic database* covering business management and administration (see *INFORM*).

abort To abandon an activity, usually because an error has been made.

abort timer A device which terminates *dial-up data transmission* if no data are sent within a predetermined time.

absolute address In computing, a string of characters that identifies a *storage* location, without further modification or intermediate address.

absolute coding *Program instruction in machine code.*

absolute loader A *routine* that reads a program into *core storage*.

absolute value Magnitude of a number, regardless of whether it is positive or negative.

absorption In communications, the loss of power of a signal (wave) during propagation through a *medium*.

ABSTI Advisory Board on Scientific and Technical Information, Canada.

abstract An abbreviated representation of the contents of a document. The two most important types of abstract are: a. indicative abstracts. These indicate the content of the document (ie what it is about), rather than its methods and findings; b. informative abstracts. These emphasize the main findings, conclusions, and, if appropriate, methods. Abstracts provided by abstracts, journals and information services will typically be a mixture of informative and indicative. The word is also used as a verb to indicate the activity of abstracting.

AC 1. Alternating current. 2. Automatic computer. 3. Analog computer.

ACARD *Advisory Council for Applied Research and Development.*

ACCC Ad Hoc Committee for Competitive Communications, US.

acceleration potential The potential difference (ie voltage) between a cathode electron emitter and the face of the tube in a *CRT*.

accent Mark placed above or below a character; usually to indicate its pronunciation (see *diacritic*).

acceptance testing Used to prove the capabilities of a computerized system by a potential user.

ACCESS Automated Catalog of Computer Equipment and Software Systems, US Army.

access 1. Used either as a verb or noun to indicate either gaining control of a system or the acquisition of data from a *storage device* or *peripheral unit*. 2. A US teleordering system.

access arm A mechanical device within a *disc drive* that positions the *read/write head*.

access barred In communications, a facility which only permits transmission in one direction.

access control In computer networks, refers to the control of system usage for the purposes of *data security*, user charging, system monitoring, etc.

accession number The number assigned to a record in a file, indicating the order of its entry.

access line A telecommunications *line* that continuously connects a *remote terminal* to a *switching centre*.

access mechanism See *access arm*.

access point The part of a *record* which is used to identify that record in a given *search* (eg in the case of a bibliographic file, the access point might be an author's surname).

access time The time taken to retrieve information from a storage device. For examples of typical access times, see *storage device*.

accordion fold Synonymous with *fan-fold*.

Accounts Index *Database* compiled by the American Institute of Certified Public Accountants, covering accounting, auditing, banking, finance, investment and related areas. It is available for *on-line searching* via *SDC*, and offers *off-line* services.

accumulator A memory location in the computer which stores data temporarily while they are being processed.

accuracy Freedom from error, or the size of an error: used in relation to *programs*, *data* and machine operations. Should not be confused with *precision*.

ACIA Asynchronous communications interface adapter. A device which *formats* and controls *data* at an asynchronous communications interface.

ACIMAIL Australian *electronic mail* service provided by Australian Consolidated Industries Computer Services.

ACK Affirmative acknowledgement sent down a *transmission line* to indicate either that a block of *data* has been received or that the receiver is ready to receive data (see *NAK*).

ACL Audit Command Language. A *high level programming language*.

ACLS American Council of Learned Societies.

ACM Association for Computing Machinery. A US based international organization aimed at advancing computer technology and its applications.

ACOMPLIS A Computerized London Information Service. An information service operated by the Library of the Greater London Council.

acoustic coupler A device capable of transmitting and receiving specified sound tones along telephone lines. It allows a computer and *terminal* to be connected via these lines, using a *modem* and telephone handset.

acoustic delay line A *delay line* whose action is based on the time of propagation of sound waves.

ACRL Association of College and Research Libraries. A US organization within the *ALA*.

action frame See *response frame*.

action message A message issued by a computer indicating the need for a user or systems operator to take some action.

active device In electronics, a device which produces *gain*.

active file A computer *file* in current use.

active matrix *LCD* technology based upon a matrix of conductors set on glass plates. Individual *pixels* can be switched on or off, giving the display *high resolution*.

activity In data processing, the percentage of records in a file that are processed in a *run*.

activity loading A way of storing records in a file so that the most frequently processed records can be accessed most readily.

activity ratio In data processing, the ratio of the number of records in a file that are in use to the total number of records in the file.

ACTSU Association of Computer Time Sharing Users, US.

ACU *Automatic calling unit*.

ADA A *high level programming language*, based on PASCAL, with important additions. It is a significant (and controversial) language, partly because of its adoption by the US Department of Defense, and its projected use in the control of nuclear power plants. It is named after Ada Lovelace, a colleague of Charles Babbage, who designed a 'calculating engine' considered to be the forerunner of present-day computers.

ADAM Automatic document abstracting method (see *automatic abstracting*).

ADAPSO Association of Data Processing Service Organizations, US and Canada.

adaptive channel location A method of *multiplexing* in which *channels* are allocated according to varying patterns of demand.

adaptive routing A *packet switching* technique for optimizing the use of available *channels* in response to varying patterns of demand.

ADB A Danish *teleordering* system.

ADC *Analog* to *digital* conversion.

added entry In cataloguing, a secondary entry (ie any entry other than the main entry).

add-on An extra piece of equipment, *peripheral unit*, or facility which may be added to the original system in order to provide additional or improved functions (see *upgrade*).

add-on conference feature Originally a Bell telephone service for telephones with more than one line. A user can put a conversation on 'hold', call another party on a second line, and then retrieve the first caller so that there are three speakers on the line.

address 1. In telecommunications, this refers to the coded representation either of the destination of data, or of the terminal from which the data originate. 2. In computers, it is a number which identifies a location in the computer's memory.

addressability The number of *pixels* which can be separately coded in a *computer graphics* display.

ADI American Documentation Institute.

ADIS Automatic Data Interchange System.

adjacency 1. In *character recognition*, this refers to print where the reference lines between two consecutive *characters* are separated by less than a specified distance. 2. In database *search strategies*, this indicates that the words sought should be adjacent to each other.

Administrative Support System A *word processing* system aimed especially at business executives.

Adonis An experimental electronic system being developed by a consortium of major European scientific publishers for the storage and supply of *full-text* documents. The service will be based on biomedical literature and will make use of *CD-ROM*. A number of major interlending centres are also taking part in the experiment, eg *BLDSC*, *CDST*, the Medical Library in Cologne and the Royal Academy of Science in Amsterdam (see *document delivery*).

ADP 1. Advanced data processing. 2. Automatic data processing (see *data processing*).

ADPE Automatic *data processing* equipment.

ADPS Automatic *data processing* system.

ADRES Army Data Retrieval System, US.

ADRS Automatic Document Request Service. A service provided by *Blaise* (a *host* information service). It allows subscribers at an *on-line* terminal to request loans or photocopies of documents from the British Library Lending Division.

Advisory Council for Applied Research and Development (ACARD) is a UK body which advises government and publishes reports on R&D policy (including new information technology).

ADX An automatic exchange in a data transmission *network*.

AEBIG *Aslib* Economics and Business Information Group.

AECT Association for Educational Communications and Technology, US.

AEDS Association for Educational Data Systems, US.

aerial In a radio communication system, this is the device which radiates the transmitted electrical signal into space. Equally, it is the device which receives the signal and feeds it in electrical form into the receivers.

AEWIS Army Electronic Warfare Information System, US.

AFIPS American Federation of Information Processing Societies.

AFNOR Association Française de Normalisation. The French national standards organization.

AFR Automatic field/format recognition: a computer *input* facility.

After Dark User-friendly software for database access developed by the host BRS. The name refers to the potential use of the service during 'off peak' periods for telecommunication.

afterflow Synonymous with *persistence*.

Agate A 5½ point typeface often used in setting classified advertisements in the US.

AGLINET Agricultural Libraries Information Network (under the aegis of the United Nations).

Agricola *Database* produced by the US Department of Agriculture, covering agriculture and related topics. Available via *BRS*, *Lockheed* and *SDC*.

Agricultural Information System (AGRIS) An international agricultural database organized under the aegis of the Food and Agricultural Organization (FAO).

AGRIS *Agricultural Information System.*

AI *Artificial intelligence.*

AIDS 1. Aerospace Intelligence Data System of *IBM*, US. 2. Automated information dissemination system.

AIRS Automatic Image Retrieval System.

AKWIC Author and Key Word In Context. A form of computerized index (see *KWIC*).

ALA American Library Association.

ALA/ISAD The *ALA*'s Information Science and Automation Division.

Alanet *Electronic mail* and information service operated by the *ALA*.

ALA print train A standard set of characters drawn up by the *ALA* for use in machine-readable bibliographic records.

ALAS Automated Literature Alerting System. A current awareness service offered within the context of an *information retrieval system*.

Albert Name given by *British Telecom* to a machine intended to combine *teletext*, *telex*, *word processing* and telephone functions.

ALGOL Algorithmic Orientated Language. A *high level programming language* used especially for scientific applications (see *algorithm*).

algorithm A procedure, or rule, for the solution of a problem in a finite number of steps. In computing it normally refers to a set of simple rules for the solution of a mathematically expressed problem, or for evaluating a function (see diagram).

START

Lift the handset and listen. Can you hear continuous dialling tone?	NO →	Something has gone wrong. Replace the handset and try again or try dialling from another booth
YES ↓		
Dial first number of the number you want. Has dialling tone stopped?	NO →	

YES ↓

Simple algorithm: using a telephone. The great advantage of this kind of problem-solving system, for computing purposes, is that it reduces the problem to a series of yes/no options, which are easily translated into binary form.

aliasing The removal of the jagged line, or 'step edge' effect, on *graphic displays* (see *computer graphics*).

ALIS A general abbreviation for automated library information system.

ALP Automated language processing (see *data processing*, *word processing* and *machine translation*).

ALPAC National Academy of Sciences' Automated Language Processing Advisory Committee, US.

alphabet length The length of a lower-case alphabet in *points*. Used to compare different designs of printers' *typefaces*.

alphageometrics A method for generating *videotex* images on a screen. *Displays* are constructed out of geometric elements, such as diagonal lines, arcs and circles (see, in contrast, *alphamosaics*).

alphameric Synonymous with *alphanumeric*.

alphamosaics A method for generating *videotex* images on a screen. *Displays* are constructed using a mosaic of dots. Alphamosaics has been chosen in preference to *alphageometrics* as a European standard for the next *generation* of videotex systems.

alphanumeric An acronym formed from the words 'alphabetic' and 'numeric'. It signifies that data may contain both alphabetical and numerical information.

alphaphotographic A technique used in *videotex* systems to generate picture quality graphics. The images are generated from stored picture elements and displayed on screen (see *Picture Prestel*).

ALS Automated Library Systems.

alternating current (AC) An electrical current, the direction of which is periodically reversed. The frequency of reversal is usually of the order of many cycles per second.

alternative mode A computing mode which permits two interacting users of systems to access shared files in turn.

ALU *Arithmetic and logic unit.*

Alvey Report An influential report prepared in 1982 for the Department of Industry (UK), assessing how Britain should respond to the challenge presented by the Japanese Fifth Generation Computer Programme. It proposed an investment of £250m into research in four priority areas: *expert systems*, the *man-machine interface*, *software engineering* and *VLSI*. In addition, it suggested that a further £19m should be spent on building up a communications network linking research groups, £58m on demonstrations and £20m on

education in advanced information technology.

AM *Amplitude modulation.*

AMACUS Automated Microfilm Aperture Card Update System. A system which uses an *aperture card* as the primary unit of information *storage*.

America: History of Life A *bibliographic database* covering US and Canadian history and affairs, available via *Lockheed*.

AMFIS Automatic Microfilm Information System (see *COM*).

amplitude The peak positive or negative value of a wave (or signal).

amplitude modulation A form of *modulation* in which the *amplitude* of a *carrier wave* is varied by an amount proportional to the amplitude of the modulating signal.

AMPS Advanced Mobile Phone Service. A US *cellular network*.

AMR *Automatic message routing.*

AMTD Automatic *Magnetic Tape* Dissemination service offered by the US Defense Documentation Center.

ANA *Article Numbering Association.*

analog Representation of information by an output signal which varies in a continuous manner with respect to the input. It is to be contrasted with *digital* representation of information.

analyst's workbench An integrated *software package* designed to assist in the various phases of *systems analysis*, ie data collection, *data analysis*, the design and support of a *data dictionary* and the production of high level *program specifications*.

AND A *Boolean operator.*

AND circuit Synonymous with
AND gate.

AND element Synonymous with
AND gate.

AND gate A *gate* that implements
the *logic* of the *AND* function. An
AND gate is used in computer logic
to combine *binary* signals in such a
way that there is an output signal
only if all input channels carry a
signal. For the case of two input
signals, this leads to the following
table:

Input 1	Input 2	Output
1	1	1
1	0	0
0	1	0
0	0	0

angle modulation See *modulation.*

ANI Advanced Network
Integration. *Data communications*
system which permits the
interconnection of various *nodes,
transmission speeds, protocols,
interfaces, formats* and makes of
equipment into a single cohesive
network.

ANIK A series of Canadian
communication satellites launched
from the early 1970s onwards.
(ANIK is 'brother' in Eskimo.)

anisochronous transmission An
electronic *signal* which is not related
to any *clock* and in which
transitions can occur at any time
(see *asynchronous transmission*).

ANSI American National
Standards Institute. It has
established many standards in the
fields of computing and information
handling which are accepted world-
wide.

answerback See *voice answerback.*

answerphone A device for
automatically responding to

telephone calls, recording any
messages for playing back later.

antenna See *dish.*

anticipatory staging A computing
technique in which *blocks* of data
are moved from one storage device
to another, with shorter *access time,*
in anticipation of being requested by
a program. Compare with *demand
staging.*

Antiope A French *videotex*
(*viewdata* and *teletext*) system. The
name is an acronym for
'L'Acquisition Numérique et
Télévisualisation d'Images
Organisées en Pages d'Ecriture'.
(The Numerical Acquisition and
Televisual Display of Images
organized into Pages of Text.) For
teletext, the Antiope system uses
full-field broadcasting and offers a
wide range of information (see
World System Teletext).

Antiope-Didon The *teletext*
component of the French *Antiope
videotex* system.

Antiope-Titan *Viewdata*
component of the French *Antiope
videotex* system. Often referred to
by the brand name *Teletel.*

AOIPS Atmospheric and Oceanic
Information Processing System.
Employs *computer graphics* to
enhance images received from
meteorological satellites (see *DIDS*).

AP *Attached processor.*

aperture card An 80-column card
(*punched card* or edge-punched
card) which has a 35 x 48mm frame
of microfilm inserted. Aperture
cards can be used to form an index,
which is sorted via the punched
holes. After sorting, more extensive
information is immediately available
on the inserted microfilm.

APILIT *Database* produced by the
American Petroleum Institute,

covering petroleum refining, storage and transportation, petrochemicals, petroleum products and petroleum substitutes. Available via *SDC*.

APIPAT As for *APILIT*, but covering patents.

APL A Programming Language; a *high level language* suitable for use on *mainframe* computers with large memories. It is sometimes used in conjunction with statistical *databases*.

apogee The point in an orbit at which a *communications satellite* is furthest from the earth's surface.

APOLLO Article Procurement with Online Local Ordering. An experimental *document delivery* system run by the CEC and *ESA*, which will use the European Communications Satellite.

Apple A US manufacturer of *microcomputers*.

application program See *applications package*.

applications package A *program*, or set of programs, designed to perform a particular application or task (as in *information retrieval*, *word processing* and *data analysis*).

applications software *Programs*, or packages (see *applications package*), designed to carry out specific tasks, or applications; as distinct from *systems software*, which controls the operation of the total computer system.

APT Automatically Programmed Tools. A computer language used for control of machine tools.

AQL Acceptance quality level. A general engineering term, usually used to refer to the performance of machines and components: in particular, their breakdown or failure rate.

architecture The way in which computer *hardware* and *software* interact so as to provide the type of facilities and performance required.

archival storage See *backing storage*.

archive Archive can be used either as a verb or noun to indicate: a. the process of storing data files in a retrievable form; b. the data files so stored.

archive diskette Synonymous with *diskette* or *floppy disc*.

ARDIS Army Research and Development Information System, US Army.

area composition In *phototypesetting*, usually refers to putting together a *page*, either by use of an automatic page *make-up program*, or by an operator calling up the necessary material for display at a *VDT*.

area search A term used in information retrieval for a search of those items within a database which make up a single group, or category (see *information retrieval system*).

ARIANE 1. A French *database* of building products and regulations. 2. European rocket used for launching satellites.

arithmetic and logic unit (ALU) The *microprocessor* in the *central processing unit* which executes the arithmetic and logical operations required by an *input command*.

arithmetic capability When applied to a word processor, refers to its ability to act also as a calculator.

ARPANET A *resource-sharing computer network* supported by the Advanced Research Projects Agency of the US Department of Defense.

ARQ Automatic request for correction. A system which provides error correction by requesting retransmission of mutilated characters (see *automatic request for repetition*).

array 1. In telecommunications, refers to an arrangement of *antenna* elements. 2. In computing, refers to an ordered arrangement of data (such as a table of numbers) identified by a single symbolic name.

array declarator Specifies the dimensions of an *array*.

array processor A powerful computer containing a number of linked subprocessors, performing similar tasks. It is designed to handle the form of *arrays*, and is used extensively for matrix and signal processing.

Art Bibliographies Modern A *database* covering literature on art from the beginning of the 19th century. Accessible via *Lockheed*.

ARTEMIS An acronym for Automatic Retrieval of Text through European Multipurpose Information Services. It is planned to be a *document delivery system* which will supply journal articles *on demand* via *facsimile transmission* or *digitized* text. Delivery will be either by a *facsimile receiver*, or as print out from a *teleprinter*. A fully integrated ARTEMIS system will require the establishment of a set of standards between *hosts*, *databases* and users. The European Commission is currently working towards this objective.

Article Numbering Association Concerned with *bar-coding* of retail merchandise.

artificial cognition The ability of a machine to sense a *character* by optical means, and then to determine its nature (by comparing it with a set of standard characters).

artificial intelligence (AI) Artificial intelligence concerns the design of intelligent computer systems: that is, systems which exhibit the characteristics commonly associated with human intelligence – understanding *natural language*, problem-solving, learning, logical reasoning, etc.

Computers are well suited to handling those forms of reasoning and problem-solving which can be clearly broken down into a series of 'logical' steps, eg the performance of numerical calculations. However, other aspects of intelligence cannot be so easily programmed: it is the goal of AI to overcome these difficulties.

The nature of the difficulties is often illustrated in terms of computer chess. The computer is programmed to consider the possible moves it could make, and the possible responses from an opponent. It then evaluates the outcome of each sequence of moves in accord with prescribed criteria, and selects the best option. A computer can 'search' thousands of moves in the time a human can only consider a few, but no computer can, as yet, beat a human chess master. The master's advantage appears to lie in a form of intelligence derived from experience, and produces an ability to draw crucial inferences from the pattern of the pieces, and the opponent's pattern of play. The reasoning subsumed within the chess master's intelligence cannot be clearly explicated into steps, and cannot therefore be incorporated into a computer program. Nevertheless, computers can now play chess and other similar types of game to a high standard. These are generally referred to as problem-solving forms of AI. Similar problem-solving techniques, based on the principles of 'search' and 'problem reduction', have a variety of more practical uses, eg in performing mathematical integration of complex equations.

Related to 'problem solving' is logical reasoning'. In exploring this field, AI techniques have been used to develop methods for searching information in a *database*, so as to test the validity of generalized statements ('theorems'). The technique has been extended to include monitoring the acceptability of theorems as information is added to the database. Such systems can also identify crucial data, eg those which are anomalous in relation to a specific theorem, so that they can be scrutinized in more detail. A further development is the so-called *expert system* – a form of computer-based consultant. It is the AI component which distinguishes the expert system from a specialized *on-line information retrieval system*, allowing a dialogue, rather than a simple interrogation of a database. The understanding of language is a further area of application for AI which is of fundamental importance to information systems. For clearly, if AI could resolve all the inherent problems, computers could receive natural language as *input*, and perform automatic translation into *machine language*, or, indeed, into other natural languages (see *machine translation* and HAMT). Somewhat similar in impact to the understanding of language is the field of visual *pattern recognition*. If computers could recognize objects (via, for example, television cameras), this would offer even greater flexibility in the input of information to computer systems. AI of this type is crucial in the field of *robotics*.

ARU *Audio response unit.*

ASA American Standards Association (formerly the USASA) has groups responsible for the establishment of standards in the field of *data processing*.

ASC Automatic sequence control. A *program* feature.

ASCA Automatic Subject Citation Alert. A computer-produced *current*

awareness service based on the *database* of the *Science Citation Index*.

ascender A typographic expression indicating that part of a lower-case character which rises above the normal body height, eg the upper part of the letters 'b' and 'h'.

ASCII (code) A US standard computer *code*, adopted in Europe, in which eight binary *bits* can be combined to represent the characters on a typewriter keyboard. Only seven bits (128 possible combinations) are necessary to describe all the characters. The eighth bit is either used for error checking purposes, or it remains unused. Most commercial VDUs and printers utilize the ASCII code.

ASDI Automated selective dissemination of information (see *selective dissemination of information*).

ASI American Statistics Index. *Databank* of American social, economic and demographical statistics, searchable via *Lockheed* or *SDC*.

ASIS American Society for Information Science.

Aslib Originally stood for Association of Special Libraries and Information Bureaux, but is now used as a name in its own right. Aslib is a British association with headquarters in London.

ASME American Society of Mechanical Engineers. Name given to a standard set of *flowchart symbols*.

aspect In information retrieval, this refers to those features of the contents of documents, etc, which are represented by *index term*, *descriptors*, etc.

aspect card A card containing

numbers which record the location of *documents* used in an *information retrieval system.*

ASPIC Author Specified Prepress Input Coding. An *electronic mark-up* system adopted by the British Printing Industry Federation (BPIF).

ASR Answer, send and receive. A *teletypewriter* and receiver used in conjunction with a computer.

ASSASSIN Agricultural System for Storage and Subsequent Selection of Information. A bibliographic *information retrieval system* available from ICI.

assemble To put together a *machine language* program from a *symbolic language* program.

assembler A computer program which transfers a *symbolic language* program into a *machine language* program. The latter can then be directly executed by the computer.

assembly language A programming language in which each statement corresponds to a single *machine language* instruction. It is normally written in some form of *mnemonic code.*

assembly listing A list produced by an *assembler* which lists a *source program*, the *machine code* equivalent and details of any assembly errors.

assigned-term indexing See *indexing.*

assignment indexing A form of *automatic indexing*, less frequently used than *extraction indexing.* Words are selected in a similar fashion as for extraction indexing, but instead of using extracted terms as index terms, the extracted terms are used in conjunction with some kind of *thesaurus*, to produce a list of index terms chosen from a *controlled vocabulary* list. In this sense index terms are 'assigned'.

associative storage Computer *storage* where locations are identified by their contents, rather than by their names, *addresses*, etc. It is also called 'content-addressed memory' or 'parallel-search storage'. In associative storage, any *keyword* used in the search is compared simultaneously with all the keywords in the store, seeking for a match. More *logic hardware* is required than with conventional storage.

asynchronous transmission A telecommunications term. Transmission of data where time intervals between transmitted characters may be of unequal length. Asynchronous communication with other devices does not require a continuous exchange of synchronization signals (see *synchronous transmission*).

AT&T The American Telephone and Telegraph Company. Claimed to be the world's largest corporation. It is the largest common carrier in the US, handling over 80 per cent of the installed telephones in the US (although serving about a third of the geographical area). Runs the 'Bell System' and Western Electric, and jointly runs the Bell Telephone Laboratories, one of the world's largest research organizations.

ATLAS Automatic Tabulating, Listing and Sorting System. A *software package* extensively used for the purposes indicated.

ATM See *automatic teller machine.*

ATS Application Technology Satellite. The name attached to a series of US communications satellites. Both audio and video channels are used, particularly for medical communication (see *satellite communication*).

attached processor A *processor* attached to a *central processor*, often sharing its memory.

attenuation In communications systems, this refers to the loss in signal strength encountered over long transmission paths.

attribute byte A *byte* of information which describes the characteristics of either subsequent data in a transmission or an adjacent *field* (ie area) on a screen (eg input area, output area or *literal*).

AUDACIOUS Automatic Direct Access to Information with On-line UDC System. An *interactive* retrieval system using *UDC* for the *coding* and search scheme (see *information retrieval systems* and *on-line searching*).

audio Capable of being heard by the human ear, ie within the frequency range 15 Hz (cycles/sec) to 20,000 Hz.

audio cassette A small cartridge containing magnetic recording tape mounted on rotatable reels. Size has been standardized to allow interchange between a wide variety of devices.

audioconferencing The use of linked telephone lines to allow a number of people to hear and speak to each other in conference. This may be done by arranging for the operator to provide a *bridge*. Sophisticated *microprocessor*-controlled equipment is now available which provides improved facilities and group-to-group communication in *duplex* mode. Audioconferencing is widely used by educational establishments such as the Open University (UK) for *distance learning*.

audio response unit A device which can connect a telephone to a computer in order to provide voice response to a user's enquiries.

audit trail A record of every transaction taken by a computer system. This will indicate, for example, when users *log in* and *log off*, the activities they might undertake, what files have been accessed and the type of access. A record of this type may serve as a deterrent to breaches of *computer security*.

AUSINET An Australian *network* offering nationwide on-line access to a range of *databases* (see *on-line searching*, *CSIRONET* and *MIDAS*).

authentication A method of checking on users of a computer system. An authentication *routine* confirms that the user (or *terminal*) is entitled to access.

authoring language *Software* which is used in *interactive videodisc* systems.

authority file A set of records identifying a standard for established forms of headings, *index terms*, or other items, which may be subsequently used for information retrieval. An authority file may also contain established cross-references. A *thesaurus* is one example of such a file.

authorization code A user's *ID* and *password*.

auto abstract Also called an *automatic abstract*, it is an *abstract* produced by a computer analysis of a document (see *automatic abstracting*).

autoanswer A device which automatically answers calls via the telephone network (see *auto dialler*).

autocall See *automatic calling unit*.

autocode A system for the computer conversion of *symbolic code* into *machine code*.

autodial See *auto dialler*.

auto dialler A device which permits automatic dialling of calls via the telephone network (see *automatic calling unit*).

autoidentifier A device by which a computer or *videotex* terminal automatically identifies itself.

auto-kerning In *phototypesetting*, the automatic reduction of the spacing between certain characters when they appear together, eg 'A' and 'V' in 'AV'.

automated bibliography A bibliography stored in a computer file.

automated dictionary A form of *automated lexicon* used in *machine-aided translation* systems. In contrast with *automated glossaries* it separately lists roots, eg inform, and affixes, eg mis-, -ed, -er, -ing, etc. Used by the *LEXIS* and *TEAM* systems.

automated glossary A form of *automated lexicon* used in *machine-aided translation* systems. In contrast with *automated dictionaries*, it contains whole words and thus presents many variations of a generic root, eg informed, informer, informing. Used by the *SMART* translation system.

automated lexicon A generic term covering all forms of *automated dictionary* (single-word entries) and *automated glossary* (multiple-word term entries, eg 'electron spin resonance'). Automated lexicons constitute the central component within a *machine-aided translation* system (see *terminology bank*).

automated stock control Use of software on a computer to check on receipt and delivery of goods, including keeping accounts and forecasting demand.

automated thesaurus A computer-based *thesaurus* used in conjunction with an *automated lexicon* within a *machine-aided translation* system.

automatic abstract Also called an *auto abstract*; it is an *abstract* produced by a computer analysis of a document (see *automatic abstracting*).

automatic abstracting High-frequency substantive words in a document are identified using the same techniques applied in *automatic indexing* (see *extraction indexing*). Sentences which are found to contain the highest concentration of high-frequency words are then identified and printed out in sequence. The product, an *auto abstract* or *automatic abstract*, does not necessarily look like a normal human-prepared abstract, but it normally gives a fairly good indication of what a document is about.

automatic calling unit A device which permits automatic dialling of calls via the telephone network: normally used in business information systems (see *autodialler*).

automatic decimal alignment A *word processing* facility that enables numbers to be aligned automatically on either side of a decimal point.

automatic decimal tab Another term for *automatic decimal alignment*.

automatic dictionary A component within a computer translation system which provides word-for-word substitution from one language to another.

automatic encryption A system in which data are entered or typed in normally but are stored or transmitted in encrypted form, this being carried out automatically by *software* (see also *encryption*).

automatic footnote tie-in A *word processing* facility which ties a footnote to the segment of text to

which it relates. If that segment of
text is moved, the footnote travels
with it.

automatic indexing The *automatic*
production of an index for
documents in a *database*. The most
commonly used techniques are
described under *extraction indexing*
(see *assignment indexing* and
automatic abstracting).

automatic letter writing A *word
processing* facility which enables
personalized letters to be produced,
by merging a mailing list file with a
file containing a standard letter.

automatic logon (log on) A facility
offered by *intelligent terminals*
when used for *on-line searching*
(see, eg, *Userkit*). The various
passwords, identifiers and *addresses*
necessary to use local or
international telecommunications
networks and *host* computers are
stored at the terminal, so that the *log
on* process can be carried out with
one, or a few, *key strokes*.

automatic message routing
Automatic directing of incoming
messages to one or more outgoing
circuits according to the content of
the message.

automatic paper carriage A device
for guiding, or holding, prior to
printing. It feeds sheets, or
continuous paper, to the writing
heads.

automatic speech processing This
term covers a number of different
processes, such as *digital
transmission* and storage of voice
messages, and *speech recognition*.

automatic stop A means of
stopping a computer operation when

an error is detected, by an automatic
checking procedure.

automatic teller machine A device
for providing an automated banking
service: eg cash dispensers, balance
reports (see *bank on-line teller
system*).

automatic window adjust A *word
processing* facility which prevents
the first line of a paragraph, or a
heading, from being the last line on a
page.

automation Process (or result) of
making machines self-acting and/or
self-controlling, by eliminating the
need for human intervention in the
process.

autoplotter A *plotter* which
produces graphical output under
computer control.

autoscore The automatic
underlining of text.

auxiliary equipment Equipment
that is not under the direct control of
a *CPU*.

auxiliary storage Computer *storage*
which is external to the computer
itself, eg *magnetic disc*, *magnetic
tape*.

availability When a computer has
its power switched on, its
'availability' is the percentage of
time it is available to the user.

AVIP See *BAVIP*.

AVLINE Audiovisual On-line. A
bibliographic database containing
citations to, and abstracts of,
audiovisual teaching packages in the
health sciences.

B

babble Interference between two or more data transmission *channels*.

BABT *British Approvals Board for Telecommunications.*

background In *time-sharing* computers, this refers to low-priority tasks which the computer only carries out when not occupied with high-priority items (the *foreground*). Thus background tasks may be carried out while data are being input for a foreground task.

background ink A reflective ink used for documents which are to be scanned by *OCR* equipment. Its high reflectivity facilitates non-detection.

backing storage Storage within a computer's main memory is both expensive and limited in amount. When the computer needs access to large quantities of data, additional storage capacity is therefore required. At present this 'backing storage' is normally held on magnetic devices, eg *tapes, discs, cards* and *drums*. While these have cost advantages over main 'core' memory, *access times* are slower.

back number Any issue of a periodical which precedes the current issue.

backplane Synonymous with *mother board.*

back-up A procedure or facility which allows a user to retain information in the event of a computer failure.

back-up (equipment) Equipment available for use as a substitute in the event of failure of the equipment normally used. Purchase of such back-up equipment is becoming increasingly common.

Backus naur form A metalanguage used to specify or describe the syntax of a *programming language.*

backward chaining A design principle applied in *expert systems.* Backward chaining systems start with the formation of a hypothesis. Rules that would lead to this state are selected from the *knowledge base* and the database is scanned for assertions that match the chosen rules. If sufficient assertions are found, the hypothesis is taken as validated.

backward channel A data transmission channel used for supervisory, or error control, signals with a direction of transmission opposite to that of general data traffic.

backward compatibility Synonymous with *downward compatibility.*

backward recovery Recovering from a system failure by reversing processes that have already been applied, thus reconstituting the *file* to an earlier state.

BACS Bankers' Automated Clearing System. Established in 1967 for processing financial transactions between the major UK banks.

BAM See *Basic Access Method.*

band 1. A range of frequencies. 2. Recording area on a magnetic tape or drum.

band-pass The range of frequencies of signals passed by a *filter* without significant *attenuation.*

bandwidth A telecommunications term. It describes the extent of the frequency spectrum within which signals can pass through a system without significant *attenuation*. Signals carrying information, eg the human voice, are made up of a number of component frequencies. For faithful transmission and reception of a signal, the bandwidth must be sufficient to pass these component frequencies. Unwanted signals, eg *noise*, can sometimes be suppressed by the use of filters of specified bandwidth (see *band-pass*).

banking In *OCR*, a misalignment of the first character of a line with respect to the left margin.

bank on-line teller system A system of *automatic teller machines* linked to a central computer in *conversational mode* (see *debit card systems*).

bar-code A type of code used on labels to be read by a *wand* or *bar-code scanner*. The main application is in labelling retail products, the wand being used to record the sale at the place and time of purchase, but it is also used to label documents in libraries.

Typical example of a bar-code: the universal product code, perhaps the most widely seen. The detailed storage of information is shown. For an example of the practical use of the code, see optical character recognition.

bar-code scanner An optical device which can read *data* from

documents bearing characters recorded in the form of parallel bars. The characters are translated into *digital* signals for storage or processing (see *bar-code*).

bar printer A *printer* with *character* heads mounted on a type bar.

barrel printer See *drum printer*.

base The number of symbols required by a number system. The decimal system has a base of 10, the *binary* system has a base of 2.

baseband A frequency *band* used for the transmission of picture and synchronization signals in television and some telephone systems.

baseplate An interface device which connects to an electric typewriter, converting it into a word processor.

BASIC Beginner's All-purpose Symbolic Instruction Code. A *high level language* designed for ease of use. It is particularly suitable for entering and running *programs on-line*. It is now a standard programming language, in a number of variant forms, for *microcomputers*.

Basic Access Method A computer access method in which each *input/output statement* causes a machine input/output operation to be performed.

basic mode link control Control of *data links* by use of the ISO/CCITT 7-bit character set for information processing interchange.

Basicode A Dutch system for transmitting *telesoftware* using coded radio signals.

Batab A US *teleordering* system.

batch A collection of computer *transactions* processed as a single unit.

batch processing A method of processing data by computer which accumulates *transactions* and processes them as a single unit (a *batch*), rather than as they arise.

baud In telecommunications, a unit of signalling speed. The speed in baud is the number of discrete signal events per second. If each signal event represents one *bit*, a baud corresponds to bits per second, otherwise the *baud rate* cannot immediately be equated to bits per second.

baud rate Baud rates are usually quoted as two figures: eg 300/300 or 75/1200. The first number represents the speed at which the originating computer can send data; the second is the rate at which it can receive.

Baudot code Standard five-channel *telex* code. The name derives from Emil Baudot, who produced the first major teleprinter code in the 19th century. In the UK, the telex code is called the Murray code.

BAVIP British Association of Viewdata Information Providers (see *viewdata* and *information provider*).

BB *Bulletin board.*

BBC 1. British Broadcasting Corporation. The state-owned radio and television broadcasting agency in the UK. 2. A *microcomputer* produced by the UK manufacturers Acorn allowed to carry the BBC name. It is widely used in schools and educational establishments.

BBIP *British Books in Print.*

BC See *Bliss classification.*

BCD See *Binary coded decimal.*

BCPA British Copyright Protection Association.

BCS British Computer Society.

bead A small *program* for a specific function (see *thread*).

beam store A *storage* device in which electron beams are used to write, or read, data.

beamwidth The angular extent over which an antenna can readily detect or transmit a signal.

bearer A high *bandwidth channel.*

BEEF Business and Engineering Enriched FORTRAN. An adaptation of the *FORTRAN programming language* to enhance its capabilities for business and engineering applications.

beginning of file label A *record* at the beginning of a *file* which gives information about the file's contents and limits.

beginning of information marker (BIM) Usually an area of reflecting material on a *magnetic tape* which indicates the beginning of the area on which information is recorded. Some systems use transparent, instead of reflecting, material, or some kind of perforation in the plastic of the tape.

Bell and Howell Newspaper Index A very large *database* (over 2,000,000 entries) covering news and current affairs items appearing in major US newspapers from 1977 onwards. Accessible via *SDC.*

bell character The member of a *character* set used to sound a bell on a *terminal* device. Also used as a *flag* in some *phototypesetting* systems (see *Bell code*).

Bell code A computer code used for *phototypesetting* commands.

Bell System The network of telephone and data circuits, *switching* offices, television and other links in the US operated by *AT&T*, its subsidiaries and associated companies.

BELTEL South African *viewdata* (*interactive videotex*) system.

bells and whistles Computer jargon used to describe an item of *hardware* or *software* which has a large number of special features.

benchmark A program designed to test and compare the performance of different computers.

BESSY Bestell-system. A German *teleordering* system.

Betamax Former name of *Beta*.

Beta (system) A type of *video cassette recording* system, developed by Sony. Uses slightly smaller cassettes than the *VHS* system.

BEX *Broadband* exchange.

bibliographic(al) Relating to the description of documents.

bibliographic coupling A method of grouping documents by examining the number of common *citations* that the documents make. Thus, if two documents each cite three other documents in common, the citing documents are said to have a bibliographic coupling strength of three (see *co-citation indexing, information retrieval techniques*).

bibliographic database A *database* containing information relating to documents (books, articles, reports, etc). The information normally covers details of authorship and title, together with place and date of publication. Some databases include *abstracts*. The content of each item is indexed to facilitate search and access (see *information retrieval systems*).

bibliographic utility A service provided by organizations such as *OCLC*, offering libraries access to *bibliographic databases*: these contain *MARC* records and can form the basis of the library's own on-line catalogue.

biconditional Synonymous with equivalence.

BIDAP Bibliographic Data Processing Program. A *software* package for the *processing* of *bibliographic data*.

bidirectional printing The direction of printing of consecutive lines is alternated so as to eliminate the need for a return to the beginning of a line. This speeds up the printing process.

Bildschirmtext A West German *viewdata* (interactive *videotex*) system.

billi- Prefix meaning one thousand million (10^9). The US billion (=10^9) is coming into use in the UK, but the UK billion (=10^{12}) is still used.

BIM *Beginning of information marker*.

binary A system in which the choice is limited to one of two alternatives, eg an on-off switch.

binary chop A method of computer searching a stored table for an item by successively splitting it in half and searching one half for the presence of the item. If found, the half is split in two once more, and the process repeated. This continues until the exact position of the item is located.

binary coded decimal Each individual decimal digit is represented by the corresponding group of binary digits. The resulting number is not the same as a number in *binary notation*. For example, the number 15 in binary coded decimal is 0001 0101, whereas in binary notation it is 1111.

binary digit A digit on the binary scale of notation; either 1 or 0.

binary notation The writing of numbers to the *base 2*, so that the position of the digits in the number designates powers of 2. For example, the number 101 represents 1 x 2^2 + 0 x 2 + 1 x 1 (=5 in decimal notation). The table of binary numbers from 0 to 10 is as follows:

decimal notation	binary notation	decimal notation	binary notation
0	0000	6	0110
1	0001	7	0111
2	0010	8	1000
3	0011	9	1001
4	0100	10	1010
5	0101	11	1011

binary number Any number written in binary notation.

binary search A method of searching for an element in a table or *serial file*; the location is successively narrowed down by halving the table or file (see *binary chop*).

bind The action of transforming two, or more, *object program* modules into a program for *execution*.

BIOS Basic Input/Output System. The part of a computer's *operating system* that deals with the *input* and *output* of data.

biosensor A device for detecting and transmitting data relating to biological activity, so that they can be processed, displayed and stored.

Biosis Previews A large *database* containing approximately 2,500,000 items. The subject range is Biology and the Life Sciences as covered by *Biological Abstracts* and the *Bio Research Index*. It is accessible via most of the major *hosts*.

BIS *British Imperial System.*

bisynchronous The continuous exchange of *synchronization* signals between communications devices.

bit An abbreviation of binary digit. It represents the smallest unit of information (corresponding to, eg 0 or 1; 'on' or 'off'; 'signal' or 'no signal'). Computers usually store information as a series of bits (see *byte*).

8-bit, 16-bit, 32-bit, etc. Refers to the amount of *data* that a computer can deal with in one *cycle* of operation. There may be a difference between the number of bits that can be processed through the *CPU* in one cycle and the number of bits that can be transferred from the *memory* to the CPU in one cycle. This difference is indicated by writing the two numbers separately. For example, an 8/16-bit computer, also called a pseudo 16-bit computer, can transfer 16 bits (two *bytes*) of data from the memory to the CPU in one cycle, but can only process 8 bits (one byte) per cycle through the CPU. It is thus little faster than an ordinary 8 bit computer. A 16/16-bit computer can both transfer and process 16 bits per cycle, and is known as a true 16-bit computer.

bit density The number of bits contained in a storage area, eg of a magnetic tape or magnetic disc.

bite Alternative spelling of *byte*.

bit location A *storage* position in a *record* capable of storing one *bit*.

bit map A way of producing high resolution computer pictures in which every *pixel* on the *screen* can be *addressed* individually.

bit parallel See *parallel bit transmission*.

bit pattern See *bit map*.

bit position Refers to a position in a bit sequence. For example, to represent 2 in binary form requires a 1-bit in the second position (10); to represent 4 in binary form requires a 1-bit in the third position (100), etc.

bit rate The speed at which *bits* are transmitted, usually expressed in bits per second (see *baud*).

B-I-T-S An *SDI* service offered by the *database* producer *Biosis*, which provides the information on *floppy disc* and other *machine-readable* media.

bit serial The sequential transmission of the bits in a group through a single channel.

bit-slice microprocessor *Integrated circuit* design that enables *microprocessors* having a short *word* length (eg 2 or 4 *bits*) to be connected and programmed in such a way as to produce a microprocessor handling a longer word length.

bit-slice processing *Microprocessors* which allow large scale parallel *data processing* (ie permit many *jobs* to be done simultaneously).

bit stream A set of related *bits* (a *bit string*) travelling along a communication line.

bit string A set of related *bits*.

bit stuffing The insertion into a *bit stream* of a dummy *bit*, often employed to satisfy the requirements of a data transmission *protocol*.

black box A device that performs a specific function, but whose detailed operation is not known, or not specified, in the context of the discussion.

black signal In *facsimile*, the signal produced by scanning the darkest areas of a *source document*.

BLAISE British Library Automated Information Service. Contains bibliographical details of all books published in the UK since 1950, and in the US since 1968. In addition, it

acts as a *host* and it provides access to a number of medical and chemical *databases*, eg *Medline*, *Chemline* and *Toxline*. BLAISE additionally offers a cataloguing service. Specially developed *software* enables BLAISE's *MARC* records to be retrieved and edited to produce local catalogues (see *BLAISE-LINE* and *BLAISE-LINK*.)

BLAISE-LINE A *BLAISE* service which provides access to a number of databases containing UK and US *MARC* records.

BLAISE-LINK A *BLAISE* service which links users to the American *National Library of Medicine* (NLM) system.

blast-through alphanumerics A set of *alphanumerics* which can be used in a *videotex* display.

BLCMP Birmingham Libraries Cooperative Mechanisation Project. A cooperative project established in the Birmingham (UK) region to give members access to *on-line cataloguing* services.

BLDSC *British Library Document Supply Centre.*

bleed Spreading of ink beyond the edges of a printed character: a problem in *optical character recognition*.

BLEND Birmingham and Loughborough Electronic Network Development. A research project, spanning the period 1980–84, which assessed the cost, efficiency and *ergonomic* implications of an information *network* based on an *electronic journal* (see *Project Quartet*).

blind 1. A piece of equipment which is unreceptive to data. 2. To make a piece of equipment unreceptive.

blind keyboard A *keyboard* which does not provide a visual display, or *hard copy* of data entered through the keyboard.

blinking A method of signalling important messages by flashing characters on a display screen.

blip 1. An unwanted signal on a display screen. 2. A document mark.

blip counting A position-sensing technique based on adding or subtracting one from a *location register*, depending on the direction in which each position mark (blip) passes a sensor.

Bliss classification A classification scheme which uses 26 alphabetic classes (A-Z), with subdivisions of each main class indicated by the addition of further letters.

blitter A *chip* which can rearrange and *manipulate* large areas of *core memory* very quickly. Used in conjunction with *graphics* to produce moving images on a computer *screen*.

BLLD British Library Lending Division, renamed *British Library Document Supply Centre* (BLDSC).

block 1. A group of information units handled as a single unit. In many *magnetic storage* devices only complete blocks can be accessed, or transferred. Block size may be fixed or variable, depending on the equipment. 2. A *half-tone* or *line drawing* printing plate.

block diagram A diagram of a system or a computer *program* in which the parts are represented by boxes, usually labelled with interconnecting lines (see *flow diagram*).

block gap Synonymous with *inter-block gap*.

blocking The creation of *blocks* from individual *records*.

block retransmission An *error control* technique in *data transmission* which involves repeating any portions of the data which contain too many errors.

block transfer The movement of data in *blocks*.

blow back 1. Full size print-on-paper copy of information stored on *microform*. 2. Image enlargement on a *cathode ray tube*.

blowing As in 'PROM blowing', this refers to programming *read-only memory* (ROM) using special equipment.

blow up An enlargement, usually of pictorial matter.

BMMG British Microcomputer Manufacturers' Group.

body The main text of a *word-processed* document.

body (size) A term used in *typesetting* to describe the size of typeface in *points*. Body is also used to describe the viscosity of printing ink.

boilerplate Standard paragraphs or chunks of text in the memory of a *word processing* system.

bold face A typeface which appears blacker than normal. Usually employed to give emphasis, eg to headings.

bomb Loss of a computer *program* due to incorrect commands.

book In the computing sense, a large segment of computer memory.

Book Machine A modified microcomputer system, produced by Prefis, which is specifically designed to handle *word processing* and *phototypeset* output.

book message A message which is sent to two or more destinations.

Bookseller Data A Danish *teleordering* system.

Boolean algebra An algebra dealing with classes, propositions, etc, associated with such operators as AND, OR, NOT, IF, THEN,

EXCEPT, etc. It contrasts with conventional algebra, which deals with mathematical relationships. Though developed in the 19th century, Boolean algebra has wide applicability in *computer* analysis of information and problems because it expresses logical relationships in a form which can be accommodated within the *binary logic* of *digital computers*. This type of logical expression and analysis is usually illustrated by means of a *truth table*. The example below asks 'if X may be true or false, and Y may similarly be true or false, which combinations of truth and falsehood of X and Y lead to a true or false Z?' In the example given, '0' corresponds to 'false' and '1' corresponds to 'true'. It can be seen that the Z postulated in this relationship is true if one of X or Y is true, but not if both X and Y are true or false. Complex logical relationships can be broken down into binary elements in this way. (The name derives from George Boole, a British mathematician, who first developed this type of algebra.)

X	Y	Z
0	0	0
1	0	1
0	1	1
1	1	0

Boolean calculus Synonymous with *Boolean algebra*.

Boolean logic Synonymous with *Boolean algebra*.

Boolean operation An operation in which the result of giving each of a number of operands one of two possible values is itself one of two values. Such operations can clearly be expressed in a *binary* form for computer analysis (see *Boolean algebra*).

Boolean operation table A table in which a *Boolean operation* is expressed: for each combination of

the one of two values of each operand, the one of two possible values of the result is shown. When the two possible values for each element are 'true' or 'false', the table is known as a *truth table* (see *Boolean algebra*).

Boolean operator See *Boolean algebra*.

boom An *antenna* frame, to which *array* elements are attached.

boot Short for *bootstrap*.

booting Short for bootstrapping, this term is usually used to refer to the transfer of a *disc operating system program* (DOS) from its *storage* on a *disc* to a *computer's* working *memory*. In computer jargon, an operator may 'boot the disc', 'boot the DOS', or 'boot DOS'.

bootstrap A method of inputting data prior to the *loading* of a computer *program*, so causing the program to be loaded.

Boris A Canadian *viewdata* (interactive *videotex*) system.

BOT Beginning of tape (see *magnetic tape*).

boxed mode A *teletext* facility which allows information from a teletext database to be displayed superimposed upon the broadcast picture appearing on a television set.

BPCC British Printing and Communication Corporation (formerly British Printing Corporation).

BPI Bits per inch: used for measuring density of data on a storage medium (see *bits*).

BPIF British Printing Industry Federation.

BPS Bits per second (see *bits*).

branch A point in a *program* where a computer must select one out of two, or more, pathways.

breadboard An experimental set up of an electronic circuit for design and operational testing.

break point The point in a computer program at which the running of the program can be interrupted, or requires the intervention of a user, systems operator or another program.

bridge 1. A computer-based device for making connections between *networks*. Bridges usually connect two or more *LANs* on a local basis. 2. A connection provided by the operator of a telephone exchange to allow *audioconferencing* over the telephone line.

bridging A lack of quality of definition in *OCR* characters, leading to an OCR system being unable to input data.

brightness ratio A measure of *contrast*. It refers to the ratio between the brightest and darkest parts of a printed paper sheet. The term is used in the context of *optical character recognition* and *facsimile transmission*.

Brisch classification A *classification and coding system* covering every facet of the activities of engineering organizations.

British Approvals Board for Telecommunications The organization which administers the standards with which equipment for connection to the UK telephone network must comply. The standards cover electrical performance and safety, as well as adherence to transmission standards.

British Books in Print A *database* of book titles currently in print, or about to be published, produced by Whitaker. It is currently supplied to users on *microfiche*, but it is planned to issue the database on *CD-ROM*.

British Imperial System System of units of measurement from which the US Customary System was developed. It uses such units as feet and inches, pounds and ounces, and pints and gallons. It is being superseded by the *SI* system in most scientific and technical areas.

British Library Document Supply Centre The major UK supplier of documents on inter-library loan.

British Telecom British Telecommunications. The UK Post Office has been split into two parts: the first (called The Post Office) dealing with conventional letter and parcel post, and the second (British Telecom) dealing with telecommunications services (telephone, telex, telegraph, *Datel*, *Prestel*, etc).

broadband Communication channel with a *bandwidth* greater than a voice-grade channel, and therefore capable of higher-speed data transmission.

Broadband Exchange Public *switched* telecommunications *network* of the *Western Union*, US.

broadcast The dissemination of information to several receivers simultaneously (usually via electromagnetic signals).

broadcast network *Network* over which a sender *broadcasts* a message, usually by broadcast packet switching. Within such networks, each message is given an *address* identifier so that receiving terminals can determine for whom the message is intended. Where a cable is used as the transmission medium, the system can constitute a *local area network* (eg *Ethernet*). The system has to provide that terminals do not begin to transmit while a previous transmission is in progress, and has to deal with those occasions on which transmission begins simultaneously from two or more *nodes*. This can be achieved by *token passing*, or each node may listen to the network and only transmit when the network is empty. If simultaneous start of transmission does occur, a collision detect procedure ensures that subsequent transmissions are appropriately staggered. This facility is called carrier sensing with multiple access/collision detect.

broadcast satellite A form of frequency allocation for *communications satellites* which identifies the *uplink* stations only.

Broadcast Satellite Experiment A Japanese *communications satellite* particularly intended to investigate direct television transmission (see *Experimental Communications Satellite, direct transmission satellite*).

BROWSER Browsing On-line with Selective Retrieval. A system which offers automatic *natural language searching* of documents in a *database*. All documents entering the database are subjected to a form of automatic *extraction indexing* which results in their characterization by *strings* of words, weighted in accord with their frequency of occurrence. An English language search query can then be accommodated, by comparing terms used in the query to those generated and weighted by the *automatic index*. Documents are selected on the basis of 'best fit', retrieved and listed in ranked order (see *LEADERMART* and *SMART*).

BRS Bibliographic Retrieval Services. A *host*, based in the US, offering access to a number of *on-line databases*.

BRS/After Dark An evening and weekend service for *home computer* users offered by the US *host BRS*. It offers access to a range of popular *databases* at cheap rates.

brush An electrical device for reading *information* from a *punched card*.

BSE *Broadcast Satellite Experiment*.

BSGL Branch Systems General Licence. Authorization granted to organizations using apparatus connected to the *PSTN*.

BSI British Standards Institution: establishes standards for measurement, nomenclature and product performance in the UK.

BSI Standardline A UK *database* which provides information on British standards.

BT *British Telecom*.

BTAM 1. Basic Terminal Access Method. *Basic Access Method* from a *terminal*. 2. Basic Telecommunications Access Method: *Basic Access Method* using telecommunications *channels*.

BT Gold Synonymous with *Telecom Gold*.

BTX An abbreviation commonly used for *Bildschirmtext*, a West German viewdata (interactive *videotex*) system.

bubble memory See *magnetic bubble memory*.

bubble sort A way of ordering items in a list. Sequential pairs of items are compared with regard to a given criterion (eg alphabetical order) and then ordered. The process is repeated until all pairs satisfy the criterion (compare *selective sort*).

bucket In computing, a place, or unit, of storage.

buffer 1. A *storage* device (typically between *input/output* equipment and the computer) where *information* is assembled to allow for differences, eg in data flow rate, in its onward transmission. 2. A circuit used to isolate one circuit from another.

buffer channel A method for interfacing devices with a computer, which contains *memory addressing* capability and the ability to transfer words.

buffering Technique whereby data or information is stored in a *buffer* for a short time prior to being released for a subsequent process (eg printing or transmission).

bug An error in a computer program or system.

bulk storage Large volume storage, for which *access times* are relatively slow (see *backing storage*).

bulk update terminal Used by a *videotex information provider* for *off-line* preparation, storage and transmission of pages to a videotex computer.

bulletin board Developed from *computer conferencing* and *electronic mail* systems. It provides general messaging facilities, together with a public information area to which participants may add comments. Access may be unrestricted or confined to specialist groups, depending on the type of information provided. Bulletin boards are operated under the control of a system operator who is responsible for editing and maintaining the files.

Bundespost The *PTT* of West Germany.

bundle A number of *optical fibres* grouped within a single protective sheathing.

bundled software *Software* provided with a computer as part of the basic price.

bureau See *computer bureau.*

Bureau of Standards US Government agency concerned with standards for measurement and performance. Should not be confused with *ANSI.*

burning Programming a *read-only memory.*

burst A set of characters grouped together for *data transmission.*

burst modem In satellite communications, each station sends high-speed bursts of data which are interleaved with each other. These bursts have to be very precisely timed, and are therefore sent using a burst modem.

burst traffic Transmission of data in bursts, rather than continuously. A simple example is the exchange of information in a telephone conversation.

bus An interconnected system path over which information is transferred, from any one of many sources to any one of many destinations, the devices involved being connected in parallel.

bus driver A power amplifier used to drive several devices using a *bus.*

business systems See *office automation.*

bustrophedon printing Synonymous with *bidirectional printing.*

byte A group of adjacent *bits*, such as 4, 6 or 8 bits, operating as a unit. For example, a 6-bit byte may be used to specify a letter of the alphabet, and an 8-bit byte may be used to specify an instruction or an *address*. Normally shorter than a word. Unless otherwise indicated a byte is normally assumed to be 8 bits long.

byte mode Synonymous with *multiplex mode*.

C

C 1. Coulomb. The *SI* unit of electrical charge. 2. See *C-language*.

© International sign indicating the copyright assignment of a document.

CAAS Computer-Assisted Acquisition System. To assist libraries in their acquisition of material.

CAB Abstracts *Database* compiled by the Commonwealth Agricultural Bureaux, UK, covering a broad area of agriculture and related sciences. The database is accessible via *Lockheed* and *ESA-IRS*.

cable One or more conductors contained within a protective sheathing. If multiple conductors are present, they are electrically isolated from each other (see *coaxial cable*).

cable casting Refers to dissemination of information via cables, eg *cable television*, instead of broadcasting, eg radio, or broadcast TV.

cable television Cable television is sometimes called *CATV* (which stands for community antenna television). This is because cable television originally described a system where a communal antenna (aerial) received a broadcast television signal. The signal was then transmitted to domestic television sets via *coaxial cable*. Today, in many systems the cable runs directly from the office distributing the program(me)s (the *head end*) to the receiving sets, and no antenna is required. The original purpose of CATV was to improve television reception in difficult areas, but it has developed at markedly different rates in different countries, and for a variety of reasons. In some countries, for example, regulatory authorities have limited its growth. In the US, an antitrust legal decision in 1968 effectively encouraged the development of CATV, and it has grown greatly since. CATV may help the spread of new information technology. The coaxial cable which carries the television signal has an *information-carrying capacity* roughly a thousand times greater than the normal telephone cable, and can be used for other purposes besides transmitting the television signal. A disadvantage is the expense of laying cables and the consequent problem of operating economically in sparsely populated regions. Not all the channels offered by modern cables are used, so other services can be provided. CATV companies already provide relatively inexpensive information services such as weather reports, news headlines, etc on these channels. Moreover, each channel can be subdivided into further channels of smaller *bandwidth*. These can be used to provide additional information, eg *data* or *facsimile transmission*.
Interactive use of CATV increased in the US after a 1972 *FCC* ruling that such systems should be constructed with a *reverse channel* capability. With this, the subscriber can respond to signals arriving at the television set by sending back signals along the cable. These signals can be fed into a computer thereby providing access to a range of new services. A main use so far has been for simple entertainment, eg subscribers can rate performers on talent shows in *real time*. However, many other services – news, financial, *computer-aided learning*, *information retrieval* from databases – are under consideration. It may also prove possible to widen the range of facilities by linking separate CATV systems together to form a larger *network*. These various proposed services overlap to some extent with those planned for

viewdata systems. One of the main differences between CATV and viewdata is that the latter is transmitted along conventional telephone lines which have a lower capacity. See diagrams of CATV.

cache memory A very high speed *buffer memory*.

CAD *Computer-aided design.*

CAD/CAM Computer-aided design and manufacture (see *computer-aided design* and *computer-aided manufacture*).

CAE Computer-aided education. A term which covers both *computer-*

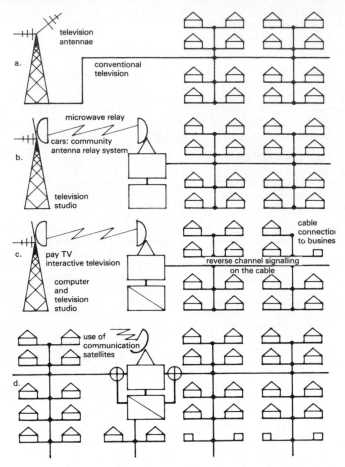

Progressive development of CATV. Initially, cable television was used for improving reception in difficult, eg mountainous, areas (a). It was then developed as an alternative to conventional television systems, with its own television origination (b). The greatest advance was made after the introduction of a reverse channel on the cable, allowing two-way communication (c). Currently, different CATV networks are being interconnected, producing nationwide coverage by CATV stations, aided by communications satellites (d).

aided instruction (CAI) and computer-aided learning (CAL).

CAFSS Content Addressable File Storage System. *ICL database software.*

CAI *Computer-aided instruction.*

CAIC Computer-aided indexing and classification (see *automatic indexing*).

CAIP Computer-Assisted Indexing Program. A *CAIC* system developed by the United Nations.

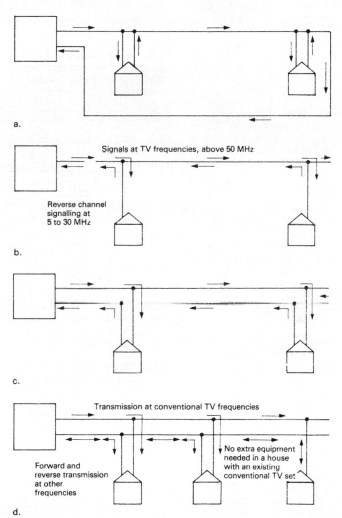

a.

Signals at TV frequencies, above 50 MHz

Reverse channel signalling at 5 to 30 MHz

b.

c.

Transmission at conventional TV frequencies

No extra equipment needed in a house with an existing conventional TV set

Forward and reverse transmission at other frequencies

d.

Reverse-channel signalling: illustrated are four different systems allowing two-way communication in CATV networks. a. A cable looping back to the cable head b. Two-directional transmission along a single cable c. Two separate cables d. Utilization of both a conventional and a two-way cable.

CAIRS Computer-assisted information retrieval system (see *information retrieval systems*).

CAL *Computer-aided* (or assisted) *learning.*

CALL Computer-assisted language learning. The use of computers as teaching machines for learning a foreign language (see *computer-aided instruction*).

call directing code A *code* directing messages between two communications *stations*.

calligraphic plotter A *plotter* which draws an image on a *CRT* consisting of lines only. It is used in *computer graphics* (see *raster plotter*).

calling In data communications, refers to the transmission of selection signals to establish a connection time between terminals.

CAM 1. *Computer-aided manufacture* 2. Computer-addressed memory.

Cambridge Ring A *local area network* developed at Cambridge University, UK.

camera-ready copy *Hard copy* manuscript (usually a typescript) of a quality and layout suitable for photographing and printing directly.

CAMIS Computer-Assisted Make-up and Imaging System.

Cancerline A group of three *databases* produced by the US National Library of Medicine. They are CANCERLIT (a bibliographic database), CANCERPROJ (covering research projects in progress) and CLINPROT (clinical protocols for treatment). Cancerline is accessible via a variety of *hosts*.

candidate key A *key* used in searching a *relational database*, that has the properties of a primary key.

CANDOC A Canadian electronic document ordering service operated in conjunction with *CANOLE*.

canned paragraphs Used in *word processing* to describe pre-recorded paragraphs which are in frequent use, and can be combined in a variety of ways.

CANOLE Canadian On-Line Enquiry. The *host* services of the National Research Council of Canada.

capacitance disc See *videodisc*.

capacitive videodisc See *videodisc*.

caps A printer's abbreviation for 'capital letters'.

CAPTAIN A Japanese *viewdata* (interactive *videotex*) system.

CAR *Computer-assisted retrieval.*

carbonless paper See *no carbon required paper*.

card A small board containing electronic components which can be plugged into a piece of *hardware* to give it an extra facility.

card (punched card) A card of standard size, thickness and shape used to input data and instructions. The most frequently used card is 7¾ inch by 3¼ inch and has 80 vertical columns numbered from left to right. Each column has 12 possible punching positions, which accommodate the encoding of *characters*, one to a column. A numeric character requires only one hole to be punched in its column (these positions are numbered vertically 0-9), while other characters require two or more holes to be punched in the columns into which they are to be entered. The pattern of positions punched for any given character is determined by the *code* used by the *card punch*. Not all equipment uses the same codes, and consistency between the codes used by card punch and *card reader* therefore has to be checked before cards can be used to *input*. In the event of inconsistency, many computers offer facilities for automatic recording and repunching of cards (see diagram).

card column One of the columns (typically 80 altogether) on a *card* into which information can be punched.

card feed A device which moves *cards* one by one into a machine where they can be read.

card punch A device which perforates cards in specific locations under the guidance either of a computer, or of a user at a *keyboard*.

card reader A device which permits the sensing of information punched on *cards* (by means of *brushes*), and then converts this information into electronic messages.

CARIS Computerized Agricultural Research Information System of the United Nations Food and Agriculture Organization.

carriage return A key, or character, which ends a line of type when activated and brings the cursor down to the start of the next line, eg in *phototypesetting*. The word has been adopted from typewriter terminology.

carrier signal A signal which carries packages, or streams, of information.

carrier sensing with multiple access/collision detect See *broadcast network*.

carrier wave An electromagnetic signal to which information can be added by means of *modulation*.

CARS *Community antenna relay system.*

cartridge A memory *chip* containing *software*. Specially packaged so that it can plug directly into a microcomputer.

cartridge disc A type of *hard disc* storage.

CAS 1. *Current awareness service.* 2. *Computer Acquisition System.*

CA search *Database* containing *keyword* and Chemical Abstract volume index entries and bibliographic citations. It is based on the entire contents of Chemical Abstracts, and therefore contains information which represents the sum of that within *CA Condensates* and *CASIA*. It is available via *BRS, Pergamon-Infoline, Lockheed* and *SDC*.

CAS files Chemical abstract service files. A generic name for several files based on chemical abstracts: *CA Condensates, CA Search, CASIA, CIN*.

CASIA Chemical Abstracts Subject Index Alert. A *database* containing the volume index of Chemical Abstracts. When mounted *on-line*, CASIA records are usually linked to the main *CA Condensates* files.

cassette A portable container for film (videocassette) or *magnetic tape*.

cast-off A term used by printers to mean estimating the number of pages a manuscript will make when it is composed (see *composition*).

CAT 1. Computer-assisted teaching training (see *computer-aided instruction* and *educational technology*). 2. Computer-aided

translation. Synonymous with *machine-aided translation*. 3. Computer-aided typesetting.

catalog(ue) A list of items arranged for easy reference.

catalogue database A *database* which provides information on major national library collections. Many national bibliographies have been mounted as *on-line* databases. They are used for subject searches, document location and ordering, and the creation of private catalogue records (see *MARC, UKMARC, LIBRIS*).

catastrophic error When so many or such large errors occur in a computer *program* that the *job* is terminated.

CATCALL Completely Automated Technique for Cataloguing and Acquisition of Literature for Libraries.

cathode ray tube An electronic display device, similar to a television picture tube, used to display information including graphics. Its surface provides the screen in *visual display units* and *word processors*. The name is often abbreviated to CRT.

cathode ray tube display unit A *visual display terminal* (VDT) in which a *cathode ray tube* (CRT) is used to display information and/or graphics.

CATNIP Computer-Assisted Technique for Numerical Index Preparation.

CATO Computer-aided telephone operations.

CATV Community antenna television (see *cable television*).

CB Citizens' band radio.

C band The frequency range 3.9-6.2 GHz (see *spectrum*).

CBEMA Canadian Business Equipment Manufacturers' Association.

CBMS Computer-based messaging system.

CBPI Canadian Business Periodicals Index. A database covering Canadian business, industry, finance and related matters. Accessible via QL and SDC.

CBT Computer-based training.

CBX Computerized branch exchange. A digital in-house branch exchange capable of handling both voice and data traffic.

CCC Copyright Clearance Center.

CCD Charge-coupled device.

CCIR Comité Consultatif International des Radiocommunications.

CCITT Comité Consultatif International Télégraphique et Téléphonique.

CCL Common command language.

CCLN Council for Computerized Library Networks, US.

CCTA Central Computer and Telecommunications Agency.

CCTV Closed circuit television.

CCU Communications control unit.

CD Compact disc.

CDC Call directing code.

CDI Comprehensive Dissertation Index. A database covering US doctoral dissertations, accessible via BRS, Lockheed and SDC.

CD-I Compact disc – interactive.

CD-ROM Compact disc – read-only

memory. CD-ROM was developed from audio compact disc technology. Because of the digital storage technique employed, compact discs can be used for the storage and retrieval of all kinds of digitally encoded data. CD-ROM is an optical storage medium, read by laser. In appearance it is the same as the audio compact disc – a 4¾ inch plastic disc coated with reflective material. It is a non-erasable, read-only device, and in common with the videodisc, is produced by a mastering/replicating process. A CD-ROM can store up to 600 megabytes of data, equivalent to about 1,000 floppy discs. The data are stored serially in 99 sections, each of which can be subdivided 99 times; all sections and subsections can be digitally labelled and located within a second. In retrieval applications, access time is slower than for floppy discs; this is a function of the Constant Linear Velocity recording technique, which means that for random access the disc is constantly being slowed down or speeded up. CD-ROM has attracted much interest from database producers. Instead of mounting the database on-line, publishers may record the information, or subsets of it, on CD-ROM for direct supply to customers who can access it locally on their own equipment, thereby avoiding telecommunications and access charges. A number of CD-ROM database publications are on the market.

CDST Centre de Documentation Scientifique et Technique de CNRS. French database producer and document supply centre.

CE Consumer electronics.

CED 1. Centro Elletronico di Documentazione. A Rome-based host linked with Euronet DIANE. 2. Capacitance electronic disc.

Ceefax The *teletext* system operated by the British Broadcasting Corporation (BBC) in the UK.

cell The *storage* for one unit of information.

Cellnet A *cellular radio* network operated by *British Telecom*.

cellular modem A *modem* which employs radio transmission techniques and therefore requires no direct connection to telephone lines. Cellular systems are prone to electrical interference, so error correction procedures are used in order to effect *data transmission* (see *cellular radio*).

cellular network A *cellular radio* service offering mobile communications.

cellular radio A form of radio transmission used particularly for mobile communications. Geographical areas are divided up into 'cells' usually about three miles across. Within each cell there is a low-power radio transmitter. Adjacent cells employ different frequencies of transmission. As a user moves from one cell to another, a computer automatically changes the receiver frequency to match the transmitter.

cellular telephone A portable telephone which uses *cellular radio* techniques to carry voice-related information to and from the *PSTN*

Celtic French telecommunications device to improve the efficiency of voice transmission by data *compression*. Uses *voice activation* to assign channels to users.

Central Computer and Telecommunications Agency Agency set up by the UK Government to advise on public purchasing policies in the fields of *computers, telecommunications* and other *information technology*.

central office A US term for telephone exchange.

Central Office of Information (COI) UK Government agency with responsibility for information and publicity.

central processing unit (CPU) The heart of a computer. It contains the *arithmetic and logic unit*, the core memory and the control unit, which directs and coordinates the operation of the computer and its *peripheral units*. It thus carries out all the arithmetic, logic and control operations.

central processor *Central processing unit.*

Centre operator The organization running a *videotex* service.

Centronics Printer *interface* used in microcomputers for *parallel transmission*.

CEPT The Conference of European Postal and Telegraph Administrations. Makes recommendations on telecommunications standards.

CET Council for Educational Technology. An *information provider* for the UK *Prestel* (interactive *videotex*) service.

CETA Chinese-English Translation Assistance Group; operating a *pure MAT* system which aids translation from Chinese to English, but not vice versa (see *pure machine-aided translation* and *machine-aided translation*).

C-format Type of magnetic cassette tape used for *storage*, particularly in *home computers*.

chain A set of data items linked by a series of *pointers*.

chain indexing The production of an alphabetic index in which each

item appears under the title of each of the terms under which it falls within a *hierarchical classification*. Terms lower in the classification are listed after the higher terms. Thus, for example, an item on Shetland Ponies may have five entries:
Shetland Ponies pp20-25
Ponies – Shetland Ponies pp20-25
Horses – Ponies – Shetland Ponies pp20-25
Mammals – Ponies – Shetland Ponies pp20-25
Animals – Mammals – Ponies – Shetland Ponies pp20-25.

chain printer A printer in which the type characters are mounted on a chain which rotates at high speed.

chain search A method of searching which leads from one *record* to another until a required record is found, or the end of the chain is reached.

channel A pathway along which signals can be transmitted. Can be used in communications to mean a path for transmitting signals in one direction only (contrast with *circuit*).

Channel 2000 See *Viewtel*.

channel bank *Multiplexing* equipment.

channel group An assembly of 12 *FDM channels* within a transmission *line*, occupying adjacent frequency bands.

character A single number (0-9), letter, punctuation mark, or other symbol, eg *, #|.

character block The group of dots in a display which, used in appropriate combinations, can produce a sequence of different characters.

character byte In *videotex*, refers to the *byte* produced by adding an odd *parity bit* to a character code.

character code A *code* used to represent a *character* in a computer, or in telecommunications.

character density The number of *characters* stored in a unit length, area or volume.

character-generator In a *CRT phototypesetter*, this is the device which forms the characters on output.

character reader A device which inputs printed *characters* into a computer (see *optical character recognition* and *magnetic ink character recognition*).

character recognition The use of *pattern recognition* techniques to identify *characters* (especially *alphanumeric*). There are several types of technique, eg *magnetic ink character recognition* (MICR), *optical character recognition* (OCR).

character set The collection of numbers, letters, graphics and symbols that can be generated by a particular system.

character skew In OCR rotational displacement relative to a vertical reference line.

character space The space occupied by a *character*, or symbol, in a *videotex*, or other display.

character spacing display A facility within a word processing system for viewing text as it would appear using print formats (ie 10 or 12 *pitch*, proportionally spaced and with right or left *justification*).

character spacing reference line A vertical line used to determine the horizontal spacing of characters (see *optical character recognition*).

character string A sequence of *characters*.

character stroke A line segment or

mark used to form characters in *optical character recognition.*

character style The way in which a character is constructed in *optical character recognition.*

charge-coupled device (CCD) A *volatile storage device* made from *silicon chips.*

check bit A *binary check digit.*

check character A *character* used in carrying out an error check, as with a *check digit.*

check digit When an item is catalogued, or classified, using a sequence of digits, a check digit is sometimes added to assist the automatic detection of errors in transcription. This check digit normally has an arithmetical relationship to the classification digits. A departure from this relationship therefore indicates that an error has been made in coding, or transcribing, the sequence of digits (see, for example, *ISBN* and *ISSN*).

checkpoint-restart A point in a program at which the status of all files, *working storage* and relevant operations is recorded. It obviates the need to rerun a whole program in the event of a *hardware* or *software* failure. Instead, the system can be directed to return to the 'checkpoint' and then 'restart'.

Chemdex A *database* structured like a dictionary containing names and nomenclature derived from Chemical Abstracts. It is accessible via *SDC.*

chemical structure retrieval *Information retrieval techniques* used to index and retrieve information about chemical compounds. There are three main methods of representing chemical structures for use with computers: a. fragment codes. Standard structural fragments of compounds are given

codes, and these codes combined to describe the structure; b. topological methods. All the atoms in a compound and their bonding are represented by tables; c. linear notation. The best known system of this type is *Wiswesser line notation.*

Chemline *Database* taking the form of an *on-line* dictionary, produced by the US National Library of Medicine and accessible via a variety of *hosts.*

Chemname A *database* produced by the Chemical Abstracts Service which takes the form of an *on-line* dictionary of chemical substance names. It is accessible via *Pergamon-Infoline* and *SDC.*

child segment Describes the relative logical position of a *segment* in a *hierarchical database.*

chip A description of a single integrated circuit. It is usually in a package between 1 and 5cm in length, and having between 6 and 40 external connections. The type normally found in computer systems is called a *logic* chip. *Analog* circuits, eg an audio-frequency amplifier, can also be made as chips.

chip architecture The arrangements of *chips* forming a *microprocessor.*

chord keyboard A small, non-conventional *keyboard*, designed to be operated with one hand.

chord keying The simultaneous use of two or more keys on a single *keyboard* to *input* a *command*. A technique used to prevent loss of data by the accidental depression of certain keys.

CI 1. *Chain index.* 2. *Cumulative index.*

CICI *Confederation of Information Communication Industries* (UK).

CICIREPATO Committee for International Cooperation in Information Retrieval among Examining Patent Offices (see *ICIREPAT*).

CICS Customer Information Control System. Software run in conjunction with *IMS* to support complex *applications software* (usually in the financial services area.)

CIM Computer input microfilm. *Microfilm* used for high-speed input of information into a computer.

CIN Chemical Industry Notes. A *database* containing business-orientated information covering the chemical processing industry. Accessible via *Lockheed* and *SDC*.

CIP Cataloguing In Publication. The provision of bibliographic data on material in the process of publication. The data are included in Library of Congress and British Library *MARC* files.

CIPS Canadian Information Processing Society.

CIRCA Computerized information retrieval and current awareness.

circuit 1. The path round which an electrical current flows. 2. In telecommunications, a means of two-way communication involving 'go' and 'return' *channels*.

circuit switched data network A *data transmission* network which uses *circuit switching* techniques.

circuit switching A telecommunications term. Individual *circuits* are interconnected through successive *exchanges* to establish a continuous end-to-end connection which provides for transmission in each direction (contrast *packet switching*). Synonymous with *line switching*.

circular file A file organized so that

as new records are added, the oldest records are automatically displaced.

CIS Congressional Information Service. Built upon a *database* containing the working papers of the US Congress: it is publicly accessible via *Lockheed* and *SDC*.

CISI Compagnie Internationale de Service en Information. A Paris-based *host* linked with *Euronet DIANE*.

citation A reference to a work from which a passage is quoted, or to a source regarded as an authority for a statement, or proposition.

citation indexing A *citation* here refers to the bibliographic reference made by one document to another. A citation index lists the 'cited' documents, usually arranged alphabetically by the author. Under each cited document are also listed those documents which have cited it subsequently. Thus, from a known document, a searcher can find presumably related documents published more recently. The most developed and famous citation index is the *Science Citation Index* (see *co-citation indexing, bibliographic coupling*).

CitiService Financial and investment information provided on the *Prestel* (UK interactive *videotex*) service.

Citizens' band radio (CB) Is intended for the transmission of messages between individuals and groups, eg businesses. It uses low power transmitters, typically giving a range of up to 20 miles. In the US, where it is far more highly developed than elsewhere, most CB radios are installed in cars or trucks, and used in much the same way as radio telephones. CB radio has become so popular that there is now over-crowding of the *frequency band* allocated for CB radio (around 27 MHz in the US). American users of CB radio have developed a vocabulary of their own, which is currently being exported to other countries. CB radio can also be used for other purposes, eg the *remote control* of electronic devices.

CLAIMS/CHEM Class Codes Assigned Index Method Search/ Chemistry. A US *database* containing US chemical and chemically related patents with equivalents for Belgium, France, UK, West Germany and the Netherlands. Accessible via *Lockheed*.

CLAIMS/GEN A *database* containing US general, electrical and mechanical patents. Accessible via *Lockheed*.

C-language A *microcomputer language* developed by Bell Laboratories in the US.

classification Any systematic scheme for the arrangement of documents, usually according to their subject (see, for example, *Dewey Decimal System*).

classification and coding systems Conventions which provide a logical and meaningful basis upon which to code information or artefacts. The aim is to identify items in a way that facilitates easy identification and selective access and retrieval (see, for example, the *Brisch, Dewey Decimal, NATO, Opitz, PERA* and *Pittler systems*).

clear To erase data from a memory.

Clinical Notes Online A *bulletin board* system provided by Elsevier Science Publishers and *IRCS Medical Science*. Clinical case studies are mounted *on-line*; users may access these details and then add their own comments and experiences.

clock 1. Equipment used in *data communications* which provides a

timebase in order to control particular functions, eg the duration of *signal* elements. 2. An electric pulse generator which synchronizes all the signals in a computer.

clone See *lookalike clone*.

close classification Arrangement of subjects in a *classification* system involving a number of small subdivisions. This is necessary for the adequate definition of documents in a specialist collection.

closed circuit television (CCTV) A form of *cable television* accessible to a limited user group. It is currently used especially in security systems and in educational applications (see *educational technology*).

closed coordinated index An index prepared on the basis of a fixed list of terms, to which no new terms are added. Possible synonyms are coordinated with the 'closed' list.

closed indexing Indexing of records by means of a restricted set of terms.

closed loop System, or form, of control in which there is automatic *feedback*.

closed user group This term appears mainly in the context of *viewdata/videotex*. It refers to a group of users who are allowed *access* to data or information which is not made available to other users of the system. The facility has been used to ensure the confidentiality of medical and financial information, to provide specialized information to those who have paid a subscription to the *information provider*, and to restrict access to transaction services to customers who have signed contracts.

Club 403 A *closed user group* on the *Prestel* (UK interactive *videotex*) service, for residents of the Birmingham area.

cluster 1. A group of *terminals* and other computer devices connected so that they operate together. 2. A mathematical process whereby objects are grouped together as members of clusters. The members of each cluster have properties in common which distinguish them from other clusters. Used in some computer *information retrieval* and *classification* systems.

cluster systems See *shared resource.*

CLV *Constant Linear Velocity.*

CM Communications multiplexor (see *multiplex*).

CMC Code for magnetic characters (see *magnetic ink character recognition*).

C MOS Complementary metal oxide semiconductor. A *transistor* used in *integrated circuits.* Employed where low power consumption is required (see *N MOS* and *P MOS*).

CNC *Computer numerical control.*

CNCPT Combined Organization of Canadian National Telecommunications and Canadian Pacific Telecommunications.

CNI Canadian News Index. A *database* giving coverage of current affairs in Canada. It is accessible via QL and SDC.

CNRS Centre National de Recherche Scientifique. French funding agency for science, and *database producer.*

COAM equipment Customer owned and maintained communication equipment – such as terminals.

coax An abbreviation of *coaxial cable.*

coaxial cable A communication cable consisting of an inner central conductor, usually of copper, insulated from an outer conductor, also usually of copper. When high frequencies are passed down such a channel, there is very low loss of energy. Several such cables can be combined into a single bundle.

COBOL Common Business Orientated Language. A *high level programming language* designed especially for the manipulation of business data. It uses terms which are related to ordinary English words.

co-citation indexing A development from *citation indexing.* Co-citation pairs documents which have been cited in common by other documents. The method rests on the assumption that the more frequently documents are found to be cited in common by other documents, the more likely it is that there is a subject relationship between the documents (see *bibliographic coupling, information retrieval techniques*).

Codabar code A type of *bar-code.*

CODASYL Conference for Data System Languages. Established and developed COBOL and DBMS standards.

CODATA Committee on Data for Science and Technology of the International Council of Scientific Unions.

code A *machine language* representation of a *character.*

codec This is an abbreviation of coder-decoder. A device which converts *analog* signals to *digital* and vice versa. It is typically used to convert analog signals to digital form for *digital transmission*, and then, after transmission, to reconvert again to the original analog form.

code conversion Different
terminals may use different *codes*.
Code conversion is therefore
necessary before these can
communicate with each other. For
example, a terminal using *ASCII*
code can only be connected to one
using *Baudot* code, if *digital* devices
in the communication network
perform the conversion. If different
line control procedures are used,
these will also need conversion
before communication can take
place.

code extension The extension of
character codes to cover a greater
range and variety of characters than
are covered by the standard codes.

code key A key on the keyboard of
a *data processing* or *word*
processing terminal which is used in
giving instructions to the computer.

coden A five-character code which
uniquely designates the title of a
periodical or other serial.

coding sheet A paper form printed
with a grid of rows and columns.
Characters can be entered into each
box on the form. The resulting
format makes it easier to transcribe
the information into machine-
readable form, eg at a *card punch* or
terminal.

coherence When applied to a
computer system, refers to how well
the system performs as a whole, and
how well this performance can be
traced to individual parts of the
system.

COI *Central Office of Information.*

COINS Computer and Information
Sciences.

cold start A complete restart
following a major computer failure.

cold type Any *typesetting*
technique that does not require the
formation of characters from *hot*

metal. Synonymous with 'strike-on'.

Colleague A *database* service, in
the medical field, introduced by the
host BRS. It is aimed at individual
users with *user-friendly software*
and *access* to full text and
bibliographic databases. A *videodisc*
option is included for the provision
of graphics and illustrations.

collision detection A *protocol* on a
packet switched network in which a
terminal monitors the network to
ensure that a channel is free for
transmission (ie that there is no
danger of a 'packet collision').

collotype A photo-mechanical
process of printing from a raised
gelatine film image on a glass
support.

colour bars Standards designed to
ensure that colour television and
computer terminal equipment work
well together.

colour blind film Photographic film
that is not sensitive to all colours:
sometimes used for *microfilm.*

colour microform See *microform in*
colour.

COM Normally computer output
microfilm (sometimes *microform* or
microfiche). Instead of producing
paper output, COM systems reduce
the same information to *microfilm,*
thus offering a number of
advantages over paper output: a.
speed – pages are produced at
speeds in excess of 2,000,000 lines
per hour (cf 20,000 lines per hour for
printers); b. economy – microfilm
cost is 20 per cent that of equivalent
paper costs; c. distribution and
storage – clearly cheaper and easier,
being less bulky. The main
disadvantage is continuing reader
resistance to the medium.

combiner 1. In *CATV*, a device
enabling two or more separate
signals to be sent down a single

channel. 2. A device enabling two signals to be transmitted simultaneously from a single antenna.

Comet *Electronic mail* system operated by British Leyland (BL) Systems.

Comité Consultatif International des Radiocommunications (CCIR) One of the three main organizations within the International Telecommunications Union (ITU). CCIR is particularly involved in examining and recommending standards for long range radio communications.

Comité Consultatif International Télégraphique et Téléphonique (CCITT) One of the three main organizations within the *International Telecommunications Union* (ITU). CCITT is particularly involved in examining and recommending standards relating to telephonic and telegraphic communication.

command Any instruction to a computer.

command language Language used in *on-line searching* to facilitate a dialogue between a user and a *host* computer. It consists of a restricted range of instructions and terms. Command languages vary from host to host, eg *Dialog* for *Lockheed* and *ORBIT* for *SDC*.

commissioning The process of running a computer system under normal working conditions, but under trial, in order to ensure that the system works according to specification.

Committee Support System Developed by *DG XIII* as a computerized means of storing, forwarding, retrieving and editing documents in any of the European Community languages.

Commodore A US manufacturer of microcomputers.

common carrier An organization which provides communications services to the general public, eg *British Telecom* in the UK, or *AT&T* in the US.

common command language A *command language* established for the searching of more than one *host*. Common command languages are particularly valuable when host computers are connected in a *network*, eg *Euronet*. The searcher can then more easily switch from host to host during a search. Such a common command language is offered, for example, as an option by several *DIANE* hosts within Euronet (see *on-line searching*).

common software Computer *programs* and *routines* which are in a language common to several computers and users.

Common Technological Policy An EEC policy dealing with cooperation between member states in various fields of advanced technology, including computer and information technology.

communicating word processors Word processors connected via a network to allow very rapid office-to-office and/or institution-to-institution communication of text.

Communication Satellite Corporation (COMSAT) Based in the US, COMSAT provides technical and operational support services for the transglobal satellite communication systems using the *Intelsat* satellite services.

communication(s) buffer See *buffer*.

communications control unit A device that controls the transmission of data over a *network*.

communications mix A combination of communication media and/or techniques.

communications satellite An artificial satellite, usually in a *geostationary orbit*, which amplifies and converts the frequency of signals received from earth stations. The resulting signal is then retransmitted back to ground-based receivers (see *satellite communication*).

communications server See *server*.

Communication Technology Satellite Canadian *communications satellite* launched in 1976. The first operational satellite dedicated to direct television transmission (see *direct transmission satellite*).

community antenna relay system *Microwave* system for the transmission of *CATV* signals to the *head end*.

community antenna television See *cable television*.

COMPAC Computer output microfilm package (see *COM*).

compact disc An *optical storage medium* on which sound (*analogue*) is recorded in *digital* form. It consists of a plastic disc, $4\frac{3}{4}$ inches in diameter, and coated with a reflective material. The audio compact disc plays on one side only and gives up to 75 minutes of music. Digital recording techniques are used, giving a dynamic range of sound corresponding to 90 *decibels* or more (as compared to 60/70 decibels with conventional analogue systems). Compact discs are read by *laser*, so there is no physical contact with the surface of the disc. Because of the digital storage technique employed, compact discs can be used for the storage and retrieval of all kinds of digitally encoded data, including computer storage (see *CD-ROM*).

compact disc – interactive A set of specifications which define how *multi-media* formats can be encoded on *compact disc* with the aim of enabling *interactive* applications to be carried out. *CD-ROM* is only one of several possibilities provided by this new application which allows the convergence of audio, video, text, *digital data* and *applications programs* on compact disc.

compaction algorithm An *algorithm* to achieve data compaction (ie reducing data into a more compact form requiring fewer *bits*). It is used, for example, in digital *facsimile transmission*.

companding Compressing and expanding. Information in *bits* can often be recoded into a more compact form for transmission, using a *compaction algorithm*. A complementary algorithm can recover the original form; the entire process represents companding.

compartment A set of related programs within a larger system.

compatibility Refers generally to the ability of two (*hardware/ software*) devices to work in conjunction: eg if a *floppy disc* can be read by a particular *word processing* system, they are said to be compatible. Computer compatibility usually means software compatibility. If a *program* can be successfully run on two computers, without alteration to the program, then the computers are said to be compatible (see *upwards compatibility*).

COMPENDEX Computerized Engineering Index. A *database* covering all branches of engineering. Accessible via most of the major *hosts*.

compile To translate a *high level language* into a sequence of *machine language* instructions for the computer.

compiler A *program* which *compiles*.

compose See *composition*.

composite video A type of *output* signal used for computer *displays* (see *RGB* and *RF*).

composition 1. Preparation of copy in a *format* which can be duplicated. 2. Filing *records* in a *storage device* (see *computer-aided phototypesetting*).

compression (techniques) See *compressor*.

compressor Any electronic device which compresses the range of a signal. The aim is to improve the proportion of wanted to unwanted signals and enhance the efficiency of transmission (see *companding*).

compunications Computers and communications. A jargon term referring to the joint use of computers and communication systems. Thus it has a similar meaning to *information technology*.

compuscript A manuscript which has been composed on a computer, usually by means of a *word processing package*, and transmitted electronically to the publisher for input to a *phototypesetter*.

CompuServe A US *videotex* service, provided by the CompuServe Information Service.

computer An *electronic* device which receives *input data*, puts them into *storage*, operates on them according to a *program*, and *outputs* the result to the user.

Computer Acquisition System A US *teleordering* system.

computer-aided design (CAD) The use of computers to aid design involves *computer graphics*, modelling, analysis, simulation and optimization of designs for production.

computer-aided instruction (CAI) Refers to the use of computers as *teaching machines*. The computer presents instructional material, and asks questions of increasing difficulty, at a rate determined by the correctness of a student's responses. If a student is unable to give correct responses, the computer is *programmed* to give additional instructional material, and to ask less demanding questions. By this method, called *programmed learning*, tuition is adapted to the needs of the individual students. CAI systems often incorporate a facility for monitoring each student's progress, thus obviating some of the need for examinations. If, however, examinations are required, a CAI machine can be programmed to administer them (see *educational technology*).

computer-aided manufacture (CAM) The use of computers and numerical control equipment to aid manufacturing processes (see *numerical control, computer numerical control* and *direct numerical control*). It can also include *robotics* and automated testing procedures.

computer-aided page make-up The use of computers to automate, or semi-automate, the formation of text and graphics into discrete pages. Automatic page make-up is easier for 'directory' type material, where acceptable page-breaks can be readily codified. Semi-automatic page make-up uses a *cathode ray tube* (CRT) to present text for manipulation by an operator.

computer-aided phototypesetting Phototypesetting means, in general, the preparation of material for printing using an optical system. A phototypesetter has four basic components: a light source, a character (type) store, a lens system, and a light-sensitive recording

medium.
Several *generations* of
phototypesetter exist, each
exhibiting an advance in technology
(examples of each type are still in
use). First-generation
photocomposers were adaptations of
traditional *hot metal* casters. The
metal melting pot and mould of the
latter are replaced by a photographic
unit. These machines were often
called 'filmsetters'. Such devices are
essentially mechanical in operation
and slow.
Second-generation phototypesetters
are also electro-mechanical in
nature, but faster. Characters are
mounted on discs, or drums. Their
speed makes it desirable that they
should be run by remote control –
for example, by computer. This
makes them the earliest generation
of computer-aided phototypesetters.
Third-generation phototypesetters
are essentially electronic, using CRT
character generators. These use
characters stored in *digital* form,
whose appearance can then be
electronically manipulated. The final
characters are displayed on a screen,
which is then exposed to a
photosensitive medium. They can be
very fast: for example, an advanced
system may set up to 3,000 lines of
newspaper column per minute.
Fourth-generation phototypesetters
have a digital character store, but
employ *lasers* for imaging, and have
good potential for graphics as well
as text.
The input devices of
phototypesetting have changed
considerably. Early types used *blind
keyboards* and material was stored
on *punched tape* (ie operators could
not see what was set until
composition had taken place).
Direct-entry phototypesetters are
now common. A variety of outputs
now exist: *paper tape, magnetic
tape, floppy discs*, etc. Text can then
be displayed (as hard copy, or on a
screen) for examination and
correction before being fed into the
computer-controlled
phototypesetter.

Word processors can be used as the
input stage to a phototypesetter: it is
becoming increasingly easy to
interface such devices, with
consequent savings in costs of
keyboarding.
The computer editing of text
followed by input to a
phototypesetter is known as *text
processing* (although this is
sometimes also used as a synonym
for word processing).

computer-aided translation (CAT)
Synonymous with *machine-aided
translation*.

computer-aided typesetting A
general term for the use of a
computer at any stage in the
typesetting, or composition, process.
At the simplest level, it is concerned
with automatic *justification*,
hyphenation, etc. At a more
advanced level, it refers to *word
processor* input to the
phototypesetting operation, or direct
to a phototypesetter, as well as
computer-aided page make-up.

**Computer and Control
Abstracts** A UK-based *database*
covering computers and control.
This includes *cybernetics*,
information science, mathematical
techniques and *software*. Accessible
via most of the major *hosts*.

computer-assisted instruction
(CAI) See *computer-aided
instruction*.

**computer-assisted interactive
tutorial system** A system in which
a *computer* is *programmed* to
perform the role of tutor in
(normally) a one-to-one tutorial. The
student uses the computer, either
passively, as a recipient of
programmed learning, or, actively, in
a mode which permits the student to
ask questions and the computer to
respond (see *computer-aided
instruction, programmed learning*
and *educational technology*).

computer-assisted (or aided) learning (CAL) 1. Another name for a *computer-aided instruction* (CAI) system. 2. The receipt of 'tuition' from a CAI system.

computer-assisted retrieval The use of computers to aid the organization and identification of documents stored on *microform*.

computer-assisted teaching Synonymous with *computer-assisted instruction*.

computer-based messaging system Any computer system which supports messaging, including *electronic mail*, *bulletin boards* and *computer conferencing*.

computer bureau 1. An agency which runs other people's work on its own computer and often offers additional types of computing assistance and consultancy. 2. A large international company which offers *host* facilities to provide access to *on-line databases*. Such bureaux were established to offer *time-sharing* facilities and have large resources of computer *storage* and sophisticated *software* which clients may use on-line. They usually specialize in statistical databases and derive most of their income from the time the client spends on-line *manipulating* the data retrieved.

computer conferencing The interchange of messages on a particular topic via a computer *network* (see *electronic mail*, *electronic journal* and *teleconferencing*).

computer graphics The use of computers to generate and display pictorial images. A user can generate these images using either a *keyboard*, or some special graphic *input* device.
The simplest approach is that of *vector graphics*. If a keyboard is used, the parameters can be entered, and the corresponding curve then appears on the screen. More than one curve can be entered and displayed simultaneously, and a variety of colours can be used.
As well as two-dimensional shapes, three-dimensional objects can be shown in perspective. Once entered, these forms can be manipulated: they can be moved, elongated, rotated about any axis, etc. These operations can be effected in some systems by using a *light pen*, applied directly to the display screen. Other systems use a *graphics tablet*: a special stylus is used to draw and manipulate forms on a tablet of semiconducting material (see *digitizing tablet* and *electro-acoustic tablet*). An alternative to vector graphics is *raster graphics*. This utilizes a matrix of *pixels* covering the display screen, so that, when a particular group of these picture cells are illuminated, they describe an image. Each pixel has its own *code* and is switched on, or off, according to the controlling *program*.
Using either vector or raster graphics, images, once entered, can be directed to a *storage device*, or transmitted to a distant *terminal*. In addition, the images can be directed to an *output device* to produce a wide variety of types of film, or print-on-paper copy (see, for example, *film recorders*, *flat-bed plotters*, *graphics plotters* and *ink jet printers*). With this flexibility, computer graphics clearly has major implications for *computer-aided design*, animation techniques, the production of audiovisual aids to communication and the electronic communication of information in graphical form (as an alternative to text or numerical form). However, the current comparatively high costs of computer graphics systems may delay their widespread introduction.

computer input microfilm See *CIM*.

computerization 1. The process of converting manual systems to ones under computer control. 2. The conversion of information held in *hard-copy* form to *machine-readable* form.

computer-integrated manufacture See *computer-aided manufacture*.

computer journal See *electronic journal*.

computer language 1. *Machine language*. 2. A language in which instructions are given to a computer by a programmer, or user.

computer letter A letter of standard form into which personal details (ie recipient's name and address) are inserted using *word processing* software. Used extensively in marketing.

computer literacy Having a general idea of how computers work and what they do.

computer mail See *electronic mail*.

computer memory See *memory*.

computer micrographics A computer system handling *CIM* and/or *COM*.

computer network See *network*.

computer numerical control Describes a situation in which a number of *numerical control* machines are linked together via a *data transmission network* and thus brought under the control of a single numerical control machine.

computer output microfilm See *COM*.

computer printout See *printout*.

computer readout See *readout*.

computer security Measures taken to protect a computer installation or computer *network* against

accidental or intentional damage, and to prevent unauthorized *access* to any of the *software* or *files* associated with it (see *data security*, *encryption*).

Computer Software Copyright Act A US Act, passed in November 1980.

computer typesetting See *computer-aided typesetting* and *computer-aided phototypesetting*.

computing amplifiers See *operational amplifiers*.

computing power A term referring to the speed with which complex operations may be performed in a computing system.

COMSAT See *Communication Satellite Corporation*.

COMSTAR *Communications satellites* provided by COMSAT General (a subsidiary of *COMSAT*) for *AT&T*, and used for internal communication within the US.

COMTEC Computer Micrographics and Technology. A Californian-based group of users and manufacturers of *COM* equipment.

concatenation Adding *records*, *fields* or *character strings* to other records, fields or character strings.

concentrator A device which divides one or more data transmission channels into a larger number. Use of the latter is allocated in such a way as to maximize the throughput of data. Incoming data may, for example, be placed in a *buffer* to achieve this aim.

concertina fold Synonymous with a *fan-fold*.

concordance program A *program* which analyses text and provides a list of words showing each occurrence and its immediate context.

Concurrent CP/M See *CP/M*.

conditioning Procedures used to ensure that the quality of data transmitted lies within specified limits.

CONF See *Conference Papers Index*.

Confederation of Information Communication Industries A UK association of organizations concerned with the UK information industry, established in response to the *ITAP* report on 'Making a business of information'. Its aim is to develop and expand national and international markets for UK information products and services.

CONFER *Software* developed by Information Management and Engineering for conference organization. A specially designed public *interface* for up to 10 *terminals* allows participants to find out who is giving papers, times and locations of sessions and use its built-in messaging system.

Conference Papers Index (CONF or CPI) *Database* covering papers presented at about a thousand conferences per annum. It is accessible via *Lockheed* and *SDC*.

configuration The layout of the *hardware* in a particular computer system.

conflation algorithm A computer procedure (see *algorithm*) of particular value as an *information retrieval technique*. Where use is made of *natural language* terms for *indexing*, problems can arise from different forms of related words, eg 'computing' and 'computational'. A conflation algorithm reduces all words with the same root to a single form by removing all the derivational or inflectional parts.

Confravision *Teleconferencing*

service offered by *British Telecom*. Two or three conference studios in different cities can be simultaneously interconnected.

connectivity The degree to which equipment may be connected for the purpose of communications or *file* transfer (see *compatibility*).

connectors The *Boolean operators* AND, OR and NOT used to connect terms used in a *search*. Some *information retrieval software* has additional operators such as ADJ (adjacent), W (width) and F (in the same field).

CONSER Conversion of Serials Project. A US project to create and maintain large *machine-readable databases* on serial publications, eg journals, periodicals.

console That part of a *data processing system* which allows the operator to communicate with the computer, usually utilizing a keyboard (see *terminal*).

constant Part of a computer *program* whose quantity or value is fixed and cannot be changed during execution of the program (see *variable*).

constant length field An entry on a document or card requiring a fixed number of *alphanumeric characters*.

Constant Linear Velocity A type of *videodisc* operation which provides increased storage capacity by using a variable speed of rotation of the disc.

Consultative Committee on International Radio (CCIR) One of the three main organizations within the *International Telecommunications Union* (ITU). CCIR is particularly involved in examining and recommending standards for long-range radio communication.

content-addressed memory See *associative storage.*

contention A situation in which two or more devices simultaneously attempt to access a facility.

continuation page A *videotex* page which cannot be separately *addressed*; it forms a continuation of the main page listed in the system's *menu.*

continuous graphics A set of *videotex* characters which are able to occupy a display fully, ie there are no gaps between. Compare with *separated graphics.*

continuous stationery A continuous piece of paper in a roll, or stacked in a *fan-fold*, with horizontal perforations to separate the pages and holes along the sides of the paper for the *tractor feed*

continuous tone Used in graphics to describe a picture with continuously varying grey tones, as in an ordinary black-and-white photograph (contrast *half-tone*).

contrast In *optical character recognition*, the difference between the reflectance of two adjacent areas (normally black text and white paper).

control block An area of storage used by a program to hold control information.

control character A *character* whose occurrence in a particular context can change a control operation. A typical example is a character that can initiate *carriage return.*

control device The device which controls the movements of the *cursor* around the display *screen.* Various means are available: controls may be issued via the *keyboard*, by using a *mouse*, *joystick* or *pointer*, or via a *touch-*screen terminal.

controlled indexing language See *information retrieval techniques.*

controlled vocabulary A fixed list of terms used to index records for storage and retrieval. The use of controlled vocabulary is normally required in *on-line searching.*

controller A device which coordinates the functioning of a set of *remote* devices (eg *VDUs* and *local printers*) and enables them to *interface* with a *host processor.*

control track In *video recording*, a track on the tape records pulses which synchronize the *head* and the drive for recording and replaying.

convergence Describes the coming together of technologies which in the past have been regarded as relatively distinct, eg computers, telecommunications, printing and publishing, to provide integrated systems. One example is the concept of the *electronic office.*

conversational language Natural language used to communicate with a computer in *conversational mode.*

conversational mode *On-line* interaction between a computer and user in the form of a dialogue. Each 'participant' responds in turn to the information or response presented by the other.

Converse A system for the *on-line* description and retrieval of *data* using *natural language.* (Developed by *SDC* in the US.)

conversion The process whereby a *file* or *database* is converted from one logical structure to another.

converter A computer *peripheral* which converts *data* from one physical form to another, eg *punched card* to *magnetic tape.*

copy A manuscript that is to be *composed* and printed.

copyright The legal mechanism by which intellectual property rights are protected. Copyright considerations apply to many sorts of work, including the spoken word, printed text and music, musical and other performances, in recorded form and computer *software*.

Copyright Clearance Center A US non-profit-making organization which offers licensing arrangements for the *photocopying* of documents.

Copyright Licensing Agency A UK organization composed of the Publishers Association, the Association of Learned and Professional Society Publishers, the Periodical Publishers Association, the Society of Authors and the Writers' Guild. It has proposed a blanket licensing scheme, under which licences would be issued to owners of reprographic equipment from whom royalties would be collected in return for blanket permission to make copies of works.

cordless telephone Portable, radio-based telephone which is not connected to the *PSTN* by wiring, but uses a radio link to nearby PSTN connections.

corecol A contraction of COmmon REvenue COLlector. One element in plans to allow users of *information retrieval systems* to find information from the databases offered by several *host* operators in one search, instead of contacting each in turn. A corecol would deal with the billing for this type of service.

core memory Synonymous with *core storage*.

core storage The computer's internal *memory* to which data and data processing instructions are sent for storage before being processed by the *CPU*. The processed data are held in core storage until transferred to *auxiliary storage*, directed to an *output device*, or erased (see *random access memory*).

corporate electronic publishing *Desktop publishing* techniques used in-house by business corporations to produce advertising literature, manuals, reports and other short-run publications.

correcting code See *error correcting code*.

corruption The unintended alteration or mutilation of data during processing, storage or transmission.

COS Corporation for Open *Systems*: an American-based consortium of computer suppliers and users concerned with facilitating interconnection between different makes of computer.

COSAP Cooperative On-line Serials Acquisition Project (see *teleordering*).

COSTAR Conversational *on-line storage and retrieval* (see *on-line searching* and *information retrieval systems*).

CPBX Computerized Private Branch Exchange (see *CBX*).

CPI *Conference Papers Index*.

CP/M Control Program/ Microcomputers. A widely used microcomputer *operating system*. CP/M was originally written for *8-bit* machines. More powerful versions are now available for *16-bit* computers and for *multi-tasking*, eg *Concurrent CP/M*, *CP/M-86* and *MP/M*.

CP/M-86 See *CP/M*.

CPM 1. Cards per minute (the rate at which a *card reader* operates). 2. *Critical path method*.

CPS 1. *Characters* per second. 2. Cycles per second (=hertz).

CPU *Central processing unit.*

CPW *Communicating word processor.*

crash The shutdown of a computer system because of a malfunction of hardware, or software (see *program crash*).

Cray-1 A *supercomputer*. One of its distinguishing features is its circular shape. It is so constructed in order to minimize the length of wiring required, and thus speed up the computer's operation.

Crecord *Database* giving comprehensive coverage of the Congressional Record: the official journal of US Congress proceedings. The database is accessible via *SDC*.

CRESS Computer Reader Enquiry Service System (for libraries).

critical path method (CPM) A management technique for scheduling and controlling large projects, particularly those which involve a large number of interdependent phases. The nature of each phase and its dependencies is incorporated into a 'network' of events, and *software packages* are widely available for the mounting of such networks within a computer. This allows progress to be monitored, 'automatic' progress reports to be written, problems, eg hold-up and resource acquisition difficulties, to be analysed, and management strategies to be simulated. Sometimes also called *PERT* or *network planning*.

CROSSBOW Computerized Retrieval of Organic Structures Based on Wiswesser. A *software* system for use with the *Wiswesser Line Notation* system to allow computer searches for information on chemical compounds.

cross fire *Interference* between *telegraph* and *telephone* circuits.

crossfoot To add across several domains of numerical information.

cross talk In telecommunications, the unwanted transfer of energy from one circuit to another.

CRT *Cathode ray tube* but the acronym is sometimes used to refer to the complete *cathode ray tube display unit.*

CRT composition A *phototypesetter* in which the characters are generated on the face of a *CRT*, rather than projected from a master grid or disc.

cryogenics The application of very low temperatures – close to absolute zero – to the use of *semi conductors* and *integrated circuits*. At these temperatures, metals lose almost all their resistance and, correspondingly, have greatly increased conductivity (see *superconductivity*).

CSDN *Circuit switched data network.*

CSMA/CD Carrier sensing with multiple access/collision detect (see *broadcast network*).

CSIPR Comité Spécial et International sur les Parasites Radiotélégraphiques (see *International Special Committee on Radio Interference*).

CSIRONET Commonwealth Scientific and Industrial Research Organization (CSIRO) Network. A *computer network* offering *on-line* access within Australia to the *databases* of CSIRO (see *on-line searching, MIDAS* and *AUSINET*).

CSS *Committee Support System.*

CTI Centre de Traitement de l'Information. A Belgium-based *host*.

CTS 1. Computer typesetting (see *computer-aided typesetting*). 2. *Communications Technology Satellite.*

cuetrack In *video tape recording*, a track on the tape on which are recorded verbal instructions and editing codes.

CUG *Closed user group.*

CULT system Chinese University Language Translation (Hong Kong). An HAMT system used to translate Chinese journals into English (see *HAMT, machine translation* and *machine-aided translation*).

cumulative index An index containing all items appearing in a number of separate indexes.

currency The degree to which information is up-to-date and therefore still valid.

current awareness service Any service that alerts users to new information likely to be of interest to them. Such information is typically bibliographic and retrieved by computers (see *selective dissemination of information*).

cursor A light indicator on a *VDU*, which shows where the next *character* is to be generated. The cursor can be moved across the screen by use of a key on the *keyboard*.

cut-and-paste The use of scissors and glue to cut up and incorporate existing material into new documents. The same principle can be applied to computerized information, by using computer *files* instead of *hard copy* as sources.

cut sheet feeder Device found on a *printer* which allows cut sheets rather than *continuous stationery* to be used (see *tractor feed*).

CWP *Communicating word processor.*

Cybernetics Theory of communications and control which accounts for the operations of systems in terms of *feedback* effects.

CYCLADES French *packet switching network.*

cycle A complete sequence of operations, at the end of which the series can be repeated.

cycle time The time required to read a *word* from the computer *memory* and write it back again. Also used in the more general sense of *response time.*

cyclic code Synonymous with *gray code.*

Cyclops audio graphics system A system originally designed by the Open University (UK) to augment the teaching of its (home-based) students. Sound and graphics are recorded on an *audio cassette*. This can either be viewed *locally*, or transmitted over telephone lines (and via a *modem* and audio-graphic *terminal*) to be received on a television set. The tape can be stopped at any convenient time to allow tutor and students to confer: messages can be sent by drawing with a *light pen* on the television screen.
The audio-graphic 'studio' and 'terminal' are now generally available, and their use for *distance learning* and industrial training is being evaluated (see *educational technology* and *computer-assisted interactive tutorial system*).

cylinder A set of aligned concentric *tracks* on a magnetic *disc pack.*

cylinder scanning A form of *scanning* used in *facsimile transmission*. So called because the object image, eg a printed page, is wrapped round a rotating cylinder which is scanned by the photosensitive device. Also called *drum scanning.*

D

DAA Direct access arrangement.

DACOM Datascope computer output microfilmer. An early output device for *COM*.

DAC system Data acquisition and control system.

DAI Distributed Artificial Intelligence.

daisy wheel printer A printer where the typehead is circular, with the characters attached round it on the ends of stalks. Such printers are commonly found as a part of *word processing* systems.

DAR Daily activity report. A computer-generated report on library operations.

DARC *Software* for *on-line searching* offered by the French *host* Télésystèmes-Questel. The *program* allows the user to search chemical abstracts by using chemical structures.

DARE 1. Data retrieval system for the social and human sciences run by *UNESCO*. 2. Documentation automated retrieval equipment. Equipment used in *automated information retrieval and document delivery systems*.

dark-trace CRT A *CRT* in which the surface does not glow brightly under electron bombardment. Instead, it is coated with a substance which produces a dark image against the white surface of the tube.

DART Diagnostic Assistance Reference Tool. A type of *expert system* being developed by Stanford University and *IBM*, to be used by a computer in analysing its own performance.

DASD Direct access storage device (see *direct access storage media*).

Daspan The data communications network facilities of the US-based multinational corporation *RCA*.

Typical daisy wheel printer.

DAT *Digital audio tape.*

data Groups of *characters* (*alphanumeric* or otherwise) which represent a specified value or condition. Data provide the building blocks of information.

data acquisition and control system A system in which a central computer is connected to a number of *remote terminals*. The computer receives data from, and transmits data to, such terminals while operating in *real time*.

data analysis A technique used to derive optimal *data structures* from an analysis of patterns of data usage.

databank Usually an alternative term for a *database*. However, it is sometimes used to refer exclusively to a collection of factual, or numerical, data, as distinct from a *bibliographic database*, which gives references to documents.

database A store of data on *files* which can be made accessible to a computer. It is designed for operation in connection with an *information retrieval system*. The word is often hyphenated (database), or spelt as two separate words (data base).

Database administrator A person who designs logical database structures, determines how they should be physically allocated on a *disc/disc pack*, monitors database performance (eg data *access times*) and seeks to optimize its performance. The term is sometimes also used to describe software designed to assist or perform one or more of these functions.

Data Base Index An internal *SDC* index, acting as a master index to all SDC *databases*. It is used to aid the selection of the most suitable database for a given search.

database management system *Software* designed to control the loading and running of a *database*.

database producer An organization which creates a *database* and makes it available commercially, often via a *host*.

database umbrella organization An organization which provides services for the creation and maintenance of *databases*. A term especially associated with *viewdata* information providers.

data capture A general term covering techniques for converting data into *machine-readable* form. These include direct input on a computer, or *word processing*, keyboard, or via *direct acquisition* devices.

data carrier A medium, eg cards, paper, *magnetic tape*, or *discs*, used for recording data.

Datacentralen Danish *on-line* information system connected with *Euronet DIANE*.

data circuit A *circuit* which allows communication between any two pieces of *data terminal equipment*.

data circuit terminating equipment Equipment located at each end of a *data circuit* which provides all the necessary functions to establish, maintain and terminate a connection. It also executes the *signal* conversion and coding between the *data terminal equipment* and the telephone line (see *modem*).

data collection platform An automatic *earth station* in a *satellite communications* system.

DATACOM 1. *Western Union* data communication service linking over 60 US cities. 2. A global communications *network* used by the US Air Force.

data communications The transmission of information in digital form via communications *networks*.

data compaction Refers to methods used to reduce the space and time required for data storage and transmission.

data compression Reducing the size of data elements by changing the way in which they are *coded*.

data concentrator See *concentrator*.

data definition language Used to define the overall logical structure of a *database* (a *CODASYL* concept).

data dictionary A listing of the names and attributes of *fields* within a *database*, defining how those fields are grouped (into *segments*) and how those segments relate to one another to form a *data structure*.

data display unit A *display* unit based on a *CRT*.

data entry Entering *commands* or information into a computer system. A variety of *input devices* may be used for this purpose.

dataflow computing A form of *parallel computer* in which the work is broken down into discrete items between which there is a controlled flow of data.

data flow diagram *Systems analysis* technique.

datagram A *packet* in a *packet switched* system that contains sufficient information to enable it to reach its destination.

data haven A country which does not operate stringent *data protection* legislation. Organizations from

countries with more stringent regulations may move their *data processing* activities to a data haven.

Data-Inform A/S A Danish *on-line* information service containing information on travel and tourism. The *database* can be searched in any one of six languages, and confirmation and invoices can be effected automatically. The service is available via *Euronet DIANE* information services.

dataline A line in a television broadcast signal used to carry *teletext* data.

data link 1. A physical connection over which data can be transmitted. 2. The physical medium of transmission, the devices, *protocols* and programs that enable data to be transferred from a *data source* to a *data sink*.

data manipulation Working on, or altering the *format* of, information retrieved from another source, usually from an *on-line database*. This may take the form of statistical analysis, the generation of reports and graphics, or the merging of material with the user's own existing data.

data manipulation language A *language* which enables an *applications program* written in a *high level language* to access and process data held on a *database* (ie it provides an *interface* between the applications program and a *DBMS*).

data network A telecommunications *network* linking *terminals*, via which data are communicated.

data packet Data divided into packets of about a hundred *bits* for transmission (see *packet switching*).

Datapac Network A commercial *network* linking *Telenet* in the US with the Trans Canada Network (ie the major American and Canadian computer networks).

Datapak Danish *packet switching* telecommunications network.

Dataphone Digital Service *Digital* data transmission system operated by *AT&T*. It is available in over 150 cities in the US.

dataplex *Multiplexed* data communications.

data plotter Synonymous with *plotter*, also sometimes called an x-y *plotter*.

data processing (DP) Includes all clerical, arithmetical and logical operations on data. Data processing in the context of information technology always implies the use of a computer for these operations.

data processing cycle The sequence of operations commonly associated with data processing (ie collection of data; conversion into *machine-readable* form; checking, or *validation*; processing, or *manipulating* the data; display and storage of results).

data processing system The computer *hardware* and *software* required to carry out *data processing* activities.

data protection Actions taken to safeguard *personal data* held on computers (see *Data Protection Act*).

Data Protection Act The UK Data Protection Act became law in 1984. Its purpose is to provide protection for individuals whose personal details are held on computer *files*. The Act follows similar legislation in Europe and North America, and is partly designed to avoid the possibility of other countries refusing to allow the transfer of *personal data*, in computer readable form, to the UK. It imposes obligations upon *data users*; they

must 'register' with the *Data Protection Registrar*, maintain 'good practice in relation to their personal data' (eg ensure that data are secure while giving the individual access to details about him/herself), and be open about the uses made of personal data.

Data Protection Authority Sometimes used to describe the office of the *Data Protection Registrar*.

Data Protection Convention Convention drawn up by the Council of Europe, laying down principles (similar to those proposed by the *Lindop Committee*) for the regulation of computer data to protect the privacy of the individual.

Data Protection Registrar A role created by the *Data Protection Act*: to maintain a public register of users of *personal data*, to publicize the Act and its operation, to promote observance of *data protection* principles, and to consider complaints about contravention of the Act.

data radio The transmission of data using radio waves. One example is *teletext*.

data reduction Transforming large bodies of raw *data* into useful, ordered, or simplified *information*.

data response The feedback *channel* for *data transmission* in a two-way system.

Dataroute Canadian digital data communications network.

data security The control of access to data held within a computer system. Usually achieved by issuing a series of confidential *passwords* to authorized personnel. *Software* then checks that the correct sequence of passwords has been entered into the computer before it will output information, or permit stored information to be changed.

data set Another name for a *modem*.

data set adapter Device for *interfacing a computer* and a *modem*. It breaks down *bytes* from a computer into *bits* for *serial transmission*. This process is reversed for received signals.

data sink Part of a terminal that receives data.

Datasolve A *host* specializing in providing access to *full-text databases*.

data source Part of a terminal that sends data into a *data link*.

Data-Star Swiss *on-line search* service offered by *Radio Suisse*.

data structure A set of specified relationships between items of data which facilitate easy access to particular *fields* when updating, or accessing, a database.

data subject Used in the *Data Protection Act* to denote an individual whose *personal data* are held on computer.

data tablet A device with which to *input graphics*. A pen-shaped stylus is moved over a flat electromagnetically sensitive board, and the pen's position over the board is monitored by a computer. In this way, it is possible to draw images directly into the computer.

data tagging A technique in the compilation of bibliographic *databases*. Data tags are *codes* that indicate and uniquely identify specified types of *data* in a *source document*. The tags are attached to the bibliographic references, and then used as an aid in searching the database.

data terminal equipment Any equipment at which a communications channel begins or ends (see *data circuit terminating equipment*).

data transfer device Transportable equipment which can accept data from a range of *word processors* and store them either on *disc* or *cassette* (see *milking machine*).

data transfer rate The rate at which data are written, read, or transmitted (normally measured in characters per second).

data transmission See *data communications*.

data user Used in the *Data Protection Act* to denote a collector or holder of *personal data*.

Datavision A Swedish *viewdata* (interactive *videotex*) system.

Datel services British *Telecom* services enabling data to be transmitted over the public switched telephone network (see *switching*) or *leased circuits*. There are six different Datel services, with varying *data transmission* rates and performance characteristics.

Datex-P The West German *public packet switched data transmission network*.

db *Decibel*.

DBAM Database access method. A general computing term covering, eg *direct access* and *random access*.

dBase II, dBase III A microcomputer-based *database management system*.

DBI *Database index*.

DBMS *Database management system*.

DBOS Disc-based operating system.

DBS Direct broadcast satellite.

DC 1. Direct current. 2. Display console (eg VDU). 3. Digital computer. 4. Decimal classification. 5. Data conversion. 6. Detail condition (specification of condition). 7. Design change. 8. Direct coupled (see direct coupling).

DCA Document Content Architecture. A standard announced by IBM in connection with SNA. DCA is intended to provide a framework for defining the format of individual documents to be used in IBM office automation systems in order to ensure that documents are portable between different systems (DIA).

DCE Data circuit terminating equipment.

DCR 1. Data conversion receiver. 2. Digital conversion receiver. 3. Design change recommendation.

DD 1. Digital data. 2. Digital display. 3. Data demand.

DDC 1. Dewey Decimal Classification, sometimes also abbreviated to DC. 2. Direct digital control. Under the control of a digital computer.

DDCE Digital data conversion equipment. Equipment for converting digital data into some other form.

DDD Direct distance dialling.

DDL Data definition language.

DDP 1. Digital data processor. 2. Distributed data processing (see distributed processing).

DDS 1. A data dictionary system. 2. Dynamic defect skipping. A technique used in the production of optical storage media which allows errors to be corrected during the writing process. 3. Digital display scope. 4. Digital dataphone service.

DDT 1. Digital data transmitter. 2. A software package designed to assist the debugging of programs.

DE 1. Display element. 2. Digital element. 3. Decision element. 4. Display equipment.

deadlock In a computer operating system, deadlock exists when two programs, or processes, are concurrently executed, but each has allocated for its own use a resource which cannot be shared. Processing then ceases until priorities are allocated.

deadly embrace Synonymous with deadlock.

debit card system A form of bank on-line teller system. Plastic 'debit cards', incorporating magnetic strips, are issued by banks to their customers. The strip records the customer's personal identification number. To use the card, the customer inserts it into a terminal and keys in the corresponding identification number. Having thus gained access to the system, the customer can, via the keyboard, deposit or withdraw funds (or implement certain other types of request). The transaction is recorded on the card, as well as in the bank's computer.

debit magnetic strip(e) reader A device for reading the magnetic strips which appear on debit cards (see debit card systems), credit cards and cards used in electronic funds transfer systems.

debug (debugging) Isolate and correct errors in a computer routine or program.

DEC Digital Equipment Corporation. A US manufacturer

and *database producer.*

decade A group of 10 items. Usually refers to *storage* locations.

decentralized system A computer system in which the *processing* functions are distributed over a number of devices (see *distributed system*).

decibel A unit used in measuring the relative power of a signal. Usually abbreviated to db.

decimal classification system One of the most widely used systems for cataloguing documents in libraries according to their subject matter. The main classes and sub-classes are designated by a number composed of three digits. Further sub-divisions are represented by numbers after a decimal point. For example, the number range 300-399 is allocated to Social Sciences; 369 = Sociology; 369.1 = Anthropology; 369.11 = Primitive Sex.

deck A set of *cards* used for a particular computer *program.* They are usually sequentially numbered so that they can be kept in order.

declarative language A *programming language* which allows sets of logical relationships (these may include *fuzzy logic*) and general principles to be declared, and then used by a computer in order to perform a task or solve a problem. Declarative languages (eg PROLOG) are being used most extensively for the development of *expert systems.*

decode The interpretation by a computer of the instructions which are input to it (see *code*).

dedicated A *program*, procedure, machine, *network channel*, or system set apart for special use.

dedicated port An access point to a communication *channel* which is

used only for one specific type of traffic.

default A particular value of a variable which is used by a computer system unless it is specifically alerted via the keyboard to use another value. For example, a computer chess player may assume its lowest level of play unless the operator keys in a higher one.

definition The degree to which detail is shown by an image. Particularly significant in *display devices* and readers, eg *optical character reader, microform reader.*

deflection plates Used to create *electrostatic deflection* in a *CRT.*

degradation Deterioration in the quality of a transmitted signal.

delay line A device for introducing a time delay into the transmission of data, eg for bringing together data arriving at different times. There are various types of delay line, eg acoustic, magnetic.

delimiter One of a pair of characters which mark the bounds, for example, of a *string* of characters.

delivery time The time interval between the start of transmission at an initiating *terminal* and the completion of reception at a receiving terminal.

delta modulation A form of *pulse code modulation.*

demand A service operated by the US Library of Congress which makes use of *optical disc* and *videodisc* technology. The Library reproduces and supplies catalogue cards to libraries all over the world. Over 200,000 images of master cards are stored on one side of an optical disc and these can be retrieved and printed out on demand using a high resolution *laser printer* at the rate of 12 copies per second.

demand multiplexing A form of *time division multiplexing* in which time slots are allocated in response to user demand.

demand processing The processing of data virtually as they arrive; ie they are not accumulated in any storage device other than an input *buffer*.

demand staging A computing technique in which *blocks* of data are moved from one storage device to another, which has a shorter *access time*, when the data are requested by a program (see *anticipatory staging*.)

demodulation The reconstitution of an original signal from a modulated one. The opposite process to *modulation*.

demodulator A device for carrying out *demodulation*.

demultiplexing The reverse of *multiplexing*.

Dendral An *expert system* used to ascertain molecular structure of organic components from mass spectrogram data.

densitometer An optical-electronic device used for measuring the density (ie degree of darkness) of photographic images.

dependent segment Description of a *segment* in terms of its relative logical position in a *hierarchical database* (ie in relation to a *parent segment*, 'grandparent', 'great grandparent', etc).

deregulation The liberalization of state-owned companies in order to allow supply of equipment and services from any source.

derived-term indexing See *indexing*.

descender A typographic expression indicating that part of a lower-case character which extends below the normal body height, eg the lower part of the letters 'p' and 'q'.

descriptor A term, or terms, attached to a document to permit its subsequent location and retrieval. Descriptors are particularly employed in computerized *information retrieval systems* (see *keyword*).

desktop computer An alternative name for a *microcomputer*.

desktop publishing (system) *Microcomputer*-based equipment which, allied to a *laser printer*, can produce finished documents with integrated text and graphics and *page make-up* accomplished *on-screen*. Equipment falls into one of two categories: purpose-built equipment, and *page-layout packages* which run on microcomputers.

destructive read-out When data are read from a *storage device*, and the record of the data in the storage device is then lost.

device independent Used to describe the ability of a computer to execute *input* and *output* functions without having to take into account the specification of the input and output devices used.

device media control language Used to map a *database* on to a *storage device*.

Dewey Decimal System A particular form of *decimal classification system*.

DFD *Data flow diagram*.

DFS German communications satellite.

DFT Diagnostic function test. A

computer *program* to test the
reliability of a system.

DG XIII Directorate-General
(Section XIII) of the Commission of
the European Communities (CEC)
which deals with the information
market and innovation. The
Department for Scientific and
Technical Communication forms
part of DG XIII. It a. makes
available research carried out under
CEC patronage and b. promotes
scientific and technical
communication in the European
community.

DGT The French *PTT* (Directorate
General of Telecommunication).

DIA Document Interchange
Architecture. A standard announced
by *IBM* in connection with *SNA*.
DIA is intended to define methods
whereby individual documents can
be stored, retrieved and manipulated
by any number of different *office
automation* systems (see *DCA*).

diacritic An accent placed above or
below certain letters in some
languages; eg 'é' and 'è' in French; 'ü'
in German. Modern *phototypesetters*
can include these accents on output,
if they are identified in the input
text *string*.

diagnostic program A *program*
used to detect equipment
malfunctions.

diagnostics Information printed out
by a computer to assist the user in
locating errors; or programs and
routines run for this purpose.

Dialcom An *electronic mail* service,
developed in the US by *ITT*. *British
Telecom* acquired Dialcom in May
1986, having previously held the UK
franchise.

Dialnet The *network* providing
access to *Dialog*.

Dialog 1. A US *host* system. 2. The

search *language* and *software* used
for *on-line access* to *Lockheed's*
databases.

Dialorder A *document delivery*
system operated by *Lockheed* in the
US. A document, identified by an
on-line search of a Lockheed
database, can be requested from a
document fulfilment agency. The
request is made on-line but
fulfilment is met by largely non-
automated methods. (*Hard copy* is
sent via the mail.)

Dialtech The *on-line search* service
associated with use of the *ESA-IRS
host* facility from the United
Kingdom.

dial-up Systems where *terminals*
have access to a computer, via a
modem attached to the telephone
network, by dialling a telephone
number for the computer.

DIANE An abbreviation of Direct
Information Access Network for
Europe. It refers to the information
services offered over the *Euronet*
system. There are currently over 300
hosts and 300 *databases*.

dibit A group of two *bits*.

dictionary Words contained in a
spelling check program. Some such
programs provide specialized
dictionaries, eg for medical text.

DID Direct inward dialling.

Didot (point) A typographic system
of measurement used in continental
Europe. Based on a *point* of 0.0148
inch (with 12 Didot points = one
cicero).

DIDS Domestic Information
Display System.

diffusing screen A translucent
screen that evenly diffuses light. It
is used in *microform readers*.

DIGICOM Digital communications
system.

digiography Suggested term for processes involving digital storage of images, text and graphics, eg in *phototypesetting*.

digital Representation of information by combinations of discrete *binary* units, as contrasted with representation by a continuously changing function which is referred to as *analog*. For example, a piano creates sound waves in discrete units of pitch, whereas the human voice can change pitch in a continuous manner. In computing, the unit used is usually a *bit*.

digital/analog converter Converts *digital* signals into *analog* signals.

digital audio tape Similar to an ordinary audio cassette in operation, but records data in *digital* format. It has similar applications to *compact discs*.

digital camera A camera which records images (*text* and *graphics*) in *digital* form. Digital cameras are used as *input devices* for *graphic information storage* and *retrieval systems*, and to record images for immediate transmission.

digital computer A calculating machine, normally electronic, which expresses all the variables and qualities of a problem in terms of discrete units (see *computer*).

digital optical recording The recording of *digital* information using optical (ie *laser*) techniques. DOR refers particularly to the *optical digital disc* (see *video disc*).

digital speech interpolation A method of transmitting voice signals more efficiently. The transmission channel is only active during the periods when the speakers are actually talking.

digital transmission The transmission of signals that vary in discrete steps with the input signal, rather than continuously. The steps are usually based on *bits*. Digital transmission is used not only for data communication between computers, but also increasingly for the representation of continuously varying signals. The reason is that digital signals can be amplified at intervals along a long-distance channel without adding *noise*. This may be compared with *analog* transmission, where amplification of the signals can increase noise and, consequently, the error rate. An example of an area of new information technology which currently employs both digital and analog devices is *facsimile transmission*.

digitize To convert a continuous variable into *digital* form (see diagram).

digitized fount A *fount* stored in a *phototypesetter* system in *digital* form.

digitizer See *graphics tablet*.

digitizing tablet A type of *graphics* tablet (for which it is sometimes used as a synonym) (see *electro-acoustic tablet* and *computer graphics*).

DIL Dual in-line. Synonymous with *DIP*.

DIMDI Deutsches Institut für Medizinische Dokumentation und Information. Performs abstracting and indexing of German medical literature for input to the *MEDLARS* and *Medline* systems, and acts as a *host* to medical *databases* in West Germany.

din A multipin audio connector based on West German standards.

DIN Deutsche Industrie Norm. A West German standards body.

diode An electronic device which

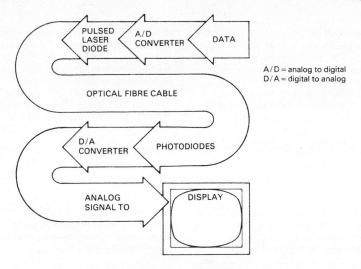

Digital transmission of pulsed light-wave signals for a one-way cable system.

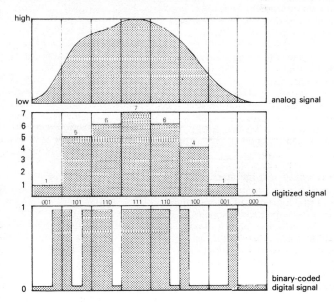

Breakdown of analog to digital conversion, the latter being transmitted in binary form.

permits current flow in one direction, but restricts it in the opposite direction.

DIODE Digital Input/Output Display System (see *digital, input/ output* and *display*).

DIP Dual Inline Package. The most common form of *chip*.

diplex A mode, or facility, that allows two signals to be transmitted simultaneously over a *channel* in the same direction.

dip switch A small switch found inside some items of computer *hardware*. The position of the switches can be altered in order to change certain hardware *parameters*, eg the *baud rate* or communication *protocol* used by a printer.

direct access The ability to go directly to a desired item in a storage and retrieval system, without having to scan any other portion of the *storage file* first.

direct access arrangement (DAA) A device designed to protect the telephone network from high voltages, or large signals, which may be produced by the attachment to the network of consumers' equipment. In the US, the *FCC* has ruled that equipment meeting certain standards can be attached to the network without a DAA.

direct access file (organization) Covers *indexed sequential files* and *direct access* files.

direct access storage devices Storage devices which provide *direct* access to the information required (see *direct access storage media*).

direct access storage media (DASM) Media capable of storing data (and *programs*) in a form such that the time required to *access* particular elements is rapid and independent both of their location, and of the location of the last data element accessed (see *memory*).

direct broadcast satellite A *communications satellite* in *geostationary orbit* used for the relay of broadcast signals (usually television) to a recipient's local receiver.

direct connection A connection to a computer, at a distance of no more than a kilometre or so away, made directly via *coaxial cable*. At greater distances, *remote access* via other channels is used.

direct coupling A way of connecting electronic circuits or components so that the amplitude of currents within each are independent of the frequency of those currents.

direct current (DC) A unidirectional current of effectively constant value.

direct distance dialling An automatic exchange service which enables a telephone subscriber to make calls to telephones beyond the local area.

direct-entry photocomposition See *phototypesetting*.

direct-entry phototypesetter A typesetter in which a keyboard is incorporated into the photo-setting unit (see *phototypesetter*).

direct inward dialling A *PABX* facility which allows automatic direct routing of incoming calls.

direct numerical control Describes a situation in which a number of *numerical control* machines are linked together via a *data transmission network*. They can then be put under the direct control of a central computer with, or without, the guidance of a human operator. If there is no human operator, the system is often described as *computer numerical control* (CNC).

directory A *record* which informs the *operating system* of the whereabouts of a *file* held in the *backing storage*.

directory database A *database* of non-bibliographic data, giving information about companies, associations, organizations, etc.

direct output *On-line output.*

direct outward dialling A *PABX* facility which allows automatic direct routing of outward-going calls.

direct plate exposure A system for the automatic processing of a printing plate, where the processor is attached to the exposure unit.

Direct Read After Write See *DRAW.*

direct transmission satellite A *communications satellite* which transmits messages to individual (ie home- or office-based) receiving sets. Direct transmission is currently being investigated for use in television broadcasting.

direct typesetting from disc The use of *word processed* information as the input stage to a *phototypesetter* (see *computer-aided phototypesetting*).

direct voice input The input of information into a device, eg a computer, directly using the human

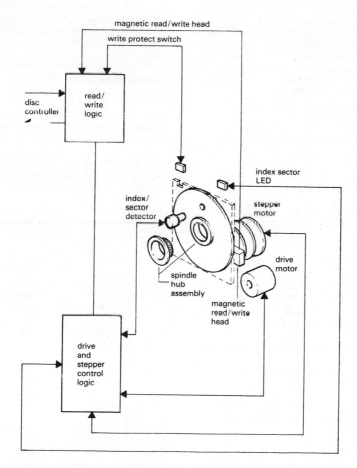

Functional components of a disc drive system.

voice, without an intermediate stage of *keyboarding* (see *speech recognition*).

DIRS DIMDI Information Retrieval Service. Information retrieval system operated by *DIMDI*.

disc See *magnetic disc*.

disc-based operating system An *operating system* in which *software* is held on one, or more, *magnetic discs*.

disc drive 1. A device which reads from, or writes to, *magnetic discs*. Also called a *disc unit*, or *magnetic disc unit* (see diagram). 2. The mechanism within a disc unit which effects the necessary movements of the magnetic disc.

disc operating system (DOS) A *program* which controls the operation of all activities related to the use of *magnetic discs* in a computer system.

Discovision An optical *videodisc* system introduced in the US.

disc pack The removable element of a *disc drive*. It includes the recording surfaces and usually the spindle on which they are mounted. Some types of disc pack include the *read/write heads* (see *Winchester disc*), while some are in the form of a cartridge.

disc reader See *disc unit*.

discretionary hyphen A hyphen inserted in a word by an operator to indicate the best place for a break if required by *justification*. If in subsequent setting it appears that the hyphen is not needed, it is removed from the output text.

disc unit A device which reads from, or writes to, magnetic discs. Also called a *disc drive* or *magnetic disc unit*.

dish (antenna) A transmitting or receiving *aerial* shaped like a dish. Typically used to receive radio and television signals from a *communications satellite*.

disk See *magnetic disc*.

diskette Synonymous with *floppy disc*.

display The production of a visual record on a television (or similar) screen. Can also be applied to the screen itself.

display background In *computer graphics*, the portion of a display image that cannot be changed by the user of the system.

display type Large type (18 *point* or more) used for headlines, etc.

distance learning Instruction where the teacher and student are not in face-to-face contact. They communicate with each other by correspondence, radio, television, CCTV, *computer-assisted interactive tutorials*, audioconferencing, etc (see *educational technology*).

distortion An undesired change in the form of a signal that may occur between two points in a transmission system.

distributed artificial intelligence A growing area of *artificial intelligence*, concerned with solving problems where several facilities are simultaneously concerned with the solution. Becoming more widespread as distributed processing systems increase in popularity.

distributed logic Systems where *logic*, or *intelligence*, is distributed in the system rather than located centrally. For example, some *word processing* systems link *intelligent terminals*, which may make shared use of other resources, eg storage, printer (see *shared logic, shared resources*).

distributed processing Processing of data at different physical locations in a *distributed system.*

distributed switching The use of small *switching* units near to subscribers' homes in some types of *cable television* system. Such units need to be smaller, but more numerous, than conventional telephone exchanges.

distributed system A computer system in which several interconnected computers share the computing tasks assigned to the system.

distribution point The point in a *cable television* system at which branch, or spur, cables leave a *trunk* distribution cable.

DJNR *Dow Jones News/Retrieval.*

DL1 Database *interrogation* language used for *databases* run under *IMS.*

DMA Direct memory access. A method for transferring data between computer *memory* and *peripheral* units not via the *CPU.* This increases speed and efficiency.

DMCL *Device media control language.*

DML *Device manipulation language.*

DMM Defense Market Measures (system). A *database* recording all US Department of Defense contract awards. It can be searched via *Lockheed.*

DNC *Direct numerical control.*

DOCDEL Programme of the Commission of the European Community for improving electronic services relating to *document*

delivery (see *EuroDocDel* and *Transdoc*).

Docfax Jargon for *facsimile transmission.*

document A medium and the data recorded on it. Most commonly refers to print on paper.

document assembly In *word processing*, the integration of different documents (or parts of them) into a single document.

documentation A permanent record of the way in which a computer system is to be operated. It includes, for example, *program* specifications and operating instructions.

documentation book A collection of all the documentation relevant to a particular *program*, or system.

document delivery (system) Most current document delivery systems rely heavily on manual methods of storage, retrieval and distribution. Documents are held as print-on-paper or *microfiche*, and distributed *on-demand* (normally in response to an inter-library loan request). Although electronic systems are currently being developed to satisfy each of the functions required of a delivery service, no large-scale, fully electronic systems are yet in operation. Some small experimental systems have been tried. For example, a range of articles indexed and abstracted for the *INSPEC database* (which can be searched on-line) are held as full (ie complete) text on *magnetic tapes*. These articles are on the database, and can be retrieved by the searcher. By switching to the full-text *file*, the relevant document is made immediately available on the user's terminal (see diagram). Such integrated systems will become more widely available in the future, as a back-up to the on-line bibliographic search facilities

document delivery (system)

currently available (see *on-line searching*). The European Commission is currently seeking the development of an integrated system (codenamed *ARTEMIS*) to operate in conjunction with *Euronet*.

At present, the major application of new technology to document delivery is in the 'request' phase. This stems partly from the introduction of fully automated document request systems in the inter-library computer *networks*. It also results from the activities of the major US *on-line database hosts* (*Lockheed* and *SDC*). They have introduced *switching* mechanisms which permit *on-line* requests to be made for documents identified during the course of a search (see *Dialorder* and *electronic maildrop*). Electronic systems for the storage

and retrieval of *full-text* documents are developing rapidly. For example, in the *Adonis* system, full-text articles are to be stored on CD-ROM. The *Apollo* project will provide a high speed digital information transfer system, with *digitized* text and graphics transmitted to distant points for local print out and display. The viability of this approach will be enhanced by development in telecommunications – in particular, the more extensive use of *satellite transmission* and high capacity *broadband optical fibres*. The range of documents available via delivery systems will be increased through the use of ever larger capacity *storage devices* (*optical disc* and CD-ROM).

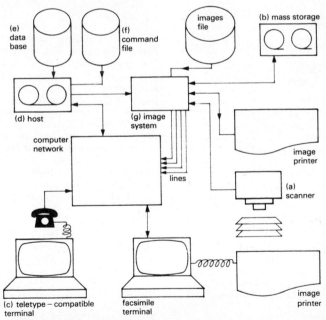

Processes involved in a typical document delivery system. Documents are digitized by an optical scanner (a) and transferred to mass storage (b) via the image system (g). By means of on-line searching, documents are ordered: (c) to (f). This order is transmitted to the image system, which forms a channel between the mass storage and the computer network. The user's document delivery terminal, connected to the network, receives and prints out the document via a facsimile terminal.

document fulfilment agency Any body which provides copies of documents requested by users. The requests may be generated as a result of on-line searching and transmitted to the agency via a computer network.

document retrieval Systems for indexing, searching and identifying documents, from which information is sought (see information retrieval systems).

docuterm A name designating a segment of data in a way which indicates the content of that segment. The docuterm is used to assist in subsequent data retrieval (see information retrieval systems).

Dolby Noise reduction system used on audio tapes.

domain 1. The resources under the control of a particular computer, or set of interconnected computers. 2. In programming, the set of values assigned to the independent variables of a function. 3. A specific area of knowledge used in an expert system.

domain dependent Refers to the structure of an expert system which can only be used in connection with a specific kind or field of knowledge. MYCIN and Prospector are domain-dependent systems.

domain independent Used to describe the structure of an expert system which can be applied to any field of knowledge (see domain and shell).

Domesday Project An interactive videodisc project carried out by the BBC. Two videodiscs have been produced which provide a comprehensive image of Britain in the 1980s. The information stored on discs includes maps, demographic data, and data collected by government and research organizations.

Domestic Information Display System A US computer graphics system which displays demographic data for the whole of the US in the form of colour-coded maps. Developed by AOIPS.

DOMSAT An Australian communications satellite system for domestic television and telecommunications.

DOR Digital optical recording.

DOS Disc operating system.

dot matrix A pattern, or array, of dots used for the presentation of characters, used in visual display units and in some printers.

dot matrix printer See matrix printer.

dot printer See matrix printer.

double density Used to describe some floppy discs which have an increased storage capacity achieved by means of a modified frequency modulation technique.

double-sided Used to describe a floppy disc on which data can be recorded on both sides of the disc.

double strike See multiple-pass printing.

doubleword Computer jargon for a bit-width of 64 bits.

Dow Jones News/Retrieval (DJNR) An on-line information retrieval system built upon a database covering business news, articles, etc, from the Dow Jones News Service, the Wall Street Journal, and other leading financial periodicals. The database is updated daily.

down Has a specific meaning within the context of computer systems. A system is described as 'down' when it is not operating, due, for example, to a fault, repairs or maintenance.

download The transfer of data or programs from one computer to another: typically from a *mainframe* to a microcomputer (see *upload*).

downstream From the *head end* of a *CATV* system toward the subscriber's terminal.

downtime The period when equipment is not operating because of malfunction, maintenance, etc.

downward compatibility The ability of a more advanced system to interact with a less advanced one (often through an intermediary system).

DP *Data processing.*

DPE *Direct plate exposure.*

DPM 1. Data processing manager (ie a person involved in managing data processing activities). 2. Documents per minute.

DPS 1. *Data processing system.* 2. Document Processing System. Developed by IBM, US.

DRAGON An *expert system* developed by *ICL* for evaluating computer workload profiles and predicting future equipment requirements.

DRAW Direct Read After Write. With optical digital discs, information once written cannot be erased. However, the DRAW technique allows immediate identification of errors. These can then be corrected by rewriting data in a new section of the disc, and erasing the *address* of the incorrect section from the computer memory. The incorrect section will then always be ignored (see *videodisc*).

DRCS Dynamically Redefinable Character Set. A method of building up *videotex* frames from a range of patterns available at the receiver.

Drexon An optical data recording material developed by the Drexler Technology Corporation. It is used in the production of *LaserCards* and *optical discs.*

Drexon DRAW Disc A *videodisc* developed by Drexler Technology Corporation. Follows the Philips *DRAW* process, but the resultant disc is claimed to be less susceptible to deterioration.

drive Any device used to load a disc (*magnetic disc, floppy disc*) on to a computer.

driver program *Software* for a computer *typesetter* which provides the commands (interspersed with text *characters*) required for the operation of the typesetter in the correct format and *code* structure.

DRL Data Retrieval Language (see *information retrieval system* and *information retrieval techniques*).

DRO *Destructive read-out.*

drop A connection between a *terminal* and a transmission *line*. For example, a 'subscriber's drop' is the line from a telephone *cable* to the subscriber's home or office.

drop line A *cable* which branches off from a feeder *line* to bring *cable television* into a subscriber's home.

drop out Refers to faulty *magnetic tape* which prevents signals from being recorded.

dropped cap In publishing, to denote an *upper case* initial letter at the beginning of a piece of text which overlaps into the text below.

DRS Document retrieval system (see *information retrieval system*).

drum Often used as an abbreviation for *magnetic drum.*

drum printer A type of *line printer,*

which prints from a drum engraved with identical characters in each print position across the drum with the full character set engraved in each print position around the drum. Synonymous with *barrel printer*.

drum scanning A form of scanning used in *facsimile transmission*. So called because the object to be imaged, eg a page of print, is wrapped round a drum, which then rotates past the optical sensing device. Used as a synonym for *cylinder scanning*.

DSA *Data set adapter.*

DSI *Digital speech interpolation.*

DTE *Data terminal equipment.*

dual-density disc A magnetic disc with twice the storage capacity of a standard disc with the same dimensions.

dual dictionary A printed *inverted file* of two identical parts. It is used in *bibliographic information retrieval* for the manual comparison of document numbers contained under each descriptor.

dual in-line See *DIP*.

dual processor A computer system based on two *CPUs*. One is normally dedicated to information processing while the other deals with system operations.

dumb terminal A *terminal* with no independent processing capability of its own. It can only carry out operations when connected to a

computer (see *intelligent* or *smart terminal*.

dump The transfer of data from one computer *storage* area to another, or, more usually, to *output*. It can also refer to the data obtained by this process. It is common practice to produce a dump whenever a computer system *abends*, so as to aid diagnosis of the abend.

duplex A method of communication between two *terminals* which allows both to transmit simultaneously and independently. A synonym for *full duplex* (contrast with *half duplex*).

duplexing The use of duplicate components, so that, if one fails, the system can continue to operate via the other.

Dvorak keyboard A form of typewriter keyboard designed to make the most frequently used keys most easily available. This can lead to improvements in typing speed and accuracy as compared with the standard *Qwerty* keyboard.

dynamic leading Continuous motion (as contrasted with line-by-line advance) of the surface receiving images in a *phototypesetter*.

dynamic RAM *RAM* in which only one *bit* can be stored at an *address*, where it is held for a fraction of a second (contrast *static RAM*).

dynamic range The range from the weakest to the strongest signals that a receiver is capable of accepting as input.

E

EAM Electrical accounting machine. An electronic machine which provides lists and totals from input data.

EAN European Article Numbering.

EAPROM Electrically alterable programmable read-only memory. Often used as a synonym for EPROM.

EAROM Electrically alterable read-only memory. Often used as a synonym for EEROM.

earth segment A term in satellite communications, referring to the earth, or ground, port, as opposed to the satellite itself. Thus earth segment costs are those of the ground receiving and transmitting stations, etc.

earth station A terminal which is able to transmit, receive and process data communicated by satellite.

EasyLink An international electronic mail service operated by Cable and Wireless.

EasyNet A menu-driven intelligent front-end system, sponsored by NFAIS, which gives untrained users access to a wide range of databases available on nine on-line hosts.

EBCDIC (Code) Extended Binary Coded Decimal Interchange Code. A standard 8-bit transmission code for the exchange of data between items of equipment.

EBR Electronic beam recording.

EBU European Broadcasting Union.

EC External computer.

ECCTIS Educational Counselling and Credit Transfer Information

Service. An information service provided by the Open University on its private videotex system, Optel.

echo Part of a transmitted signal reflected back with sufficient amplitude and delay time to be recognizable as interference. Echoes can be used to check the accuracy of data transmission.

ECHO European Commission Host Organization. A European host system offering information about the European community.

echo check Method of checking the accuracy of data transmission by returning the received data to the sending point for comparison with the original message.

ECMA European Computer Manufacturers' Association.

E-COM The US Postal Service's electronic mail system.

Econet A UK communications network which can be operated over a limited distance, and allows computers to share resources, eg printers. The system is primarily intended for schools and colleges, but can also be used in business.

ECS 1. European Communications Satellite. 2. Experimental Communications Satellite.

ECSTC Eighteenth Century Short Title Catalogue. A catalogue database with wide coverage of 18th century English and other language material, provided by BLAISE-LINE.

E-cycle See machine cycle.

edge card A circuit board with contact strips along one edge. Can be plugged into a microcomputer to provide extra facilities.

edge connector The socket into which an *edge card* is inserted.

edit The process of removing, or inserting, information by the intervention of an operator when a *record* is passed through the *computer*. Also used as an abbreviation for text *editing*.

editor Besides the usual connotation, this term is used in information technology to mean: a. *software* which aids the *editing* of a *file*, normally by a user at a *terminal*; b. a *routine* which edits in the course of a *program*.

editorial processing centre (EPC) The concept of editorial processing centres first appeared in the 1970s. It refers to a system in which new information technology is shared by a number of journals. Such resource sharing is intended to produce savings in costs and to reduce the time-delays in publication experienced by conventional journals. The key elements of the concept are to capture authors' manuscripts in *machine-readable form* at an early stage; to avoid unnecessary re-typing; to use the computer for assistance in editing; to use *terminals* and *telecommunications* when communicating about submitted manuscripts; to introduce *computer-aided typesetting*; to monitor schedules more efficiently, and to aid financial management. Studies of EPCs suggest that four types might be distinguished (minimum, intermediate, advanced and maximum) depending on the extent to which new technology is incorporated. The diagram shows a suggested 'intermediate' configuration, in which authors' manuscripts, and editors' and referees' comments are typed in an appropriate form to be read into a computer via an *optical character recognition* (OCR) device. In contrast, a minimum configuration makes less use of the computer, and

the advanced and maximum configurations make use of a computer within the EPC with *visual display units* (VDUs). EPCs have been the subject of a number of experiments, but do not actually exist in the fully integrated form described above. The phrase editorial processing centre is now often used more loosely to describe any centralized editorial facility using new technology and responsible for the production of several journals (see diagram and *electronic journal*).

EDP 1. Educational *data processing*. 2. Electronic *data processing*.

EDPE Electronic *data processing* equipment.

EDPM Electronic *data processing* machine.

EDPS Electronic *data processing system*.

educational technology The development, application and evaluation of systems and techniques for improving the process of human learning. The term may refer to the social and psychological aspects of the learning process but it is also applied to the development of devices and systems to assist: a. face-to-face teaching, eg films, tape-slide presentations, and *computer graphics*; b. *distance learning*, eg broadcast lectures, CCTV, *video cassette* teaching packages and *computer-assisted interactive tutorials*; c. self-instruction, eg *teaching machines*, *computer-aided instruction*, and *interactive videodisc*. Educational technology and information technology have interacted extensively. Information technology provides the basis for much educational technology, but, equally, educational technology has contributed to such areas as the design of *user-friendly* systems. In particular, it has emphasized the use and design of *menus* as a means for gaining access to any required facility within a computer-based information system (see *computer-aided instruction* and *CYCLOPS audio graphics system*).

Educational Telephone Network Educational *audioconferencing* service run by the University of Wisconsin.

EEC/COMEXT A *numeric database* produced by the Statistics Office of the EEC, covering trade between the EEC countries and the rest of the world.

EEC/CRONOS A *numeric database* produced by the Statistics Office of the EEC, which contains 700,000 time series on economy, industry, trade, finance, energy, agriculture and labour for the EEC countries.

EEPROM Electrically erasable programmable *read-only memory*.

EEROM Electrically erasable read-only memory. *Read-only memory* which can be erased by passing an electrical current through it and then reused, ie new data entered. Often used as a synonym for *EAROM*.

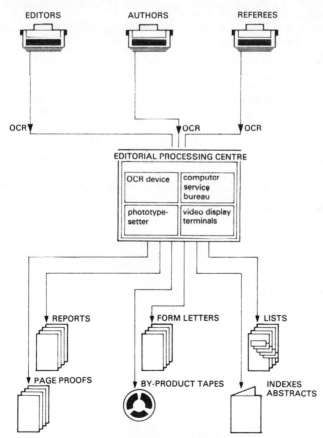

Flow of material through an editorial processing centre which employs a computer service bureau.

effective time The actual time for which a piece of equipment operates.

EFT *Electronic funds transfer.*

EFTPOS Electronic funds transfer at *point of sale*: see item 'd' under *electronic funds transfer.*

EGA *Enhanced graphics adapter.*

EHF Extremely high frequency. Radio waves above 30 GHz (see *spectrum*).

EHOG European Host Operators Group. A group of six European *hosts* who are working towards a *gateway* system which would provide interconnection between them and the *databases* they offer access to.

EIA Electronic Industries Association (US). Amongst other things, produces recommended standards (RS) on a variety of electronic fields (see, for example, *RS232*).

EIES Electronic Information Exchange System (pronounced 'eyes'). An experimental computer *network* supported by the US National Science Foundation to evaluate the impact of information technology on personal communication. It connects members of professional groups to one another, offering them *electronic mail*, *teleconferencing*, and a facility to maintain and update personal electronic 'notebooks'.

elastic buffer (or store) A *buffer store* which can hold a variable amount of data. Such a store is often used in *digital transmission switching systems.*

ELECOMPS A *databank* of electrical components searchable *on-line* via *ESA/IRS.*

Electrical and Electronics Abstracts A UK *database* containing *abstracts* of papers published in all fields of electrical engineering and electronics. It is accessible through most of the major *hosts.*

electro-acoustic tablet A type of *graphics tablet* in which the position of the pen, or stylus, is determined by measuring the time it takes pairs of pulses to reach the stylus' contact with the tablet surface (see *computer graphics*).

electromagnetic delay line A *delay line* whose action is based on the time of propagation of *electromagnetic waves.*

electromagnetic wave Electrical and magnetic vibrations at right angles to each other which travel together through space (see *spectrum*).

electron beam recording A *COM* output method, where a beam of electrons is directed onto a sensitive film.

Electronic Blackboard A device developed by Bell Laboratories to sense and transmit chalk markings on a normal-sized blackboard of special construction. Display is via a *VDU* or television.

electronic composition Any computer-assisted method of *composition*, normally leading to output in page form.

electronic data processing *Data processing* performed by electronic machines.

Electronic Directory Service A *videotex* service operated by the French *PTT* in which free *Minitel terminals* are issued to telephone subscribers for accessing the electronic version of the telephone directory.

electronic document delivery systems See *document delivery.*

electronic funds transfer (EFT) A method for transferring funds from one account to another using computers and telecommunications. At least four types of EFT are currently in common use: a. transfers between computers at different banks; b. transfers between banks and other organizations, eg industrial firms; c. public access to *terminals* providing banking services, eg *machine-readable* cards for obtaining money from cash dispensers; d. cards for making direct debit payments for goods and services via an electronic link.

electronic glass A transparent solid which is electrically conducting. It is used in a variety of information technology products, eg touch control *input devices*, using a finger instead of a *light pen*; visual display devices.

Electronic Industries Association See *EIA*.

Electronic Information Exchange System See *EIES*.

electronic journal In its simplest form, it is the all-electronic counterpart of a conventional print-on-paper scholarly journal. The concept originated in experiments based on *computer conferencing* systems. The approach currently envisaged is based on a large *mainframe computer*, which acts as a central store.
The sequence of events might be as follows. An author prepares a research article at a computer or *word processing* terminal, and may then inform selected colleagues of its existence (using an *electronic mail* or message facility) inviting their comments. These colleagues 'call up' the article on their own *terminals*, and transmit comments to the author, either directly, or via a central electronic store. The author views these comments, and, if necessary, revises the article. The article is then submitted to an

editorial office via a telecommunications link. The editor of the journal views the submission and, if appropriate, chooses referees to judge its acceptability for the journal. The referees carry out this examination at their own terminals. As with most conventional scholarly publications, the referees' comments may then be transmitted via the editor to the author – over the electronic network – and the article may be accepted, rejected, or revised. Up to this point, no user of the network, other than those chosen by the author and editor, has had access to, or knowledge of, the article. Once the article is accepted, it can be 'published' (ie made available via telecommunication links) to the subscribers to the electronic journal. They are alerted to its existence, and can call all, or part, of it up on their terminals. In this form, paper is not needed at any stage.
The flexibility of electronic communication means that the procedures of print-on-paper journals can be varied to determine which are best suited for the new medium. For example, each article might be structured so that the reader could then follow a variety of routes through its contents. Where a reference is made to other work, the user might be able to retrieve the work referred to immediately via a *document delivery system*. Again, the organization of the journal might be modified, with both editorial and refereeing activities more widely distributed among contributors.
The electronic journal is increasingly being regarded as but one facet of the facilities offered by an electronic communication *network*. For a particular scholarly community, these may include: a newsletter, probably compiled centrally; a 'paper fair', where authors can input articles for comment from other participants; a message capability (person-to-person, or for all participants) (see *BLEND* and *Electronic Magazine*).

Electronic Magazine An *electronic journal* produced jointly by Learned Information and *ESA/IRS* with assistance from the EEC. Subjects covered include *electronic publishing, library automation* and *on-line retrieval*. There is no printed equivalent.

electronic mail A general term covering the electronic transmission, or distribution, of messages. Electronic mail can be distinguished from most areas of telecommunications by its capability for 'non-real time' use.
Unlike a telephone conversation, messages can be transmitted at one time, for reception or reading at a later time. The delay can be brought about by the transmission system employed: for example, a 'store and forward' system which may have a central facility which stores received messages and subsequently transmits them down another line. Alternatively, messages may be stored at the receiving end, to be read at the convenience of the recipient.
Most telephone networks are heavily used only at peak periods, and may be relatively little used at other times. A typical network may be only 20 per cent utilized. Electronic mail permits the usage of this spare capacity, transmitting in the 'off-peak' periods. This may be of particular value for business mail, much of which is already generated by computers for eventual insertion into other computers, eg orders, invoices, receipts, etc.
For the most part, electronic mail will involve the *digital transmission* of messages. However, the term can also include *facsimile transmission*, most of which still takes place by *analog transmission*. A combination of facsimile transmission and telex or *teletex* makes possible electronic mail systems able to handle both text and graphics.
Electronic mail can be carried by a variety of devices - for example, by communicating *word processors* and

transmission is not limited to telephone networks, since any telecommunications link can theoretically be used. Thus some see particular use for electronic mail over cable TV (*CATV*) links. An electronic mail system which is controlled by a central computer, or *minicomputer*, and is intended for a limited set of users can be considered to be a *computer conferencing* system. *Electronic funds transfer* can also be subsumed under the electronic mail heading, since it may deal with the transmission of messages in 'non-real' time. Electronic mail services are now commercially available, eg *Dialcom* in the US and *Telecom Gold* in the UK.

electronic mailbox See *mailbox system.*

electronic maildrop A *document delivery system* operated by *SDC* in the US. A document identified by an *on-line search* of an SDC *database* can be requested, on-line, by means of a *switching* mechanism. The requests are currently met by fulfilment agencies who use largely non-automated methods (*hard copy* is sent via the mail). 2. Old name for *ORBDOC.*

electronic mark-up The insertion of special *codes* in text prepared on a *word processor* which are recognized and interpreted by a computer in order to output via a *phototypesetter* or *laser printer* with the minimum of operator intervention (see *generic coding*).

electronic message systems A general term, first used to describe communication via *terminals* in a communications *network*. It now covers a number of specialized services, such as *electronic mail, teleconferencing,* videotex and communication between *word processors.*

electronic office A general term

(equivalent to 'Office of the Future') used to describe a technologically feasible office environment which makes maximum, or optimum, use of information technology. Thus an electronic office would use electronic means for text and data handling, communication, information storage and retrieval facilities (see *work station*).

electronic point of sale Describes electronic *terminals* used at retail outlets to record financial transactions as they occur (see *barcode* and *universal product code*).

Electronic Post A service offered by the UK Post Office for reducing long distance delivery times. Bulk mail is transmitted directly between connected computer *terminals*. The individual letters are reproduced at the receiving terminal and complete their journey through the normal delivery system.

electronic printer Although the term could apply to any computer *printer*, it is used more specifically for devices which hold a *magnetic tape* record of the text and reproduce it via *digitized founts*.

electronic publishing Sometimes refers to any computerized publishing activities. This can include, for example, use of word processing for author origination and publisher's editing, leading to the transmission, or transfer, of a document in *machine-readable* form, for input into a *phototypesetter*. (In such a case the final product is print-on-paper.) However, another use of the term electronic publishing restricts it to publishing activities which result in the distribution of information in electronic form, through, for example, a *videotex* system.

Electronic Publishing Abstracts A database compiled by *PIRA*.

electronic publishing system 1. A computerized system which facilitates the production of a conventional (print-on-paper) product (see *desktop publishing*). 2. The use of computers and telecommunications to distribute information electronically.

electronics The design and construction of electrical circuits containing devices (such as *transistors*) whose operation depends on the behaviour of electrons.

electronic speech recognition See *speech recognition*.

electronic stylus An *input device* which allows images to be drawn. It can take the form of a *light pen* or a purely electronic device used in conjunction with, for example, a *graphics tablet*.

electronic switching system A *digital* telephone *switching* system which provides special services, such as speed dialling, call transfer and three-way calling.

electronic tutor A *computer* which provides *programmed instruction*.

electrophotographic printing There are two main types: a. indirect, where the photosensitive material is part of the *printer* mechanism and the image is transferred to paper; b. direct, where the photosensitive material forms part of the coated paper used as the recording medium.
In *laser* electrophotographic printing, *digital* information is fed to a laser which creates an image (in the form of a *dot matrix*) on a photoreceptor belt, or drum. This image is *toned*, transferred to paper and fused.

electrosensitive printing A method of printing where an electric current passes through a writing stylus to remove, or chemically modify, the top coating (often a wax) on a specially prepared paper.

electrostatic deflection Deviating a beam in a *CRT* by means of an electrostatic field created by *deflection plates*.

electrostatic printing/ reproduction A non-impact printing method whereby electrostatic charges are produced on paper in the design to be copied. Liquid or dry *toners* are attracted to the charged areas, which then become visible. Heat is used to fuse the toner to the paper (see *xerography*).

ELF Extremely low frequency. Less than 100 *Hz* (see *spectrum*).

Elhill *Software* written originally for the US National Library of Medicine to give *on-line* access to its *databases*. Now also used by *BLAISE* and a variety of smaller information suppliers. Elhill offers a search language similar to *ORBIT* (see *on-line searching*).

elimination factor The fraction of the total number of records in a file not retrieved by a *search*.

em A unit of measurement in printing corresponding to the width of a *lower case* 'm'. It is equal to two *ens*, also called a pica and equal to ⅙ inch.

EM 1. End of medium. A *character* in a *string* of *machine-readable data* which indicates the end of the medium on which the data are being recorded. 2. Excerpta Medica. 3. Electronic mail.

email Abbreviation of *electronic mail*.

embossment In *optical character recognition*, a measure of the distance between the non-deformed part of a document surface, and a specified point on the printed character.

EMIS Electronic Materials Information Services. A *database* on materials properties and materials supply. Published by *INSPEC*.

EMMS *Electronic Mail and Message Systems*.

EMOL *Excerpta Medica* On-line. A medical *on-line search* service (see *Excerpta Medica*).

EMS *Electronic Message System*.

emulator *Hardware* or *software* which makes a system appear, to other hardware or software, as another system, eg a *word processor* may be able to emulate a *telex*, or a computer of one type may be able to appear to software as a different type of computer.

emulsion In general, a colloidal suspension of one liquid in another. In *micrographics*, it refers to a layer of light-sensitive chemicals in a very finely divided state held in a suspension of gelatine. The emulsion is supported on a base of paper film, glass or plastic to make a *microform*.

EMYCIN *Expert system*, based on *MYCIN* with medical aspects removed; used as the basis for some other systems.

en A unit of measurement in printing, corresponding to half the width of a corresponding *em*, but the same height.

encode To use a *code* to represent *characters*, or groups of characters.

encypher See *encryption*.

encryption The *coding* of data to protect their privacy, particularly when transmitted over telecommunications links.

end pages Videotex pages which contain information: as distinct from those pages which aid the user in locating this information.

end-point determination The process in *speech recognition* for determining the beginnings and ends of words.

end-user A term in information technology to describe the 'final' user or consumer of information.

end-user processing The involvement of non-*data processing* personnel in the development and running of their own computer systems.

end-user searching *On-line searching* carried out by the person who requires the information rather than a trained intermediary. In order to cater for *end-users*, many *database hosts* now offer *intelligent front-end systems* which facilitate access and help to formulate *search strategies*.

Energyline A US-based *database* covering all aspects (engineering, economic, social and political) of energy exploitation. Accessible via *ESA-IRS, Lockheed* and *SDC*.

enhance See *upgrade*.

enhanced audioconferencing An *audioconference* which is made more efficient by the use of electronic transmission of graphic material via *facsimile, videotex* or *electronic blackboard*.

Enhanced graphics adapter An *expansion card* for the *IBM PC* which provides *high resolution graphics* – a facility not found on the standard *PC*.

envelope 1. A *byte* to which a number of additional *bits* have been added for control and checking purposes. 2. The amplitude variations of an *amplitude modulated* carrier wave.

Enviroline A US-based *database* covering all aspects of environmental science, ecology,

pollution, etc. It is accessible via *ESA-IRS, Lockheed* and *SDC*.

EOF A computer statement indicating the end of a file.

EOJ A computer statement indicating the end of a job.

EOM End of message indication when transmitting a signal.

EOR 1. End of record. 2. End of run.

EOT Indicates the end of transmission.

EPA See *Electronic Publishing Abstracts*.

EPB Environmental Periodicals Bibliography. A US-based *database* covering all aspects of environmental sciences. It is accessible via *Lockheed*.

EPIC Exchange Price Indicators. The *database* of the London Stock Exchange. It incorporates information from international agencies, eg Reuters, Extel, with information from its own sources, the price reporters who tour the floor of the market, and staff who compress business news. Epic is made available through the *Topic* information system.

epitome A precise summary of a document.

EPO *European Patent Office*.

EPOS *Electronic point of sale* device.

EPROM Erasable programmable read-only memory. *PROM* which can be erased for reprogramming.

EPSON Leading manufacturer of *dot matrix printers*, under its own and other trade names.

Epub An *electronic publishing* service offered by *Telecom Gold*.

equalization In telecommunications, compensating for *distortion* introduced during the transmission of data.

erasable optical disc *Optical discs* currently in use are *WORM* devices, and are non-erasable. A number of *prototype* erasable discs have been produced but problems remain to be solved in mass production.

erasable storage Any *storage* medium which can be reused, normally by recording over previous entries, eg an audio cassette.

ergonomics The study of human-machine interactions.

ERIC Educational Resources Information Center. A *database* covering education and educational resources. It is split into two main files: a. Current Index to Journals in Education (CIJE); b. Resources in Education (RIE). The database is accessible via *BRS*, *Lockheed* and *SDC*.

Erlang A measure of the traffic on telecommunication circuits. It is obtained by multiplying the number of calls which the circuits carry in one hour by the average duration in minutes of the calls, and dividing the product by 60.

error A *status word* indicating that the computer has detected an error, and awaits a correction.

error control Any system capable of detecting errors and (in the more advanced systems) of correcting them.

error correcting code A *code* that assists in the restoration of a word that has been mutilated in storage or transmission.

error detecting code In telecommunications, a *code* in which each signal is constructed on the basis of a set of rules so that any departures can be detected.

ESA *European Space Agency.*

ESA-IRS European Space Agency – Information Retrieval Service. A *host* providing *on-line* access to some 20 *databases*, mainly scientific, from its headquarters in Italy.

Esanet The *network* providing access to *ESA-IRS*.

ESC Escape *character*. A character in a computer data *string* which leads to an exit from a *code*.

escape character Synonymous with *escape code*.

escape code *Code* used with text input to indicate that the following *character* (or characters) will represent a *function code*.

ESI Externally specified index. A feature which enables a computer system to become a central message *switching* centre for a variety of remote devices. It provides automatic routing of messages to and from a main store without disturbing the *program* sequence of the *central processor*.

ESPRIT European strategic programme of research in information technology. A CEC initiative to stimulate collaborative research amongst European IT manufacturers. Five priority areas are identified: advanced *microelectronics*, *software* technology, advanced information processing, *office automation* and *computer-aided manufacture*.

ESS *Electronic switching system.*

ETB End of transmission block. Indicates the end of transmitting a *block* of *data*.

Ethernet A *local area network* developed by Rank Xerox to facilitate communication between electronic office equipment (computers, word processors, complete *work stations*, etc), either locally or internationally.

ETIS-MARFO European and Technical Information Service in *Machine-Readable* Form.

ETX End of (transmission) text. An *ETB* message used when the data being transmitted represents text.

EUP *End-user processing.*

EURIPA The European Information Providers' Association was formed in 1980 to promote and provide a forum for the European information industry.

EURODICAUTOM European Automated Dictionary. A *pure MAT* (*machine-aided translation*) system, operated by the European Commission, which uses a *terminology bank* to assist translation of scientific and technical documents, in particular those relating to steel manufacture.

EuroDocDel *Document delivery* experiment set up as part of the *DOCDEL* programme. Its purpose is to evaluate the use of electronic technology as a means of access to the documents, legislative texts and reports issued by the main institutions of the European Community. A central store of the *full-text* documents was held on *magnetic tape* and *optical disc*. Documents could be ordered via *electronic mail* with copies delivered by *facsimile transmission*.

Eurolex An *on-line search* service giving access to case law, legislation and treaties in the UK and Europe.

EUROLUG European On-line *User Group.*

Euronet A European *packet switching* network for the

transmission of *digital* information. It has been established by the European Commission, with entry points in each of the member states. It aims to offer fast, reliable data transmission at an appreciably lower price than existing international tariffs allow (pricing is not dependent on distance). The information search and retrieval services offered through the Euronet system are called *DIANE* (see diagram).

European Article Numbering Relates to *bar-coding* of retail merchandise.

European common command language See *common command language.*

European Communications Satellite A *communications satellite* programme, run by *ESA*, which is intended to provide Europe (and possibly other countries) with a satellite communications system similar to those under development in the US (see *Orbital Test Satellite*).

European Patent Office (EPO) Based in Munich and the Hague, it has created a central *database* of patents which can be accessed in member states of the EEC via either Euronet, or the public telephone network.

European Space Agency A West European organization involved in communication technology as: a. a *database host* (see *ESA-IRS*); b. a launcher and operator of *communications satellites*.

Eurotra A *pure MT* system being developed for the Commission of the European Communities.

EUSIDIC European Association of Scientific Information Dissemination Centres. An association formed by information suppliers to promote applied technology of information

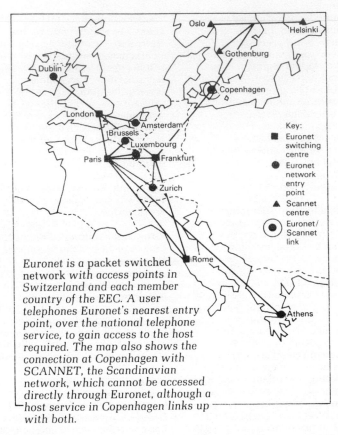

Euronet is a packet switched network with access points in Switzerland and each member country of the EEC. A user telephones Euronet's nearest entry point, over the national telephone service, to gain access to the host required. The map also shows the connection at Copenhagen with SCANNET, the Scandinavian network, which cannot be accessed directly through Euronet, although a host service in Copenhagen links up with both.

storage and retrieval, as it relates to large *databases*.

EUSIDIC Guide A European guide to *databases* which are accessible *on-line* in Europe. It includes those which are made available via non-European *hosts*, such as *Lockheed* and *SDC*. The title comes from the name of its sponsor (see *EUSIDIC*).

Eutelsat An organization formed by the European *PTTs* to coordinate the interests of the main users of European *communications* satellites (such as *OTS* and *ECS*).

evaluative database A *database* which provides the *full-text* of documents together with expert evaluations of their contents.

EVE European Videoconferencing Experimentation project. Programme of the Commission of the European Community to establish the various compatibility standards required for an EEC *videoconferencing* network.

event Any occurrence which influences the content of a *data file*.

Excerpta Medica A large medical *database* compiled in the Netherlands and accessible via *Lockheed*.

exchange A unit, normally established by a *common carrier*, to control the passage of communications in a particular geographical area.

execution The performance of operations listed in a computer *program*.

executive system Sometimes used as a synonym for *operating system*.

exhaustivity An *indexing* term. It measures how completely the concepts within a document have been indexed. The greater the proportion of concepts covered in the index, the greater the exhaustivity.

expandor An electronic device which expands the volume range of a signal. Used in a *compander*.

expansion bus A pathway of parallel wires connected within a computer into which *expansion cards*, *peripheral units* and other such devices may be plugged (see *bus*).

expansion card See *card*.

experience curve A synonym for *learning curve*.

Experimental Communications Satellite A series of Japanese communications satellites (see *Broadcast Satellite Experiment*).

expert system A particular development of *artificial intelligence*. It combines the storage capacity of a computer for specialized knowledge with its ability to mimic the thought processes of a human expert. The *program* for the latter follows a similar learning pattern to a human being's. The computer is provided with a general set of rules instructing it how to reason and draw conclusions. On the basis of these, it decides which items of information are needed, and continues requesting these, until a conclusion can be reached. In building up an expert system, close interaction is necessary between the computer and the human expert, since the latter's judgement is often based on subconscious lines of reasoning which may be difficult to elicit. An expert system consists of two parts: a. the *knowledge base* - this is a collection of facts, relationships and rules which embody current expertise in a particular area; b. the *inference engine* - this is the 'reasoning' core of the system which infers logical conclusions from the knowledge base. Most expert systems have an additional component which explains to the user how the system arrived at a particular conclusion or decision.

Several expert systems are already in use; the number is growing rapidly as computing costs fall. Two areas where expert systems have been operating for some time are: a. medical diagnosis. The common pattern here is that the system is provided with a range of symptoms, and is taught how to diagnose diseases from them. An extension of this, under development, is to allow a computer to interrogate a patient directly concerning symptoms using either *keyboard* input, or *direct voice input*; b. geological prospecting. Here the computer compares the geographical and geological characteristics of an area with its memory of the corresponding characteristics in areas where minerals have been found. Particular effort is being put into the development of expert systems for the detection of oil deposits. The development of expert system *shells* has extended the range of application into different areas, and a number of 'simpler' expert systems are being developed. Most shells are *domain independent* and allow the user to construct an expert system for different types of knowledge base.

Since expert systems are typically used by people who are not computer specialists, they need to employ sophisticated *interfaces*, written in *high level programming languages*.

explode A technique used in *on-line searching* where the search is extended from a specified *term* to include all the terms below it in the same hierarchy.

extended character set A *character set* which incorporates characters and symbols not normally included in the conventional English alphabet.

extension memory *Memory* contained in *external storage* (see *backing storage*).

external label A non-*machine-readable* label attached to the outside of a *storage device*: used to describe the contents of that device. Compare with *internal label*.

external memory Synonymous with *extension memory*.

external storage See *backing storage*.

extraction indexing The most common form of *automatic indexing*. A document in *machine-readable* form is scanned by a computer and words are extracted which comply with a prescribed formula written into an extraction *program*. This program normally directs the computer to extract those words or phrases which occur most frequently, while applying a *stop list* to eliminate common non-substantive words. Less common approaches use relative, as opposed to absolute, frequency as the extraction criterion, and some programs include allowance for word positions and even typeface, eg giving more weight to boldface or italics.

Extravision US national *teletext* (broadcast *videotex*) system provided by CBS Inc.

F

face A particular style of *character*, eg in *optical character recognition* (OCR) (see *typeface*).

facsimile See *facsimile transmission.*

facsimile laser platemaker A device which uses *facsimile transmission* to transmit a complete page, eg of a newspaper. The transmitted image is used to make a printing plate directly, eg for use in *remote printing locations.*

facsimile transmission A system which can transmit a representation of the form and content of documents over a telecommunications link. It is distinguished from other message systems in that the recipient receives a complete copy of the original document, not just its information content. It is distinguished from most video systems in that it is concerned with static, not moving, images (see *still video*). Current advances in facsimile transmission (fax) techniques suggest that it will be an important method for *document delivery* in the coming decades. Historically, fax has been an *analog* system, and most current machines are still of this form; but *digital* machines, which can transmit more rapidly, are becoming commoner. Most commercial fax systems use an electro-mechanical *scanning* technique to convert the tonal variations of the document to be transmitted (the 'subject' copy) into an analog electrical signal. Scanning can be performed by moving the document, the scanner or both. This causes a spot of light from the scanner to traverse the whole document. Most systems use the reflected light to produce the analog signal. Depending on the equipment, the document to be transmitted may be wrapped around a cylinder (*cylinder scanning*), or left flat (*flatbed scanning*).

The diagram illustrates some of the basic differences between facsimile (whether analog or digital) transmission and conventional digital communication of data. First, the facsimile system has to scan a lot of white space to transmit the letter V, whereas a digital system can put the letter V into binary code, and transmit it as only a few pulses. For transmitting the content of textual information, traditional facsimile transmission has therefore often appeared slow and cumbersome. To some extent this is compensated by the fact that, if an error is made in the transmission process, it is highly probable that the letter V will remain recognizable. In a digital system, a single error could result in the printing of an entirely different character. Facsimile transmission has been available for many decades, and has found some important applications, eg for newspaper printing. However, the development of digital facsimile has opened up new possibilities, making it a potentially important part of new information technology. In a digital facsimile, the analog information is converted to digital form. Using *data compression* techniques, this can be sent over telecommunications links much faster than is possible in the conventional analog system. After transmission and reception, the image must be recorded. Most fax recorders are again either flatbed, or cylindrical. The main process may depend on electrolysis, electrical resistance, pressure, electrothermal or electrostatic forces, though other types of recording processes, eg photographic, are also used. Receiving and sending fax terminals must be *compatible*, so

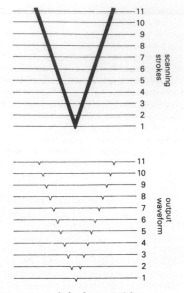

Scanning of the letter 'V' for facsimile transmission (top) and the resulting output (bottom).

standardization is particularly important. The recommendations of the *CCITT* are followed to ensure this. So far there are three main levels of fax equipment, called Group 1, Group 2 and Group 3. Group 1 was the earliest standard, and corresponds to about six minutes to transmit an A4 sheet. Group 2 takes about three minutes per sheet. Group 3 uses digital techniques, and can transmit a sheet in less than a minute. Group 4 facsimile has not yet been standardized, but is expected to be considerably faster than Group 3.

FACT 1. Fast Access Current Text Bank. An experimental electronic library (at the University of Missouri, US). It produces medical documentation in *facsimile* copy from *microfiche* over a telephone network. 2. Fully Automated Cataloguing Technique. A system used by Library Micrographic Services Inc, US. It combines

computer control of documents, storage on *microfilm* and *COM*.

fail-safe system A system which protects data against *corruption* or loss in the event of a failure.

fail-soft system A system that continues to operate, as best it can, following a failure.

FAIRS 1. Federal Aviation Information Retrieval System, US. 2. Fully automatic *information retrieval system*.

false code A *code* producing an *illegal character*.

false drop The retrieval of an unwanted *item* from a *file*, or *database*, as a result of an error in the specification of a request, or *search term*.

false retrieve Synonymous with *false drop*.

family A set of print files generated by a particular *job*.

FAMULUS A *bibliographic* retrieval *software package* in widespread use among educational and research establishments. It was developed by the US Department of Agriculture's Forest Service.

fan-fold The conventional way of folding continuous feed paper for a printer, by folding successive portions backwards and forwards.

farad A unit of *capacitance*.

Farmlink A *closed user group* on the *Prestel* (UK interactive *videotex*) service, offering information on farming products and supplies, farm management advice and meteorological information.

FAST Federation Against Software Theft. Group of *software* suppliers who are jointly investigating ways of preventing software *piracy*.

fast access storage 'Fast' here is used in a relative sense: whether a storage device is counted as fast depends on the operating speeds of other devices in the system. For examples of access times, see *storage device.*

fast picture search A feature of more sophisticated *video tape recorders.* It allows the viewer to run quickly through a tape to find a specific point in the recording.

father file (or tape) See *grandfather.*

fault tolerant Equipment which will continue to operate despite the occurrence of an isolated fault (see *fail-soft system*).

fax Abbreviation for *facsimile transmission,* or facsimile communication.

FAXCOM Canadian *facsimile transmission* service.

FBR Full bibliographic record. The provision for each document of the following information: author, title, place and date of publication, and page numbers.

FCC Federal Communications Commission.

FCS Facsimile communications system (see *facsimile transmission*).

FD Full duplex.

FDM Frequency division multiplexing (see *multiplexing*).

FDOS Floppy disc operating system.

FDS Field Definition Sheet. Documentation which describes the permissible values, purpose and derivation of data held in a *field.*

FE Format effector.

feature extraction As the name implies, this covers techniques for extracting significant features from a signal. For example, in *speech recognition,* it refers to methods for determining the *amplitude* spectrum of the incoming speech signal. These transform the *spectrum* into input recognizable to a computer. Also called pre-processing.

Federal Communications Commission (FCC) US Government regulatory body for telecommunications.

FEDLINK Federal Library and Information Network. A US *computer network* facilitating *on-line* cataloguing.

FEDREG Federal Register. A *database* covering US Federal Government regulations, proposed rules and legal notices. It is accessible via *SDC.*

feed 1. The process of entering data into a computer. 2. The part of an *antenna* where a signal originates, or is received.

feedback Return of a part of the output from a system to its input in order to control the output to within predetermined limits.

feeder cable A *cable* which branches off from a main trunk line in *cable television* in order to serve a group of users, eg all those along a street.

feeder line See *feeder cable.*

FEP *Front-end processor.*

ferro-electric display *LCD* employing polarized glass which can be used for both computer terminals and colour televisions. These displays have a faster *refresh rate* than *CRTs.*

FET Field effect transistor (see *MOS*).

FF 1. *Flip-flop.* 2. *Form feed.*

fibreoptic cable Fibreoptic cables are between one and two orders of magnitude smaller in diameter than ordinary *coaxial cables* with the same information-carrying capacity. They are light and crush-resistant, and therefore easy to store and install. They also have advantages in performance. They are electrically isolated, so sparks and short circuits are avoided: they neither radiate signals, nor pick up interference.

fibre optics See *optical fibres.*

fiche see *microfiche.*

FID International Federation for Documentation. The initials are taken from the French version of the name.

FID/OM FID Committee on Operational Machine Techniques and Systems.

FID/TM *FID* Committee on Theory and Method of Systems, *Cybernetics* and Information Networks.

FID/TMO *FID* Committee on Theory, Methods and Operation of Information Systems and Networks.

field In computing, this refers to a section of the computer record which is designated for the storage of specified information. For example, in a *bibliographic database*, a field might cover the data positions where the dates of publication of each document are recorded. A fixed field has a defined, unvarying length, whereas a variable field can be assigned different lengths.

fifth-generation computer The coming generation of computers, with greatly increased processing power which facilitates the running of sophisticated *user-friendly artificial intelligence software*. The proposed technology is based on parallel processing and programming languages, such as PROLOG, which define logical relationships between statements and allow a declaration (as opposed to the conventional procedural) approach to programming.

file Refers, in general, to any organized and structured collection of information. The data in such a collection are organized into *items,* and structured so as to facilitate the type of access required.

file control system A system designed to aid the storage and retrieval of data without restricting the type of *input/output* device (see *file*).

file conversion The process of converting a *file* from one medium to another, or one *format* to another.

file interrogation program A *program* designed to examine the contents of a computer *file.*

file inversion See *inverted file.*

file maintenance Control of *files* to ensure that their contents are correct.

file management Supervision and optimization of work in progress on a computer.

file management program Computer *program* which assigns, or recognizes, labels identifying data *files,* and enables them to be called from *storage* as required.

filemark An identification mark to indicate that the last *record* in a *file* has been reached.

file name A series of *characters* used to identify a *file.* The file name is often composed of a *code* which indicates the nature, ownership and/or status of the file.

file protection ring A detachable

ring used in conjunction with a *tape drive* unit to protect data on a magnetic tape. In some systems, write-permit rings are used: these only allow a tape to be updated when the ring is present. In other systems write-inhibit rings are used: these only allow a tape to be updated when the ring is removed.

file security The means by which access to computer *files* is limited to approved operators only. The implementation of file security usually involves the use of *passwords* (see *data security*).

file server *Software* which collects and consolidates data from several terminals interacting with a central computer (see *server*).

filial page A term used in *viewdata* to denote the *page* which is immediately below a *parent page*.

Filmorex system A system for electronic selection of *microfilm* frames.

film recorder *Output* device used to produce *COM* and/or to produce record on film of *computer graphics* displays.

film setting Often used as a synonym for *phototypesetting*, though it should only be used where the output is on film rather than paper.

filter A device used in telecommunications. It allows signals of specified frequencies to pass without significant *attenuation*, whereas other frequencies are strongly attenuated. The range of frequencies passed is known as the *band-pass* of the filter (see *spectrum*).

fine index A detailed index to a restricted area of information. Normally used in conjunction with a *gross index*, which covers a broader area in less detail.

fine mode A feature of some *facsimile transmission* machines which provides high quality reproduction by slowing down the printing process and increasing the number of dots per square inch.

FINTEL Financial Times Electronic Publishing. Group of *databases* available for *on-line searching* (some on *viewdata*) covering business information. Produced by the British newspaper 'Financial Times'.

firmware A computer *program* written into a *storage* medium from which it cannot be accidentally erased. Often stored in *read-only memory* (ROM) which is designed so that it cannot be overwritten. The term also applies to the electronic devices containing such programs.

FIRST Fast interactive retrieval system technology (see *information retrieval system* and *interactive*).

first line form advance A printing facility used in conjunction with a word processing system. As soon as an end of page is recognized, printing stationery is advanced to the position for the first line of new page.

FIU Federation of Information Users, US.

fixed decimal Format in which numeric data can be held.

fixed field See *field*.

fixed-head *Read-write* heads which are kept stationary.

fixed-head disc A *disc memory* with one *read-write head* for each track.

fixed point A number stored and manipulated in the computer with the decimal point in a fixed position (compare *floating point*).

fixed satellite A method of

allocating *frequency bands* for
satellite communication on an
international basis which identifies
all the sending and receiving
stations (see *broadcast satellite*).

FIZ-Technik
Fachinformationszentrum Technik.
A Frankfurt-based *host* linking with
Euronet DIANE.

flag Additional information added
to data (normally to each *item*) in
order to characterize, or provide
information about, the data (or
item). Sometimes called a marker,
pointer, sentinel or tag. Can also be
an indicator in a *program*, used to
test some condition set at an earlier
point in the program; or a character
indicating that the following code
does not have the normal meaning.

flag code Synonymous with *escape
code.*

flat-bed plotter An *output device*
for *computer graphics*. It uses a pen
on a mechanical arm to draw images
in several colours on paper. The
paper is held on a flat surface (flat-
bed).

flat-bed scanner A *scanner* used in
facsimile transmission.

flat-bed scanning A technique used
in *facsimile transmission.*

**flexible manufacturing
system** (FMS) The addition of
robot-controlled transport of work
from one machine to another.
Guidance is provided by *numerical
control* machines linked into a
computer numerical control system.

flexography A *letterpress* rotary
printing process using flexible, eg
rubber or photopolymer, plates.

flicker A visual sensation produced
by rapidly alternating light and dark
images, when the frequency of the
alteration is too slow to allow
persistence of vision to give an

impression of continuous
illumination.

flip-flop A *circuit* which can be in
one of two states (and so can
represent *binary* logic).

flippy Double-sided *floppy disc*
(but sometimes used as a synonym
for floppy disc).

flippy-floppy See *flippy.*

floating point Refers to the position
of the decimal point in numbers
stored in a computer. For example,
instead of storing 111.23 and 1112.3
in this form, they may be stored as
1.1123×10^2 and 1.1123×10^3.

flooding A *packet switching*
technique in which multiple copies
of a packet are sent through a
network. This permits speed and
reliability of arrival at the price of
inefficient use of transmission
capacity.

floppy Synonymous with *floppy
disc.*

floppy disc A disc made of a
flexible material, eg plastic, coated
with a magnetic surface. Such discs
are relatively cheap to make and
easy to handle but they have a more
restricted *storage* than a *hard disc*.
Floppy discs may be 8, 5¼, 3½ or 3
inches in diameter. 5¼ inch is the
commonest size for *microcomputers*,
although many machines nowadays
use the 3½ inch *microfloppy*. The 3
inch *microfloppy* is used by only a
few manufacturers. The 8 inch size
is now largely redundant for
microcomputers, although it is still
used in some *dedicated word
processors* (see diagram).

floppy tape Microcomputer
memory in the form of a cartridge of
continuous loop *magnetic tape.*

flowchart See *flowcharting,
systems flowchart* and *program
flowchart.*

a. Floppy disc in its protective cover.

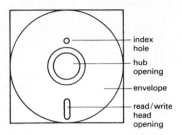

b. Soft and hard sectored discs. Soft sectored discs have only one index hole, the position of the sectors being determined by timing the disc's rotation. Hard sectored discs have many index holes and sectors are located by counting them.

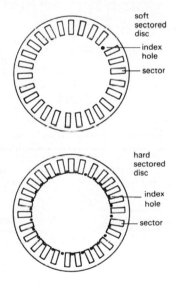

c. The recorded surface of a disc, illustrating the storage of information in bytes.

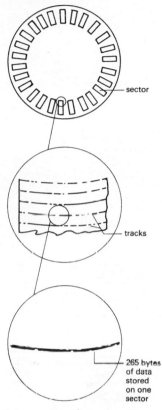

d. Cross section through a disc.

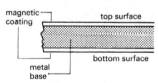

flowcharting A technique for representing a succession of events by means of lines (indicating interconnections) linking symbols (indicating events, or processes). There are two main types: *systems flowcharts* and *program flowcharts* (see diagram). The first type aims to show the relationship between events in a *data processing system*, while the second aims to break down a problem into the logical components which are analysable by programming commands.

flowchart symbol Conventional diagrammatic representation of different events shown on a *flowchart*. The shape of a symbol denotes the type of event (see *systems flowchart* and *program flowchart*).

flow diagram

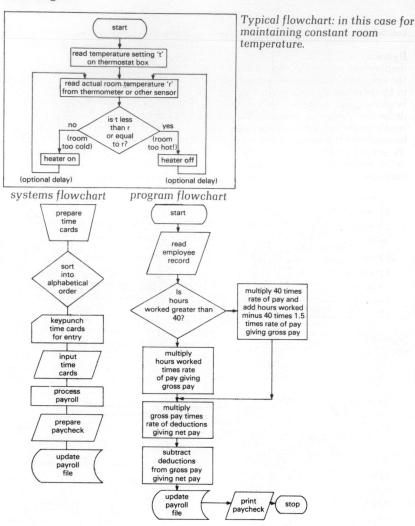

Typical flowchart: in this case for maintaining constant room temperature.

Comparison of systems and program flowcharting, here applied to payrolls.

flow diagram Synonymous with *flowchart*.

flow direction The direction of a *flowline* on a *flowchart*. This shows which of two connected events is the antecedent and which the successor.

flowline A line drawn on a *flowchart* to show the relationship between two events.

flush The removal of some data, eg a *record*, from a *file*.

flush left See *justify*.

flush right See *justify*.

flutter A recurring variation in the speed of a moving medium, eg *magnetic tape*. It is more of a problem for *analog*, than for *digital* recording (see *wow and flutter*).

flyback In a *cathode ray tube* display system, at the completion of the scanning of a line, the beam has to be deflected rapidly to the beginning of a new line. This deflection is the line flyback. When a whole *frame* has been scanned, the beam is deflected back to the top of the screen for a new frame. This deflection is the frame flyback (see diagram).

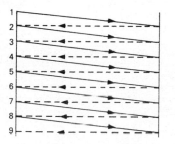

Scanning on a cathode ray tube: the dotted line illustrates line flyback.

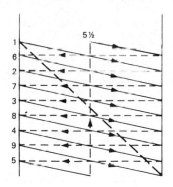

Scanning on a cathode ray tube showing interlacing, which reduces flicker. Dotted lines show line and frame flyback.

flying spot scanning A technique for scanning a surface. A spot, moving at high speed across the face of a *cathode ray tube*, generates light which is then focussed on the document to be read. Used in *OCR* and *facsimile transmission*.

FM 1. Facilities Management. User of external assistance in handling an institution's *data processing* requirements. 2. *Frequency modulation*.

FMS *Flexible manufacturing system*.

Focus Committee Established in 1981 by the UK Department of Industry, to coordinate all British national and international standardization activities relating to information technology.

folio Number appearing at the top or bottom of a page.

font US spelling for UK *fount*.

footer Information placed at the bottom of a *page*, usually for identification purposes.

footprint 1. The area of the Earth's surface to which a satellite can transmit. A satellite in *geostationary orbit* can have a footprint up to one-third of the surface of the Earth (see *satellite communications*). 2. The amount of space taken up by a microcomputer or terminal on a desktop.

foreground In *time-sharing* computers, refers to high priority tasks which are carried out in preference to those of low priority (*background*). Refers in *word processing* to a computer activity which the operator can identify and use.

foreground colours The colours of characters displayed on an *alphamosaic videotex terminal*.

foreign exchange service A service connecting a customer's telephone to an *exchange* which does not normally serve the customer's area.

forgiving system A *user-friendly* system which allows inexperienced users to make mistakes without disastrous consequences.

formant Human speech covers a range of frequencies. For vowel sounds, the frequency *bands* in which acoustic energy is concentrated are called the formants. Sensitivity to formants is thus important in *speech recognition* and *speech synthesis*.

formant frequencies In speech, the frequencies at which the energy of the acoustic wave peaks. They correspond to the acoustic resonances of the mouth cavity (see *speech recognition*).

formant synthesis See *speech synthesis*.

format 1. A predetermined arrangement of data. It may refer, for example, to: a. the layout of a printed document; b. the arrangement of data in a *file*; c. the order of *instructions* in a *program*. 2. A set of *typographical* commands available at a *keyboard*. 3. As a verb, to give a *floppy disc* the magnetic outline required by the computer's *operating system* before data can be recorded on it. This is usually achieved by putting the disc in the *disc drive* and entering a single command.

format effector *Character(s)* in a *string* of *machine-readable* data which are included to determine the layout, or position, of information being transferred to an *output device*.

form feed The mechanical device which positions and advances paper in a printer; or a command from a computer to a printer instructing that printing should commence or recommence on a new sheet of paper.

form feed character A *control character* representing a *form feed* command.

form letter A standard letter produced in multiple copies by a word processor, with names and addresses of recipients either keyed in one at a time, or automatically accessed from a word processing mailing list.

Forth A *high level language* designed to have as many commands as possible in 'plain English'.

FORTRAN An abbreviation for formula translation. A *high level* computer *language*, extensively used for scientific and mathematical programming.

forward chaining A design principle applied in *expert systems*. The *knowledge base* is scanned, searching for rules whose conditions match a question about a problem in hand. The rule is applied and the searching is continued until sufficient matching for a solution is found (contrast *backward chaining*).

forward channel A *data transmission* channel used for supervisory, or error control signals. It carries information in the same direction as the channel(s) carrying user information.

forward error correction An *error control* technique in *data transmission* which involves sending the information twice and using the best parts to reconstruct the original data.

FOSDIC Film optical sensing device for input to computers. A device which can be used to *input from microfilm* into a computer *memory*.

FOTS Fibreoptics transmission system. See *optical fibre*.

fount A complete range of characters, spaces, etc, of one *type* size and design.

fount disc In *phototypesetting*, a glass or plastic disc containing the

master *character* images which are
used to form typeset characters. Can
also refer to master characters
stored in *digital* form on a *magnetic*
disc.

Fourier analysis An analytical
mathematical technique for
expressing the waveform of a signal
as a sum of related harmonic waves.

fourth-generation computer The
majority of contemporary
computers, using *VLSI* technology.

**Fourth Generation Language –
4GL** A *very high level language*,
which can automatically generate
program instruction lines from
relatively simple commands input
by a user who is not an expert in
programming.

fox message A standard message
used to test that information is being
transmitted satisfactorily. The same
message is used to test *keyboard*
operation as it includes all the
letters in the alphabet. It comes in a
number of variants, but a typical
form is: 'The quick brown fox
jumped over a lazy dog's back'.

fragment codes See *chemical
structure retrieval.*

frame 1. In *videotex*, refers to one
screenful of information (several
frames may have the same page
number). 2. In computing, an
arrangement of *bits* across the width
of a magnetic or paper tape. 3. In
packet switching, a sequence of bits
identified by an opening
synchronizing character (see
synchronizing signal).

frame-based Used to describe
expert systems in which knowledge
is represented as a series of frames.
Frames are similar to *records* in a
database, each frame having a
general theme or title and a series of
slots (akin to *fields*) which are filled
by the available knowledge.

frame flyback See *flyback.*

frame grabber A technique for
storing and regenerating a video
frame from a *videotape* signal. This
avoids the continuous head-to-tape
contact required by *freeze frame*
operation.

framing code A *teletext* code used
to synchronize a receiving set within
the broadcast signal.

framing control *Video tape
recorder* control which allows a
recorder to accept tapes produced on
other machines.

free indexing language See
information retrieval techniques.

free running mode An arrangement
which facilitates simultaneous
multi-user access to a *database.*

free-text searching A term used in
on-line searching to denote: 1. a
system whereby all the *fields* in the
records can be searched; 2. a system
which allows the use of *natural
language* searching rather than
terms from a *controlled vocabulary.*

freeze frame The continuous
reproduction of a stationary frame
on *videotape* or *videodisc*. In effect,
the video cassette or videodisc
player continually re-reads the
frame (see *frame grabber*).

frequency See *spectrum.*

**frequency division multiple
access** A *frequency division
multiplexing* technique, which
allocates frequency *bands* in
response to fluctuating patterns of
demand, so as to achieve optimum
use of carrying capacity.

**frequency division
multiplexing** See *multiplexing.*

frequency modulation The
modulation of a *carrier wave* by
means of changes to its frequency.

frequency reuse A *satellite communications* technique for increasing carrying capacity by simultaneously using the same frequency *bands* for signals travelling on distinctly different paths (eg North-South and East-West).

frequency shift keying *Frequency modulation* used in the transmission of data.

front end A *terminal* or *input device* used to create or load data and/or instructions.

front-end processor A computer dedicated to communications functions which acts as an interface between a *host processor* and a *network*. It carries out such functions as accessing *lines*, formatting data for transmission and *queueing*.

front-end system A small computer connected to a large (*mainframe*) computer. Used to handle slow *peripherals* for which the power of the mainframe is not required. Relieves the mainframe of tasks which involve delays.

FSK *Frequency shift keying.*

FSTA Food Science and Technology Abstracts. A UK-based *database* accessible via *Lockheed* and *SDC*.

FTET Full-time equivalent terminals. A measure of *terminal* access to a computer system which allows for the number of hours each terminal is available for *on-line* access.

FTS Federal Telecommunications System. A network used by Federal Agencies in the US.

full duplex A term used in telecommunications to indicate simultaneous and independent transmission of a signal in both directions along a communication *channel* (see *half duplex*).

full-text Used to describe a *database* or *information retrieval system* in which the full text of source documents is held in *machine-readable* form.

full-text searching The *on-line* searching of a *full-text database*.

full-travel keyboard A *keyboard* which uses typewriter-style keys with a mechanical, rather than *touch sensitive* movement (see *tactile keyboard*).

fully connected network A *network* in which each *node* is directly connected with every other node.

functional unit An element within a computer system capable of performing a distinct specifiable task.

function code A *code* which controls the operation of a *typesetter*.

function keys Specific *keys* on a *terminal* keyboard which allow the user to issue a series of commands at a single key stroke. These keys can either be designated by the user, or come already programmed in purpose-built terminals. Examples of such terminals are those used in making airline reservations and handling stock market data.

fuzzy logic In the context of computing, logic based on probabilities of statements being true, rather than statements being true or false. Used in the development of some *expert systems*.

G

G Giga. Prefix denoting one thousand million (10^9).

gain The ratio of the strength of an output signal to the strength of the corresponding input signal.

galley proof In hot-metal composition, this is the first *proof*, used for editing in-house and by the author. The document was subsequently produced in *page proof* form. Modern methods of composition normally go to the page proof stage directly, but galleys may sometimes be produced.

Gallium Arsenide A material used in the production of *semiconductor* substrates.

GAM Generic Associative Memory.

gangpunching Punching information which has been read from a master *card* onto a sequence of other cards.

gap An interval left between *blocks* of data on a *magnetic tape*. It allows the tape to be stopped and started again between *reading* and *writing* processes.

garbage Meaningless, or unwanted, data.

gas plasma display A flat panel *display* which can be used as an alternative to a *CRT*. It relies on a dot pattern that can be formed anywhere on the display.

gate The basic building block of *digital* electronics, and therefore of any digital *computer*. A gate recognizes only two possible *input* states. Its *output* state can take only one of these two possible values (see *NAND*, *NOR* for examples of gates).

gateway 1. *Software* which allows users of a *viewdata* (interactive *videotex*) system, such as *Prestel*, access through a viewdata *terminal* to external computers and their *databases*. Data from these computers must be *formatted* into *pages* suitable for viewdata terminals. The first software of this type was designed for the West German viewdata system, *Bildschirmtext*. 2. A *network interface* which allows users of one service access to another service. Gateway facilities usually provide connections on a *long-haul* basis to external computer systems, other *local area networks*, satellite services, etc.

GDT Graphic display terminal.

Geac A *turnkey library automation system*.

GEM Graphics Environment Manager. An icon-based *operating system* for *microcomputers*, written by Digital Research.

GenCode A standard for generic coding produced by the Graphic Communications Association (GCA).

general purpose interface bus The name given to an *IEEE* interface bus standard for microcomputers.

general purpose language A programming *language* whose use is not restricted to a single type of computer, or to a small range of computers. *BASIC*, *COBOL* and *FORTRAN* are examples of such widely applicable languages.

general purpose program A *program* designed to perform a standard operation, but which requires the user to input parameters and/or values to describe his or her particular requirements.

general purpose scientific document writer A computer *output device* capable of producing documents in *hard copy* at the level of complexity required for scientific text (ie including graphs, mathematics, etc).

generation 1. In reference to the devices used in new information technology, the term represents the level of development reached. Thus the earliest computers are referred to as *first-generation computers*: discussion now centres round the need to produce a *fifth-generation computer*. First-generation computers employed valves; second-generation – individual *transistors*; third-generation – *integrated circuits*; fourth-generation – *LSI*. 2. In reprographic terminology, 'generation' is used to indicate the number of stages required to reach a given point in the reprographic process.

Generic Associative Memory One of a new generation of *processors*. Unlike the conventional *chip* in which each component must be connected by a path to every other component with which it may need to communicate, these new processors set up pathways through the circuits as and when they are required by *programs* (see *ULA*.)

generic coding Applied to the preparation of text in *machine-readable* form, eg on a *word processor*, so that the resulting file can then be used for a variety of purposes. For example, it may be used for *interfacing* with a *typesetter* for *hard copy* production, or for input into a database. For this purpose standard 'generic' codes must be used in the original input which can then be recognized by a variety of devices. The American Association of Publishers is currently engaged on a generic coding project, as is the British Printing Industries Federation (see *ASPIC*). The Graphic Communications Association (GCA), an affiliate of the Printing Industries of America (PIA), has produced a standard for generic coding, *GenCode. SGML* has now gained acceptance as an *ISO* Draft International Standard.

generic mark-up See *generic coding*.

Geoarchive A UK-based *database* covering a wide range of earth sciences. It is accessible via *Lockheed*.

Geonet An *intelligent front-end system* being developed by *DIANE*. The service is based on an *electronic mailbox* system and will facilitate access to European on-line *hosts*.

Georef A UK-based *database* covering a wide range of earth sciences. It is accessible via *SDC*.

geostationary orbit If a satellite is placed in orbit at some 35,700 km above the earth's equator, it completes one orbit each day. In consequence, since the earth is rotating at the same rate, the satellite remains stationary above the same point on the equator all the time. A geostationary orbit cannot be maintained above any part of the earth except the equator, and, even there, slight perturbations may tend to shift a satellite from its initial position (see *communications satellite, satellite communication*).

geosynchronous satellite An artificial satellite in a *geostationary orbit*.

ghost A shadow, or weak additional image, eg on a television screen.

GHz Gigahertz. A frequency of one thousand million hertz (cycles/sec).

GID A West German *on-line* information service which acts as a *host* for a variety of *databases*. The service is available via *Euronet DIANE*.

GIDEP Government-Industry Data Exchange Program, US.

giga- Prefix denoting one thousand million (10^9). Abbreviated to G.

gigabyte One thousand million *bytes*.

Gigadisc An *optical disc* produced by Thomson-CSF with a storage capacity of one *gigabyte*.

GIGO Garbage in, garbage out. A computing term referring to incorrect *output* resulting from incorrect *input*.

GIRL Generalized Information Retrieval Language. A search language developed by the US Defense Nuclear Agency.

GKS See *graphical kernel system*.

global (function) 'Global' is used in computer terminology to mean 'complete'. Thus a global search means a complete look through a *file* for a particular item (see *global editing function*).

global editing function A *word processing* activity that interacts with an entire document (ie data *file*).

global search and replace An *editing* function in *word processing*. The user can specify a *character string* in the text and also a replacement for it. The *software* will then automatically substitute the new character string for the old wherever the latter appears in the files. Used for updating documents kept in *storage*, eg by substituting a new reference number for an old one in a file of standard letters.

glossary command See *glossary function*.

glossary function In *word processing*, commonly used phrases kept in *storage* which can be inserted at any point in a document by the operator. The phrases are called up by executing a *glossary command*.

golf-ball Popular description of the spherical type-head found on the *IBM* electric typewriter.

GMT Graphics *mouse* technology.

GPC General purpose computer. As distinct from one constructed for a particular purpose only.

GPO 1. Government Printing Office, US. 2. The former name (General Post Office) of the UK post and telecommunications agency. It has now been split into 'The Post Office' and *British Telecom*.

GPSDW General purpose scientific document writer.

GPSS General Purpose Simulation Program. A *high level programming language*.

grammar checking program *Software*, used in conjunction with *word processing* programs, which provides assistance with the style of textual documents. Such software checks for subject-verb disagreement, wrong case of pronoun, noun-modifier disagreement, incomplete sentences, inappropriate punctuation, etc.

grandfather A way of cycling tapes in a *data processing* centre to provide back-up in the event of failure. The master tape in one processing run becomes the back-up tape in the next run ('father') and the second reserve ('grandfather') in the subsequent run. Only when a new 'son' has been created is the 'grandfather' tape released for reuse.

granule A storage element in the *tracks* of a *magnetic disc.*

graph A graphical representation of a relationship by means of dots, lines, curves, etc.

graph follower An *optical scanning device* which reads *data* from a *graph* and translates them into *machine-readable* form.

graphic(al) Pictorial, or representational, display, eg in new information technology, a computer with a graphics capability. It is to be contrasted with textual presentation (see *graphics*).

graphical kernel system A device-independent *software* standard for graphics, covering over 150 function specifications, as well as requirements for the interfacing of graphics *hardware* and *software.*

graphic arts quality A text which is produced with the *typeface* and range of *characters* normally found in traditional hot-metal *composition.*

graphic data reduction The conversion of *graphic* material into *digital data.*

graphic display terminal 1. A *VDU* which allows the user to display *graphics* material. 2. In *phototypesetting* it has the more specific meaning of a VDU which permits the phototypeset matter to be viewed as it appears on the *fount disc.*

graphics *Graphic* material produced (in new information technology) as a result of *data processing* (see *computer graphics*).

graphics character A shape which can be used in building up more complex images. They are either provided by the computer, or can be created by the user.

graphics character set The 127

different shapes that can be generated in one of the 960 rectangles which together comprise a *videotex frame.*

graphics insertion A *phototypesetting* technique which allows text and *graphics* to be handled together in a single operation.

graphics mode A mode of *VDU* operation which facilitates the display of graphics. The term is frequently used in the context of a *videotex* display.

graphics peripheral An item of *hardware,* connected to a computer and used to *input* or *output* graphics information. *Input devices* include *graphics tablets* and *light pens; output devices* include a wide variety of *visual displays, plotters* and *printers* (see *computer graphics* and *peripheral unit*).

graphics plotter A device which provides hard-copy *output* of graphics displayed on a screen, eg a *VDU,* used particularly in conjunction with *computer graphics.* There are two main types: *drum* and *flat-bed* (see *printer plotter*).

graphics tablet A device for inputting graphics. Using a *stylus,* diagrams, maps, charts or free-hand drawings can be created, and appear instantaneously on a display screen. The tablet can also be used to manipulate the image, or to direct it to a *storage device* for subsequent recall, or transmission. Tablets are normally made of a grid of wires partially embedded in a thin substrate. When a tablet is touched by its stylus, the wires are brought into electrical contact. This produces a pulse which enables the computer to register the position of the stylus. A graphics tablet is sometimes referred to as a *digitizing tablet.* There are types which operate on other principles, eg an *electro-*

acoustic tablet (see computer graphics).

graphic structure input A method of input for on-line searching of a database containing details of chemical structures, eg CAS on-line. It allows the user to phrase a search query by constructing the required structure on an intelligent graphics terminal. Structural features are either selected from a menu, or by manipulation of a cursor from a keyboard. When the required structure has been composed, the database is searched for any corresponding chemical structures and details are listed (see chemical structure retrieval).

graunch Computer jargon for an unexpected error.

gravure A method of printing from an etched, or sunken, surface (also called 'Intaglio'). It is mainly used for long print runs of illustrated magazines.

gray code A binary code in which numbers are given the following binary expression:

Decimal	Natural Binary	Gray Code
0	0000	0000
1	0001	0001
2	0010	0011
3	0011	0010
4	0100	0110
5	0101	0111
6	0110	0101
7	0111	0100
8	1000	1100
9	1001	1101
10	1010	1111
11	1011	1110
12	1100	1010
13	1101	1011
14	1110	1001
15	1111	1000

gray scale See grey scale.

Green Thumb The first federally funded videotex system in the US. It is an experimental system supplying information to farmers (prices, weather, etc).

Gremas code A code for chemical structure retrieval.

grey literature This term is often used for 'semi-published' literature: that is, literature which is not formally listed and priced, but is nevertheless in circulation, eg institutional reports. Such literature is often particularly difficult to trace. Hence, inclusion of grey literature in databases available for on-line searching greatly improves its bibliographic control, and so its availability (see SIGLE).

grey scale A range of different tones in a continuous tone image. A digitized grey scale may record anything from 8 to 255 or more different density levels.

grid 1. A device used for measuring characters in optical character recognition. 2. In phototypesetting, a carrier for the master character images which are to be scanned. 3. A device used for text alignment in making film images.

gross index An index with wide coverage, but little fine detail. Having located the appropriate domain in a gross index, a user then searches a fine index to locate specific entries.

group A combination of data elements which are logically related, but do not constitute a record. Also called a field.

Group (1, 2, 3, 4) The name used to describe facsimile transmission equipment conforming to the recommendations of the CCITT, eg Recommendation T2, 'Standardization of Black and White Facsimile Apparatus', covers 'Group 1' systems.

grouping The collation of data which come under the same classificatory heading.

group mark *Character* which indicates the beginning, or end, of a set of *data*.

group SDI A *selective dissemination of information* (SDI) service in which group, rather than individual, profiles (see *user interest profile*), are set up and matched against additions to a *database*. The database provider defines a set of standard profiles. Users subscribe to one, or more, of these. This approach offers less precision than can be obtained with individually tailored profiles. However, Group SDI is obviously cheaper for the subscriber, since the cost of each *run* is shared.

GSI *Graphic structure input.*

GSIS Group for the Standardization of Information Services, US.

GT&E General Telephone & Electronics. A large US *common carrier*.

guard band 1. A blank strip separating tracks on a *magnetic tape*. 2. In telecommunications, an unused *band* of frequencies between two allocated *channels*. In both cases, the purpose of the guard band is to prevent interference between adjacent locations.

guide A device that identifies the tape path in audio or *video recorders*.

gulp Computer jargon for a small group of *bytes*.

H

H Henry. *SI* unit of inductance.

Hacker's Handbook A publication which describes simple methods of *hacking* into computer systems using a *microcomputer* and a *modem*.

hacking Commonly used term for breaching *computer security* via a *remote terminal* usually by unauthorized use of someone else's *password*. Hacking is not always done with criminal intent – the motive is often the challenge of breaking into a supposedly secure system (see *Trojan Horse*).

HAIC Hetero-Atom in Context. *Indexing system* used for heterocyclic chemical compounds in the *CA database*.

HAL Harwell Automated Loans system. The computerized loan system of the Library, UK Atomic Energy Authority at Harwell.

half duplex In telecommunications, transmission of signals along a communications *channel* in both directions, but not simultaneously (see *full duplex*).

half-height Used to describe *hard disc* and *floppy disc drives* which take up only half of one of the slots allocated to them in a *microcomputer*'s main system box.

half-tone A print which appears to be continuous, but actually consists of small, closely spaced spots of varying size. Typically used for illustrations in newspapers.

half-word Half of a computer *word*. For example, in a computer that works on 16-*bit* words, a half-word is 8 bits.

Hamming code A method of

achieving data integrity (named after its inventor) by detecting and correcting transmission errors. It is a term used in *teletext*.

handler Part of, or an adjunct to, a computer's *operating system*. It controls the operation of *peripheral units*.

handoff A 300 millisecond break in transmission encountered in mobile communications based on *cellular radio*. Cellular networks are divided up into a number of discrete cells, each with its own low power radio transmitter. Handoff occurs when a *cellular telephone* moves out of one cell and into another.

handshaking The exchange of alerting signals between transmitting and receiving points prior to full transmission between the two.

handwritten input Ways of capturing handwriting for computer storage. There are two methods of doing this. The simpler involves scanning the writing; the image is transferred to the computer as the output of a series of *high resolution* scans, which can be re-assembled in the correct order to produce a *facsimile* of the original. In the second method *input* is achieved by using a *digitizing tablet* as the writing surface. As each character is formed, the X and Y coordinates through which the writing instrument passes are sensed and converted to a *bit pattern*. The computer analyses this pattern using techniques similar to those of OCR and recognizes the *character* (see *graphics tablet*).

hangover A lack of definition in areas of different tone, as received at a *facsimile* receiving station.

hard copy Normally synonymous with print-on-paper (ie text and graphics recorded on sheets of paper).

hard disc A *magnetic disc*, used for bulk storage of computer data. Hard discs offer much larger storage capacities than *floppy discs*, but have to be handled more carefully. They may need to be operated in a clean (filtered air) environment. *Mainframe* computers typically employ hard discs. The alternative name 'rigid disc' is sometimes used.

hard sectoring The physical marking of *sector* boundaries on a *magnetic disc* by punching holes in the disc. Contrast with *soft sectoring*. In hard sectoring, all available space can be used for data *storage*.

hardware The mechanical, magnetic, electronic and electrical devices which make up a computer.

hardwiring Permanently wired electronic components capable of *logical decisions*. *Intelligent terminals* operating without *software* are hardwired. The *program* logic cannot be changed in a hardwired computer (except by replacing the circuit boards or memories). Not to be confused with a *dedicated* computer, which is a general purpose computer assigned for a specific task.

Hartley A unit of information content. It is equal to one decadel decision (ie the designation of one of ten possible, and equally likely, values or states).

hashing The allocation of unique *keys* to database *records*. Each key is associated with a hash value - a set of integers. An *algorithm* is used in order to obtain a conform distribution of record *addresses*. The use of these addresses enables *information retrieval* to be effected more speedily.

Hayes-compatible Used to describe *modems* which are *compatible* with the Hayes modem - a de facto standard in the US.

HCI *Human-computer interaction.*

HD 1. *Half duplex* (also abbreviated to HDX). 2. *High density.*

HDCL *High level data control link.*

HDTV High definition television (see *HDVS*).

HDVS *High Definition Video System.*

HDX *Half duplex* (also HD).

head A device which reads, records or erases information on a *storage* medium.

head crash A failure in a magnetic *disc reader*, resulting from the *head* touching the surface of the *disc*. (It should float just above the surface.)

head drum The part of a *video recorder* which contains the rotating *heads*.

head end Control centre and central distribution point for a *CATV* system.

header 1. Information placed at the top of a *page*, usually for identification purposes. 2. The initial part of a message which contains the information necessary to direct the message to its destination(s).

header file In *information retrieval systems*, the *file* containing the complete records of a particular *database*, usually in order of accession.

header label A label that precedes data *records* on a *file* and contains descriptive information about the file.

header sheet An instruction sheet

for an *OCR* device which informs it of the *format*, etc, to be expected on subsequent sheets.

heading card A card containing significant information which is used in printing headings, eg relating to *index terms*.

head rotor A rotating drum with one or more recording, or reading, heads mounted on its periphery. It is used in *video tape recorders*.

helical scanning A technique by which the *head* in many *video recorders* reads information from a *tape*. One or more heads are mounted on a drum which rotates at high speed. The tape is wound on the drum helically (so requiring a corresponding *scanning* pattern). Although the tape moves at a relatively slow speed, the head-to-tape speed can be quite high.

helical waveguide See *waveguide*.

Hermes A proposed electronic *document delivery* service based on *teletex* and sponsored by the UK Department of Trade and Industry. The project was shelved in 1985. One of the reasons behind this decision was the lack of available teletex equipment on the market.

Hertz *SI* unit of frequency (= one cycle/second). Abbreviated to Hz.

heterogeneous computer network A *network* composed of different computers (ie produced by different manufacturers) (see *homogeneous computer network*).

heterogeneous multiplexing Use of a *multiplexed* system in which *channels* are operated at differing transmission rates (*bits* per second).

Heurisko An *expert system* developed at Stanford University, US. It has a variety of applications from the design of three-dimensional semiconductor chips to war games.

heuristic 1. Solving a problem by means of trial and error. 2. In *expert systems*, a rule which will increase the probability of attaining a particular goal.

hexadecimal code A data *code* which uses the base 16 (as compared with a base 2 for a *binary* code, and 10 for a decimal code).

hexadecimal keyboard *Keyboard* with 16 *keys*: 0-9, plus A,B,C,D,E and F to represent 10-15. These keyboards (also called *hex pads*) are often used in conjunction with *microprocessors* (see *hexadecimal code*).

hex pad See *hexadecimal keyboard*.

HFFC symbols Horizontal form flow chart symbols: used for *flowcharting*.

HICLASS *Hierarchical classification*.

hidden lines In *computer graphics* display, lines that are hidden from view when a three-dimensional object is displayed on a screen.

hierarchical classification A framework for designation in which terms are arranged according to a hierarchical principle: ie the classification splits items into initial sets, and then successively splits these sets into ever finer sets (see, for example, *decimal classification*).

hierarchical computer system (network) A *network* of *computers* forming a system in which control and processing functions are allocated hierarchically, along the lines of supervisory responsibility.

hierarchical database A *database* in which information is held in a hierarchy of *segments*.

High Definition Video System A proposed television standard with 1125 lines and wide screen. Because it requires a higher *bandwidth* signal, equivalent to about four current channels, it may be limited to *cable television* or satellite systems.

high density The provision of a relatively high *storage capacity* per unit storage space, eg in *bits* per inch.

high level data link control A set of *ISO protocols* for *data link* operations.

high level language A *programming language* which allows users to employ a notation with which they are already familiar, eg it may include such terms as: if, then, print, +, etc. Each natural language instruction actually corresponds to several *machine code* instructions. The most common high level languages are *ALGOL, BASIC, COBOL, FORTRAN* and *PASCAL*.

high level programming language See *high level language*.

high level protocol A *protocol* concerned with the functions permitted within a *network* (compare *low level protocol*).

high performance equipment Equipment producing signals of a quality suitable for transmission via telephone and *teleprinter* circuits.

high resolution (graphics) Graphic displays are composed of a large number of individual dots (*pixels*). The smaller the dots and the greater their density, the more detailed the images can be. A high resolution display should be able to show at least 280 dots horizontally and 192 dots vertically on a standard screen.

High Sierra Group US initiative to introduce standards for *CD-ROM*, comprising the *IIA, NISA* and a composite group of manufacturers and software companies. The group took its name from the hotel in which they first met.

high speed Within the context of data communications, data transmission rates in excess of 9,600 *bits* per second.

high speed local network Specialized network used to provide high speed data communication between devices such as *mainframes* and *mass storage* systems.

high speed printer A computer *printer* which can operate sufficiently rapidly to be compatible with *on-line* printing.

high speed reader An *input device* capable of obtaining data very rapidly from an input medium, eg *card* or *tape*, or from a *storage device*. High speed card readers operate at 1000 cards per minute, or more. High speed *punched paper tape* readers operate at 500 *characters* per second, or more.

highway Synonym for *bus* or *trunk*.

HiNet A *local area network* developed by Digital Microsystems.

HI-NET A *teleconferencing* service offered by Holiday Inn of America throughout their chain of hotels.

HISAM Hierarchical Indexed Sequential Access Method. This refers to a method of organizing a *database* for *disc storage*.

Historical Abstracts A *bibliographic database* covering world history from 1450 to the present. It is accessible via *Lockheed*.

hit In *information retrieval systems*, a hit occurs when an enquiry is successfully matched with a record in the database: ie a *search term* is matched with an *index term* or *keyword*.

hit-on-the-fly printer A *printer* where the type does not stop moving during the impression time. The need to stop and start is avoided, so saving time and wear.

hit rate The number of *hits* achieved during an *on-line search*. Using a sample set of documents and standard search procedures, the hit rate is used as a measure of the usefulness of a *database*.

HMOS High speed metal oxide *semiconductor*. Used in making certain types of *read-only memory*.

HMSO Her Majesty's Stationery Office. The UK Government publishing office.

holding time The length of time a communication *channel* is in use for an individual transmission.

Hollerith code A standard code for *card punching*.

hologram See *holography*.

holographic storage Holograms are currently being developed as high capacity information *storage* devices. A 4 x 6-inch *microfiche* could hold as much as 200 million *bits* of information in 20,000 holograms (see *holography*).

holography The creation of three-dimensional images of objects using light produced by *lasers*. A typical arrangement for producing one type

of hologram (also called a holograph) is shown in the diagram. The beam of a laser is split into two. One part is reflected on to a photographic plate. The other is directed on to the object (in this case, a transparency) and the light transmitted to the same photographic plate. The two beams produce an interference pattern on the exposed plate which is then developed to produce the hologram. If the hologram is now placed in the path of the reference laser beam, a reconstructed image of the original object is produced.

In the long term, it may be possible to use moving holographic images as an educational, or entertainment, medium, eg 'holographic television'. For communications, 'holophones' have been proposed, where speakers at distant locations can see three-dimensional images of each other. In the short term, holographic techniques may find application in information storage (see *holographic storage*).

home The starting point for a *cursor* on the screen of a *VDT*.

homebanking See *telebanking*.

home computer A *microcomputer* intended primarily for use in the home. Generally, the home computer has an 8-bit *processor*, uses cassette tape as an alternative storage medium to *floppy discs*, and may use a conventional TV set instead of a separate *monitor*.

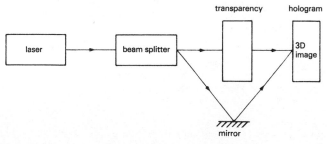

Block diagram illustrating the principle of holography.

home information system A system which allows the home to be used as a centre for electronic control and communication. It is normally envisaged under this heading that activities such as domestic accounting, education, energy management, shopping and banking will be carried out from the home using equipment based on the *chip* (see diagram).

Homelink A *telebanking* service provided by the Nottingham Building Society which operates on the *Prestel* (UK interactive *videotex*) service.

homogeneous computer network A *network* composed of computers of a similar type (see *heterogeneous computer network*).

homogeneous multiplexing Use of a *multiplexed* system in which all *channels* have the same transmission rate (bits per second).

horizontal raster count The number of horizontal divisions in a *raster* (see *raster count*).

host (sometimes also called an information spinner, information vendor, or on-line retailer). A host is an entrepreneur who makes available a number of *databases* through his/her own computer. Users are charged for access to these databases (usually via *on-line searching*). Conversely, the database compilers are paid either a commission or a fixed rental. Host computer is also more generally used as a synonym for *host processor*.

host printing Centralized or *remote printing* using a printer which is not driven by the same *controller* as the *terminal* which requests the print.

host processor The main computer in a *network*, or *distributed*

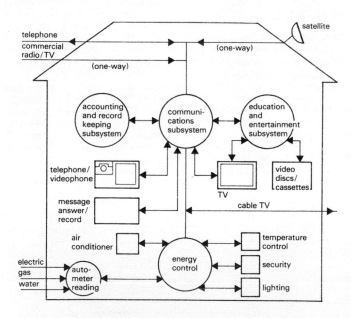

Integrated information system such as can be incorporated into a domestic dwelling, making use of a wide range of information technology inputs.

processing system. It performs the main *applications* workload of the system and may be assisted in its communications role by a *front-end processor.*

hot metal (composition)
Mechanical *composition* in which metal *type* is cast anew for each job, and then melted down for reuse. Monotype is a typesetting device which casts single type characters. A linecaster, either an Intertype or Linotype, casts one complete line at a time.

hot spot A bright spot in the centre of a projected image. A term used in the display of *microform.*

hot zone An area of adjustable width adjacent to, and to the left of, the right margin on a word processor. Any word starting in the hot zone may exceed the system's permitted maximum line length, and the user is therefore given the option of hyphenating, overrunning, or beginning a new line.

house corrections The corrections of errors introduced at the printers either by an operator at the keyboard, or by a malfunction of the *typesetting* equipment.

housekeeping Routine maintenance of *programs* and other contents of a computer.

HSELINE A *bibliographic database* produced by the Health and Safety Executive in the UK.

HSLN *High speed local network.*

HSM High speed memory. Memory which has very short *access time* (see *RAM* and *storage devices*).

HSP *High speed printer.*

HSR *High speed reader.*

human-aided machine translation (HAMT) A *machine*

translation system in which human intervention is only needed to resolve semantic or syntactic ambiguities, and problems arising from non-literal usage. The computer carries out the basic processing of *source* and *target language* texts. The major advantage of HAMT systems is that they do not require truly bilingual operators. Monolingual operators with some competence in both source and target languages are sufficient. The main disadvantage is that HAMT systems are only practical (in terms of cost-effectiveness) with *computer algorithms* powerful enough to require infrequent human clarification. Otherwise, HAMT systems cannot compete with conventional and *machine-aided translation* (pure *MAT*) systems (see *junction grammar* and *Mind*).

human-computer interaction An area of research which brings together a number of different disciplines, including computer science, psychology and *ergonomics.* Its aim is to develop an understanding of how people and computers communicate, in order to make the use of computer systems easier and more natural.

human window Refers to the facility within an *expert system*, or other computer-based system, to explain how, or why, decisions have been reached.

hybrid computer A *computer* system which combines *digital* and *analog* computers. Its main advantage is the combination of a digital computer's *storage* facilities with an analog computer's speed of *data* integration.

hybrid computer system A system which combines *analog* and *digital* devices.

hybrid interface An interface between a *digital* and an *analog* device.

hybrid network 1. The *network* of a *hybrid computer system*. 2. A *cable television* network carrying a variety of different types of service (ie in addition to television programmes).

hyphenation Breaking a word at the end of a line, so that the line can be both left- and right-*justified*.

Hz *Hertz*.

I

IAA International Aerospace Abstracts (see *NASA*).

IAC Information Access Corporation. A US *database* producer and *host*.

IACBDT International Advisory Committee on Bibliography, Documentation and Terminology, *UNESCO*.

IACDT International Advisory Committee for Documentation and Technology, *UNESCO*.

IAD Initiation area discriminator. A type of *cathode ray tube*.

IADIS Irish Association for Documentation and Information Services.

I & A Indexing and abstracting (see *indexing* and *abstract*).

IARD Information Analysis and Retrieval Division of the American Institute of Physics.

IBA Independent Broadcasting Authority, UK.

IBIS International Book Information Service. A UK *current awareness service*. It mails information on recently published books to subscribers, whose areas of interest are held on computer files. It is also an *information provider* on *Prestel*.

IBM International Business Machines. The world's largest computer manufacturer.

IC *Integrated circuit*.

ICIC International Copyright Information Centre, *UNESCO*.

ICIREPAT International Cooperation in Information Retrieval among Examining Patent Offices. Based in Geneva, its objective is to promote international cooperation in the documentation and retrieval systems operated by national patent offices. Also known as *CICREPATO*.

ICL International Computers Ltd, Britain's largest computer manufacturer.

icon Screen images on some advanced microcomputers. The image will resemble some familiar office object (eg a file, or tray, or document), and represents a work area in the computer. This area is activated by moving a *cursor* or screen pointer to the icon (eg using a *mouse*), and then pressing a *key* (which may be incorporated in the mouse).

ICR International Council for Reprography.

ICSSD International Committee for Social Sciences Documentation and Information.

I-cycle See *machine cycle*.

ID Identification. A unique set of *characters* which are assigned to a computer user and employed during a *log-on*.

IDA *Integrated Digital Access*.

IDC Internationale Dokumentationsgesellschaft für Chemie. A joint venture of 12 chemical companies in West Germany, Austria and the Netherlands. Its aim is to develop and operate a computerized *information storage and retrieval system* for chemical information.

IDD International *direct distance dialling*.

IDDS International Digital Data Service. A *data transmission* service.

idea processor *Software* which integrates *text editing* and text management or manipulation. Also known as an 'outline processor'. Material is organized in the form of an indented outline of topics and subtopics. These can be expanded in order to incorporate pieces of text which are pulled into the document from the *database*. The document may be viewed in full, or 'collapsed' to show only the headings of each section (see *text database management system*).

identification The coded name assigned to an item of *data*. It normally consists of a series of *characters*.

identify To assign a *label*, either to a *file* (ie to create a *file name*), or to *data*.

idle character A *control character* sent down a *line* when there is no information to be transmitted.

idle time Time during which a machine is ready for operation, but is not in actual use.

IEC *International Electro-technical Commission.*

IEEE Institute of Electrical and Electronics Engineering, US.

IEEE-488 A standard *interface* for connecting devices to a microcomputer.

IEEE 802 A number of committees set up under the auspices of the *IEEE* to establish standards for various kinds of *LAN* technology. They include:

802.1	*Internetworking* and *architecture* addressing
802.2	*Logical link control*
802.3	*CSMA/CD* (Ethernet)
802.4	*Token bus*
802.5	*Token ring*
802.6	*Metropolitan area networks*
802.7	*Broadband LAN* advisory group
802.8	*Fibre-optic LAN* advisory group

IERE Institution of Electronic and Radio Engineers, UK.

IFD International Federation for Documentation. Also known as FID.

IFIP International Federation for Information Processing.

IFIPS International Federation of Information Processing Societies.

IFRM See *International Frequency Registration Board*.

IIA Information Industry Association (US).

IIASA International Institute for Applied Systems Analysis. An international group of 17 organizations which uses *computer conferencing* and *teleconferencing* to coordinate its research activities.

IIC *International Institute of Communications.*

I Inf Sc Institute of Information Scientists. A UK professional body, also known as *IIS*.

IIS See *I Inf Sc*.

IKBS See *intelligent knowledge-based systems*.

ikon Alternative spelling for *icon*.

ILL *Inter-library loan.*

illegal character A combination of *bits* (a *false code*) which a computer is unable to recognize as representing a *character*.

illegal operation An operation that a computer is unable to perform.

image data tablet See *data tablet*.

image dissector 1. A mechanical, or electrical, device which detects the light level in *optical character recognition*. 2. A detector for scanning the image produced by a photo-cathode.

image printer A *printer* which uses optical technology to compose the image of a complete page from *digital input*. The final copy is usually produced as print on paper. Unlike an *intelligent copier*, an image printer cannot produce prints directly from *hard copy*.

image processing The processing of images using computer techniques. This can cover a variety of processes, including enhancement of images, extraction of particular features, *digital* storage of images for transmission or later retrieval, etc.

IMDS International Microform Distribution Service (see *microform*).

immediate processing Synonymous with *demand processing*.

impact printing A conventional means of printing in which a hard die hammers an inked ribbon on to the paper. It is used, for example, in typewriters, many *dot matrix printers* and *line printers*.

imposition A printing term. The placing of several pages together on a sheet with correct margins, so that, when the sheet is folded, the pages will appear printed in the correct sequence and position.

IMRADS Information management, retrieval and dissemination system (see *information retrieval system*).

IMS Information Management System. An *IBM* mainframe *operating system*.

IMS-DB *IMS database software*.

IMS-DC *IMS* denotes a data communication system. IMS-DC supports on-line access to *databases* run under *IMS-DB*.

IMS-VS *IMS* with *virtual storage*.

incompatibility See *compatibility*.

indent Additional space inserted before the first word in a line.

index At the most general level, an index consists of a series of identifiers each of which characterizes a document, *abstract*, or other piece of information. These identifiers can be arranged in a variety of ways to suit user needs. Examples are indexes of authors, titles, dates, countries, institutions, report numbers.
The most complex indexing operation is usually the production of subject indexes. The type of indexing system used is often called the index language (see *information retrieval system* and *indexing*).

indexed sequential file (organization) A *sequential file* on *disc* which has indexes to indicate the physical location of a *record* with a given *key* (or value for a *secondary index* field).

indexing The process by which 'labels' are produced for documents, or for information. These labels are used for subsequent retrieval of the original document, or information (see *information retrieval techniques*). Many of the items contained in a document can be used to provide indexing terms, eg author, author affiliation, subject, providing a wide variety of *indexes*. In derived-term indexing, the indexing terms are taken from the document itself. In assigned-term indexing, the indexer assesses the document and decides what terms to apply to it. Thus *natural language* indexing is 'derived-term'; whereas indexing using a list of subject-headings is 'assigned-term'. In pre-coordinate indexing, the indexer combines more than one term to describe a document, and the document can be found listed under the combination of terms. In post-coordinate indexing, the indexing terms are assigned individually, and the searcher uses his/her own combination of terms. Most advanced computerized information systems, particularly *bibliographic databases*, are post-coordinate. Classification systems can be regarded as pre-coordinate indexing systems, where the terms are arranged according to their subject relationships (see *automatic indexing*).

index page In *viewdata* (interactive *videotex*) systems, the *page* which gives the routing instructions for finding specific subjects or information.

index register A device for automatically changing *addresses* of computer *instructions* whilst still storing the instructions in the *memory*.

index term A term used to classify a document, or item, in a *database* (see *keyword, information retrieval system* and *techniques*).

indicative abstract See *abstract*.

inexact reasoning Facility within an *expert system* which permits inclusion of imprecise rules and provides a means for manipulating combinations of such rules as necessary.

INFCO Information Committee of the *International Standards Organization*.

inference engine Part of an *expert system* which enables inferences to be drawn from a *knowledge base*.

inferior A synonym for *subscript*.

INFOL Information Orientated Language. A *high level language* developed by the Control Data Corporation, US.

INFORM Also called *ABI/ INFORM*. A US *database* containing business information. It is accessible via *BRS, Lockheed* and *SDC*.

informatics A word derived from the French 'informatique'. It covers the study of information and its handling, especially by means of *new information technology*.

information Data processed and assembled into a meaningful form.

information abstract See *abstract*.

information broker A professional intermediary who provides customized information packages on a commercial basis. Brokers offer *on-line searching, document delivery* and information management expertise.

information channel The *hardware* linking two *terminals* in a *data transmission* link.

information feedback Data received by a *terminal* are retransmitted to the sending terminal for checking.

information intermediary See *information broker*.

information provider This term is used mainly in the context of *viewdata* (interactive *videotex*) systems. It describes an individual or organization providing material for the *database(s)* involved.

information retrieval system An information retrieval system basically provides information to users in response to their requests. In information technology, the term refers to the methods and processes whereby computer *files* containing information can be searched for particular *items*, in response to the definition of particular user needs. Since the performance of an information retrieval system is necessarily related to the ways in which information is stored and categorized, the expression 'information retrieval system' is normally used to include data and file compilation and *storage*, in addition to the search for, and delivery of, information items. More specifically, the performance of a retrieval system depends on the ability to maintain a consistent and clear boundary definition to its coverage, to gather information within that boundary, and to develop *indexing systems* which provide the closest possible coincidence between the classification of items within the *database* and the description of their information needs by users (see *completeness, relevance*). This initial classification of additions to the database is sometimes carried out manually, by allocating multiple indexing terms (often called *keywords*) to each incoming item. Alternatively, and with increasing frequency, automatic indexing methods are used. These have greatest applicability for *bibliographic databases*, where a document's content can be indexed by means of *key-word-in-context* terms. These are allocated by the computer on the basis of an analysis of individual words, and groups of words, in document titles. Items once indexed, are entered on files. Several different types of file organization are commonly used, the simplest of which is the *serial file*: a sequential listing of items with no indication of the links between them. While economical in storage space, a sequential search of a complete database can require a great deal of computer time. This problem is most frequently overcome by creating *inverted files*: an inverted directory is used to store, for each applicable keyword (or indexing item) the corresponding

set of document or item identifications and locations. Files can be held on a variety of different storage media; the form chosen depending on the type of file organization adopted and the amount of data contained. *Magnetic tape* is usually used for serial files, since the whole file has to be searched to meet each user request. If, however, index terms can direct the search to particular items, eg via inverted files, then *direct access storage devices*, eg *magnetic drums* and *magnetic discs*, can provide a far more rapid response. The actual search of a database can be carried out either *off-line* or *on-line*. Off-line systems have cost advantages and have proved useful in servicing *selective dissemination of information systems* and other current awareness services. They also feed into many secondary services. On-line searching has the advantage of being *interactive*, permitting 'browsing', and giving immediate results. Information retrieval systems are thus increasingly going on-line (see *on-line searching*).

information retrieval techniques Most existing computer information retrieval (IR) systems are actually systems for the retrieval of bibliographic references to articles, books, reports, patents, etc. But there are IR systems for retrieving numerical and business data, and, with the advent of *videotex*, a wide range of information of all kinds is available via computer. Various techniques can be used to extract information from these systems. Their characteristics can be described in terms of bibliographic retrieval. There are many ways of characterizing a document, eg by author name, or subject: these are the identifying 'labels' of the document. The essence of most IR is the matching of these 'labels' with enquiry 'labels' used by the person who is interrogating the system.

When the labels match, there is said to be a 'hit'; and the user can then retrieve the bibliographic references to the matching documents. Some very sophisticated systems have been developed on the basis of this relatively simple concept. The documentary labels typically employed for retrieval include: name of author, or authors; an article/book title; a number, eg *ISBN*, patent number, report number; a *Copyright Clearance Center* number; a publisher's name; a place of publication; a volume number and a part number (for *serials*); page numbers; a date of publication; a date of submission and a date of acceptance, eg for research papers; the form of publication, eg paper or *microform*; author affiliation; the body providing funds for the work; the language of the document; an *abstract* or summary; a list of references or *citations* to other documents or work; contents list, index, glossary, etc. Then there are items from the contents of the document, eg the text itself, data, tables, figures, captions.

In addition there are labels which can be added to the document – entered either in the course of publication, or by an indexer prior to entry of the bibliographic description into the *database*. Examples of these are: a classification code, eg *UDC* and/or a classification specific to the database system; index terms or phrases describing the contents; data or other *flags* indicating the presence of some kind of information, eg numerical data in the contents. In principle, all these items, both inherent and added, could be used as 'labels' to be matched against enquiries. In practice, no system makes use of them all. Searching a database consists of formulating an enquiry by combining the labels of interest in a way that the computer can understand. This is normally done by *Boolean logic*, which basically consists of AND, OR and NOT.

Suppose we wished to find out whether our database includes any documents on land reptiles or freshwater fish (except trout). We would express this as: ((freshwater AND fish) OR (reptiles AND land)) NOT trout. The exact formulation will depend on the structure of the database, and its associated *command language*. The database may be arranged in a *serial file*, where each *record* represents a document, or it may be in *inverted file* form, where each record contains some indexing term (or label) with a list of the documents to which that label applies. In a serial file search on a particular topic, each item must be searched in sequence; whereas in an inverted file only those records headed by the labels of interest need be accessed and searched. An inverted file usually requires the use of a subsidiary file, which gives a description of each document found in the search.

The terms that can be used in a search expression may be restricted by the nature of the database and by the *indexing language* used. For example, the terms denoting the subject content of a document (often called *descriptors*) may be controlled, so that problems due to synonyms, etc, are less likely to arise. Thus, in an *uncontrolled* (or free, or natural) language system, a search done on the phrase 'heart failure' would not retrieve items that used the expression 'cardiac failure' or 'cardiac arrest'. An essential aid to such bibliographic control is a listing of all the terms to be used, and their relationships. This is called a *thesaurus*.

Controlled language indexing has the advantage of synonym control. It can also help to restrict (or expand) a search in a controlled way, using the known relationships between the indexing terms. It has the disadvantage that the index can become rapidly out of date, and the corresponding danger of not being fully comprehensive.

Some systems use both controlled

and natural language indexing, whilst others allow variations of the search terms themselves, eg truncation, or *weighting*. It can be seen that the retrieval technique has an intimate relationship to the indexing system. There are many such systems which are, or can be, applied to computer retrieval (see *word/character frequency techniques, citation indexing*).

information science The study of information – its generation, communication and organization.

information spinner See *host*.

information storage and retrieval system See *information retrieval system*.

information storage and retrieval techniques See *information retrieval techniques*.

information technology The acquisition, processing, storage and dissemination of vocal, pictorial, textual and numerical information by means of *computers* and *telecommunications*.

information theory Theory concerning the measurement of quantities of information, and of the accuracy of information transmission and retrieval.

information transfer module (ITM) A device (developed by *ITT*) which permits intercommunication (ie provides an *interface*) between telephone, *telex* and data *terminals*. ITM converts the signals of each system into a form recognizable by either of the other two.

information vendor See *host*.

INFRAL Information Retrieval Automatic Language. A special computer *language* providing the ability to construct *bibliographies* from indexed information.

infrared Electromagnetic waves in the *band* between approximately 0.75 and 1000 micrometers. Certain types of transmission, eg via *fibreoptic cables*, employ these waves.

in-house line A privately owned, or leased, line connected to a public network.

in-house system A communications *network* which is either contained in one set of buildings, or which, at least, does not use *common carrier* facilities.

INIS International Nuclear Information Service. This relies on a *database* covering all aspects of nuclear science and technology (technical, economic, social and political) compiled by the International Atomic Energy Authority in Vienna. *On-line* and *off-line* search services are offered.

initialization The process of setting the initial values of variables at the commencement of a *program's* execution.

initial program load The procedure which causes an *operating system* to commence its operation.

inking A way of drawing lines on a *computer graphics* display; it involves moving a pointer across the display screen to trace the line.

ink jet printing A jet of liquid, issuing from an orifice, will break into droplets, if it is vibrated at an appropriate frequency. A charged electrode is placed near the jet, so that each droplet carries a charge. These charged droplets are then deflected by an electrostatic field. The deflection can be varied so that the ink drops can be directed to particular parts of a paper sheet. Ink jet printers are controlled by digitally-stored information. A main feature is that each printed copy can differ, since the printing is individually controlled (see diagram).

ink smudge/ink bleed Smudging of printed *OCR* characters which can prevent them subsequently being read.

ink squeekout The displacement of ink from the centre of a printed *OCR* character.

ink uniformity In *optical character recognition* (OCR), this refers to the variations in light intensity over the surface of characters.

in-line processing Synonymous with *demand processing*.

Inmarsat A marine version of *Intelsat* designed to provide *satellite communications* systems for the merchant navies of the world. The initial talks establishing Inmarsat were held in 1979.

Inpadoc The largest computerized patents *database* in the world, it is estimated to hold 98 per cent of the world's currently published patent documents. The annual number of updates is around one million items. The database is accessible via *Pergamon-Infoline* and *Lockheed*.

INPI Institut National de la Propriété Intellectuelle. The French Patent Office.

INPI-1 *Database* produced by the French Patent Office, covering French patent information. It is accessible via *Télésystème*.

INPI-2 *Database* produced by the French Patent Office, covering European patent information. It is accessible via *Télésystème*.

in-plant system Synonymous with *in-house system*.

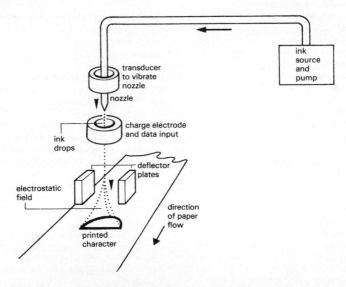

Diagrammatic portrayal of the process of ink jet printing. The jet of ink is directed onto the surface of the paper sheet, to form the required character, by breaking it in to droplets under vibration of the nozzle transducer, charging the droplets by passing them close to an electrode and then deflecting them very accurately by an electrostatic field that is directed by the computer data source.

input Information received by a computer, or its *storage devices*, from outside.

input bound A system where speed of performance is restricted by the capability of the *input* system, eg a *phototypesetter* able to work at over 1000 *characters* per second, but limited to 500 per second by a *paper-tape* input.

input device Any item of equipment which permits data and instructions to be entered into a computer's central *memory*, eg *MICR*, *OCR*, *keyboards*, *terminals* and *light pens*.

input limited Refers to a situation where the input speed is the factor which limits the rate of processing (see *input bound*).

input/output controller A device with an independent *data processing* capability. This offers additional independent paths between the *central processing unit* and its *peripherals*. It thus increases the number of *input/output channels* available to the system and speeds up its operations.

input/output control system The *hardware* and *software* which handle the transfer of data between the *main storage* and *external storage devices*.

input/output statement An instruction which results in a transfer of data between *main storage* and *input/output devices*.

input unit Synonymous with *input device*.

inscribe The preparation of a document which is to be read by *optical character recognition*. It usually involves recomposition of some of the characters in the document.

INSIS Inter-Institutional Integrated

Services Information System. A proposed information system linking the *CEC* to key national ministries and parliaments. The system aims to combine several services: telephone, *telex*, *teletex*, *fax*, *electronic mail*, *teleconferencing* and *word processing*.

INSPEC Information Services: Physics, Electrical and Electronics, and Computers and Control. Provides databases in these subjects which are made available for *on-line* searching via a variety of *hosts*. INSPEC also offers *magnetic tapes* for sale, and *SDI* services.

INSTARS Information storage and retrieval systems (see *information retrieval system*).

instruction A command (usually in the form of a *character* string) to a computer to carry out some operation.

instruction repertoire See *instruction set*.

instruction set The range of different *instructions* which an operator can use with a particular computer.

instrument In telecommunications, this is often used in the specific sense of a device used to originate and receive signals, eg telephone handsets, computer *terminals*.

Intaglio A printing method from a recessed image. Used for *gravure*, but also refers to copper-plate, die stamping, etc.

integer Whole number.

integrated circuit See *chip*.

integrated database A *database* in which there is no *redundancy*.

integrated data processing Refers to the interlinking of a variety of different data processing operations to form a large integrated processing system. The aim is to share resources, minimize the number of data entry operations, and eliminate unnecessary duplication.

integrated device A device which is an integral part of some other piece of *hardware*, with which it operates. For example, a microcomputer could contain an integral *disc drive*, *VDU* and *modem*.

Integrated Digital Access A *digital* exchange line which, as part of the implementation of an *ISDN*, will eventually replace the *analog* exchange line.

Integrated Services Digital Network A *digital transmission network* which is able to integrate voice, data and other services over a common transmission medium. An integrated telecommunications network carrying both voice and data must be completely digital, with sufficient *bandwidth* to handle the large amounts of information involved. The aim is to allow any communications device – telephone, *facsimile* or computer – access to the network through a standard wall socket and to transmit *digital* information to other devices similarly connected. The concept of an *ISDN* was proposed by the *CCITT* in 1984. The full standards are still in preparation but some telecommunications companies are installing systems which anticipate a full ISDN (see *System X*).

integrated software package A *software package* which combines a number of functions normally treated as separate programs. Such packages usually offer *word processing, spreadsheet, graphics* and *database* facilities, with the possibility of transferring information from one function to another.

integration A single cycle of

operations within an *interactive routine*.

integration testing The process whereby checks are made to ensure that the introduction of a new application on to a *multi-tasking* computer system does not adversely affect other (pre-existing) applications.

integrity With respect to data, can refer either to the preservation of files for their intended use, or the validation of data as both self-consistent, and consistent with the information that they represent.

integrity testing The process whereby checks are made to ensure that changes to one area of a system do not adversely affect other areas of that system.

intellect A *programming language* to help provide natural language methods of database searching.

intelligence 1. Describes the *data processing* capability of a computer. 2. The ability to learn and to improve a system in *artificial intelligence*.

intelligent copier Any copying device that uses a *microprocessor* to control its functions. Such copiers can often not only produce and collate copies made from print on paper, but can also accept *digital information* as an *input*, and use it directly to produce *hard copy*.

intelligent front-end system A system which acts as an intermediary between the *end-user* and an existing, external computer system, such as a *database management system* or a *document retrieval* system. An example of the use of intelligent *front-end systems* is in *on-line searching* in order to allow the inexperienced user access to *hosts* employing different *command languages*. Such systems often employ *menus* which allow the search strategy to be formulated in stages and the choice of database and host is made by the system.

intelligent knowledge-based system Synonymous with expert system.

intelligent terminal A terminal which can be used to perform local data processing without the help of a central processor.

Intelmatique The international marketing agency of the French PTT.

Intelpost A US and UK facsimile transmission service offered by Intelsat.

Intelsat International Telecommunications Satellite Consortium. The name Intelsat refers both to a communications satellite organization and to the satellite that it launches. The organization is currently the largest civilian system in this field. It was established in 1964 by 11 nations, and now has over a hundred member countries. Its first communications satellite – Intelsat I (popularly known as 'Early Bird') – was launched in 1965. The current model – Intelsat V – has a capacity some hundred times that of Intelsat I, in terms of channels available. Several are kept in geostationary orbit simultaneously, and handle both telephone and television channels. The different nations' share in Intelsat depends on their proportionate use of the system. In consequence, the US has been the leading shareholder to date (via Comsat), followed by the UK (see satellite communication).

interactional (interactive) mode Synonymous with conversational mode.

interactive The use of a computer, or other device, in real time in such a way that the operator can control its activity.

interactive routine A program, or that part of a program, which achieves a result by repeating a series of prescribed operations until a predetermined state is reached.

interactive video The combination of video recording with a computer (usually a microcomputer) (see interactive videodisc).

interactive videodisc The integration of videodisc technology with microprocessor controls (usually a microcomputer). The videodisc is controlled externally by a program on the microcomputer. The user can determine what is seen on the screen by entering commands via a keyboard or touch screen.

interactive videotex See videotex.

inter-block gap A space left in a file, between records or blocks of data, to allow a tape drive to accelerate, or decelerate.

Intercept Strategy Recommendations provided by the Department of Trade & Industry concerning the Open System Interconnection (OSI) standards. Full standards may take a considerable time to be ratified, although the basic technical content is often agreed upon in advance. The Intercept Strategy is intended to provide guidelines on the likely content of standards nearing completion so that organizations can have a head start in their implementation.

interface Used as a general term to describe the connecting link between two systems. Most frequently refers to the hardware and software required to couple together two processing elements in a computer system. Also used to describe the recommended standards for such interconnections. For example, Interface-CCITT is an international standard for the interface between data processing terminals and communication equipment.

interfaker Jargon for a junction box which allows connection between two other devices whose plugs have different pin allocations.

interference Confusion, or loss of clarity, caused by unwanted signals, or *noise*, in a communication system.

interlacing In TV *scanning*, the technique of interposing two fields to reduce *flicker*.

interleaving 1. A programming technique in which segments of a first program are inserted into a second program, so that both programs can be executed simultaneously. 2. A technique for *accessing* data from two or more *storage devices*, so that they can be processed simultaneously.

Inter-library loan (ILL) The exchange of information in *hard copy* or *microform* between libraries.

Interlink A *value added service* operated by Unilever Computer Services (UK).

interlock A computer device to prevent unauthorized access to, or change of, data, eg *log-in* procedure.

INTERMARC International Machine-Readable Catalogue (see *MARC*).

intermediate copy A copy of a document which serves as an intermediate stage in producing a final copy, eg a photographic white-on-black negative from which a black-on-white copy can be made.

intermediate storage Synonymous with *working storage*.

internal label A *machine-readable* label on a *storage device* providing information on the contents of that device (eg the data on a *disc*). Compare with *external label*.

internally stored program A *program* stored in a *ROM*.

internal memory *Memory* to which the *central processor* of a computer has *direct access*.

International code Another (usually American) name for Morse code.

International Economic Abstracts A Dutch *database* covering business and economics information. It is accessible via *Lockheed*.

International Electro-Technical Commission An international organization, based in Geneva, which recommends international standards for electrically operated equipment. It works with *ISO* in this specialized area.

International Frequency Registration Board (IFRB) One of the three main organizations within the *International Telecommunications Union* (ITU). IFRB is particularly involved in registering and standardizing the radio frequencies used internationally.

International Institute of Communications UK-based, but with international trustees, officers and Advisory Council, IIC analyses social, political, cultural and legal issues relating to communication (particularly electronic communication). It aims to assist governments and industries in the formulation of policies for handling new information technology.

International Network Working Group A working group of *IFIP*; discusses *network standards* and *protocols*.

International Nuclear Information System See *INIS*.

International Packet Switching Service IPSS is a public automatic switched data service providing access between UK data terminals and computer systems abroad (and vice versa). The service features packet assembly and transmission of data, and leads to compatibility between otherwise incompatible equipment (see packet switching).

International Special Committee on Radio Interference Committee set up by the IEC to establish standards for telecommunications equipment, with particular reference to the control of radio interference.

International Standards Organization A body which attempts to establish international standards and to help coordinate national standards.

International System See SI.

International Telecommunications Union (ITU) The ITU is the telecommunications agency of the United Nations. It has three main components – CCIR, CCITT and International Frequency Registration Board.

internetworking The interconnection of separate, heterogeneous computer networks to form large communications domains.

interpreter A computer program which controls the execution of another program which has not been previously compiled or assembled.

inter-record gap See inter-block gap.

interrogation The process of searching a database. The search statements are formulated in order to carry out an on-line search.

interrupt A signal to the CPU which indicates that priority must be given to another activity, eg it may be necessary to interrupt the running of a program in order to provide a printout.

intersatellite link The transmission of messages between communications satellites (rather than from satellite to earth station).

Interstream One A service offered by British Telecom which provides a link between the PSS networks and the UK telex system.

Intrafax Closed circuit facsimile transmission system leased to US Government Agencies, military and industrial corporations by Western Union.

invariant field See field.

inverted file A form of file organization frequently used for databases in information retrieval systems. When items are added to a database, their attributes are identified by means of index terms. Such index terms are then brought together to create an inverted file, so called because it lists all items possessing that attribute. Thus, for example, in a bibliographic database an inverted file might be set up for all items (here titles of articles) containing the word 'oxygen'; or on a police records database, an inverted file might be created for all items (here persons) who had ever been charged with theft. Inverted files occupy more storage space than is required for serial files holding an equivalent amount of data. But the creation of inverted files obviates the need for serial searching, and so greatly reduces access time (particularly important for on-line searching).

INWG International Network Working Group.

I/O An abbreviation of input/ output.

IOB Inter-Organization Board for Information Systems and Related Activities, UN.

I/O bound A *data processing* operation dominated by *input/output* operations.

I/O buffer A temporary *storage* area for computer *input/output* (see *buffer*).

IOC (or I/OC) *Input/output controller.*

IOCS *Input/output control system.*

IoD Information on Demand. US organization offering a *document delivery* service.

I/O equipment All equipment which *reads input* or *writes output*.

I/O port An *interface* socket which enables an external *input/output device* to be connected to a microcomputer.

IP *Information provider.*

IP terminal A *terminal* which can be used for creating, or updating, *videotex pages*.

IPA International Pharmaceutical Abstracts. A US *database* accessible via *Lockheed*.

IPC Industrial process control (see *numerical control*).

IPG Information Policy Group of the Organization for Economic Cooperation and Development (OECD).

IPL 1. *International program loading*. 2. Information processing language (see *language*).

IPSS *International Packet Switching Service.*

IR Information retrieval (see *information retrieval system* and *information retrieval techniques*).

IRCS Medical Science A *full-text* database of 32 medical and biomedical journals published by Elsevier. There is simultaneous availability of the *on-line* and the printed versions.

IRE Institute of Radio Engineers, US.

IRL Information retrieval language (see *information retrieval system*, *on-line searching* and *search language*).

IRMS Information Retrieval and Management System provided by *IBM*, US.

Iros A US *teleordering* system.

IRRD International Road Research Documentation. A *database* produced by the Organization for Economic Cooperation and Development (OECD) in Paris. It covers roads, traffic, vehicles, traffic safety and related topics. It is accessible via *SCANNET*.

IRT Institute of Reprographic Technology, UK.

ISAM Index sequential access method. A way of accessing data from *index sequential files*.

ISAR Information storage and retrieval (see *information retrieval systems*).

ISBD International Standard Bibliographic Description. An internationally used convention for the description of documents, established by the *ALA*.

ISBD (CM) *ISBD* for cartographic materials.

ISBD (G) General *ISBD*.

ISBD (M) *ISBD* for monographs.

ISBD (NBM) *ISBD* for non-book materials.

ISBD (S) *ISBD* for serials.

ISBN International Standard Book Number. Each book published is allocated its own unique number (ISBN), consisting of 10 digits. These are made up of: a group identifier (linguistic, geographical, national or other relevant group); a publisher identifier; a title identifier; and a *check digit*, used to help identify errors in transcribing the number. The ISBN is used to aid the location of a book within a library, or *information retrieval system*, and it can also be used in *teleordering* (see *ISSN*).

ISDN *Integrated Services Digital Network.*

ISDS *International Serials Data System* (of *UNISIST*).

IS file *Index sequential file.*

ISI Institute for Scientific Information. US compilers of *bibliographic databases*, most notably the *Science Citation Index* (see *SCI Search*).

ISL *Intersatellite link.*

ISMEC *Information Service in Mechanical Engineering.* A US-based *database* covering all aspects of mechanical engineering. It is accessible via *ESA-IRS, Lockheed* and *SDC.*

ISO *International Standards Organization.*

ISR 1. Information storage and retrieval (see *information retrieval system*). 2. Index to Scientific Reviews: *current awareness service* based on the *Science Citation Index.*

ISSN International Standard Serial Number. Each *serial* title published is allocated a unique number (ISSN) consisting of eight digits (in two groups of four). The first seven digits constitute an unambiguous title number for the serial whilst the eighth is a *check digit* used to help identify errors in transcribing the number.
The ISSN is used to aid communication between publishers and libraries, to aid *inter-library loan* and *document delivery systems*, and in the maintenance of *bibliographic databases* (see *ISBN*).

ISSP Information System for Policy Planning. A US Government system which serves the Office of Management and Budget (incorporates *DIDS*).

ISTIM Interchange of scientific and technical information in *machine language.*

IT *Information technology.*

italic A sloping *type fount.*

ITAP Information Technology Advisory Panel (UK) (see *CICI*).

item A unit of information relating to a single document, person, etc, contained within a *database.*

item size The number of *characters* in a unit of data.

iteration 1. Repetition of a series of instructions until some preset condition is satisfied. 2. In *data analysis*, describes a variable number of like data items.

ITM *Information transfer module.*

ITT International Telephone and Telegraphic Corporation (US).

ITU *International Telecommunications Union.*

IVIPA International Videotex Information Providers' Association.

IWP International Word Processing Organization based in the US (see *word processing*).

J

J Joule. SI unit of energy.

jacket Has a specific meaning in *microform*, when it refers to transparent plastic envelopes used for the insertion of short strips of *microfilm*.

jack plug See *jack socket*.

jack socket A connecting socket used for terminating the wiring of a circuit. Access is gained by inserting a jack plug.

JANET The *Joint Academic Network*.

JAPATIC Japan Patent Information Center. Produces the *database*, and acts as *host* for the Japanese PATOLIS patent search service.

JAS Japanese Awareness Service. An on-line *database* covering Japanese scientific and technical literature, produced by Engineering Information Inc.

JAWS Just another work station. Refers to any large screen graphics *work station* which runs the *Unix operating system*.

JCL *Job control language*.

JICST Japan Information Center of Science and Technology. Japan's largest *database* producer and *host* (see *JOIS*).

jitter Raggedness in copy received over a *facsimile transmission* system.

job A specific piece of work to be *input* to a computer. Each job normally requires a number of *runs*.

job control language A language understood by a computer's *operating system*. It allows users to

tell the computer how a *job* should be controlled within the system.

job-orientated language A computer *language* which is designed for the specific needs of a particular type of *job*.

job-orientated terminal A *terminal* designed for a particular type of job, eg checking and making flight reservations, conducting stock market transactions.

Joint Academic Network A *wide area network* established for the use of all UK universities and some polytechnics. It replaces an earlier network set up by the Science and Engineering Research Council (*SERCNET*) and its purpose is the sharing of computer resources among the university research community.

JOIS Japanese On-line Information System operated by *JICST*. The present service (*JOIS II*) enables users to retrieve bibliographic information on-line in Kana (Japanese symbols), Kanji (Chinese characters) or English from the JICST database. JOIS II also gives access to some major non-Japanese databases.

Jordanline A *text-numeric database* giving information about UK companies, including detailed financial data.

Jordanwatch A *text-numeric database* made available by *Pergamon-Infoline* (see *Jordanline*).

journal 1. Periodical publication (see *electronic journal*). 2. A list of messages sent and received by a terminal. 3. A record of all the changes made to a set of data.

joystick A lever whose motions

control the movement of a *cursor*, or it can be used to *write* on a *VDU*. The name derives from the analogous lever used to control the movements of an airplane.

JSP Jackson Structured Programming: a common technique used to structure data and its processing.

J-tree See *junction grammar*.

judder Vibration within *facsimile transmission* equipment, leading to the distortion of transmitted images.

jukebox A device which automatically selects a retrieved item from a range of storage devices, such as *videodiscs*, *optical discs*, *microfiche*, held in a central store. Jukeboxes are often used in conjunction with *computer-assisted retrieval* systems.

junction grammar (JG) A model of language structure used for analysing sentences in *machine translation*. It allows each sentence to be broken down into its syntactic elements (subjects, verbal predicates, objects, etc). These are arranged as a structured array

resembling a family tree (called a *J-tree*). The meaning of a sentence is then derived from the relationship between the meanings of individual elements in the J-tree (see *machine-aided translation* and *HAMT*).

justification See *justify*.

justification range Text is usually *justified* by introducing variable word spaces. The justification range defines the permitted minimum and maximum space which can be inserted between words in a line.

justification routine A computer *program* that enables a *phototypesetter* to produce *justified* material.

justify To adjust the positions of words on a page of text so that the margins are regular, with lines beginning (and/or ending) at the same distance from the edge of the page. Type can be aligned on the left, with a ragged right margin (flush left); or, less often, aligned on the right with a ragged left margin (flush right); or, as is customary in traditional printing, the type can be justified by aligning both margins.

K

k An abbreviation for kilo, denoting a thousand (10³). When referring to *storage capacity*, is generally used to mean about a thousand. For example, a 64k *word* store actually contains 65,536 words.

Kansas City Audio Cassette Standard A standard convention for encoding data on *audio cassette* tapes.

kb Kilobyte.

kcs One thousand (k) characters per second. A unit of *data transmission* speed, eg 50 kcs –50,000 *characters* per second.

KDEM Kurzweil Data Entry Machine. An *OCR* device which converts *hard copy* into *digital* information.

KEEPS Kodak Ektaprint Electronic Publishing System. An *electronic publishing* system produced by Kodak. A typical *configuration* includes several text entry *terminals*, a scanner to *digitize* graphics, a graphics *work station* for creating pages with text and graphics in place, and a *laser printer*.

kern In *hot metal*, this is any part of the type that extends beyond the main body. In *phototypesetting*, an overhang between adjacent characters must be correctly overlapped. This process is called either 'kerning', or 'mortising'.

kerning See *kern*.

key 1. A marked button, or lever, which is depressed (or touched) to register a *character*. 2. A group of characters used in the identification of an *item*, and to facilitate access to it.

keyboard A device equipped with an ordered array of *keys* (1.), which are manually operated to encode data or instructions (see diagram).

keyboarding Entering text, or data, via a *keyboard*.

keyboard lockout A property of a *keyboard* such that the keyboard cannot be used to send a message over a *network* whilst the required circuit is engaged.

keyboard send/receive A *teletypewriter* transmitter and receiver which transmits from the *keyboard* only.

keyboard-to-disc system Synonymous with *key-to-disc*.

keyboard-to-tape system Synonymous with *key-to-tape*.

KEYFAX A US broadcast *videotex* system which transmits via satellite to *cable television* companies.

key letter in context See *KLIC*.

keypad Either a hand-held *keyboard*, or a subsection of a larger desktop keyboard, which has fewer keys than a full *terminal* keyboard and is used to provide electronic input.

key phrase in context See *KPIC*.

key punch Synonymous with *card punch*.

key stroke The operation of a single key on a *keyboard*.

key stroke verification The re-*keyboarding* of data to check the accuracy of initial data entry.

key-to-disc A data entry technique in which data are sent directly from a *keyboard* to a disc file.

key-to-tape A data entry technique in which data are sent directly from a *keyboard* to a magnetic tape-based file.

keyword A substantive word in the title of a document (or other item within a *database*) which can be used to classify content. Such words provide access to the item when they are used as *search terms* (see *information retrieval systems*). For example, the keywords in the title, 'The Influence of Smoking on Lung Cancer', would be 'Smoking', 'Lung' and 'Cancer'.

keyword and context See *KWAC*.

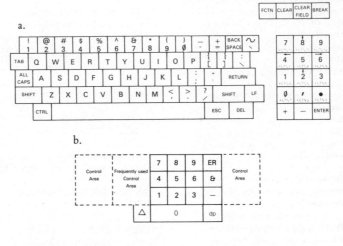

Four types of keyboard: a. A conventional, typewriter style keyboard for a word processor; b. c. and d., three keyboards from ECMA Standard 23, which show keyboards generating the ECMA 7-bit coded character set. (b) is used exclusively for numerical data; (c) is an alphanumerical keyboard for predominantly numeric data; and (d) is for predominantly alphabetic data.

keyword in context (KWIC) A form of *automatic indexing*. As items are added to a *database*, *keywords* are extracted from their titles (or from *abstracts* or portions of text). Common words which are not indicative of content, eg and, of, the, etc, are eliminated by means of a *stop list*.

For each keyword a list can then be generated which shows the context within which it appears in each item. An entry in a KWIC index normally consists of lines of text printed in such a way that the keyword appears in a central column (in alphabetical order), with context to left and right. A document reference number is entered for each line (contrast, *KWOC*).

key word out of context See *KWOC*.

kilo A prefix signifying one thousand (10^3).

kilobaud A measure of data transmission speed: a thousand bits per second (see *baud*).

kilobyte One thousand *bytes*, frequently used in the context of *floppy disc* storage capacity.

KiloStream A high speed *digital* communications service operated by *British Telecom*. KiloStream channels are used to link *System X* exchanges and may be accessed via a direct hard-line connection or *dial-up PSTN* lines.

KiloStream Plus An updated version of *KiloStream*. It is being used by the Inland Revenue to modernize PAYE (Pay As You Earn) tax operations.

KISS Keep it simple sir. Computer jargon – refers to *programming* activities. ('Sir' is sometimes replaced by 'stupid'.)

KIT Key Issue Tracking. A US *database* which provides a

constantly updated index of currently important topics.

KLIC Key letter in context. An *indexing* system for producing *permuted* lists of terms. All terms are sorted by each letter in every term. The remainder of the term is also displayed. Similar to *KWIC* indexes, but based on letters instead of words.

klu(d)ge A slang term to describe an unsatisfactory combination of component parts in a system. Derogatory, possibly derived from German 'klug' (smart, witty). Also used to refer to an arrangement of pieces of equipment which, although made to work in conjunction with each other, were not intended to do so.

knowledge base Part of an *expert system* containing statements (facts and assumptions) and a set of rules describing the relationship between such statements.

knowledge-based systems See *intelligent knowledge-based systems*.

knowledge engineer An *expert systems software engineer* who works with a specialist in a particular domain to establish a *knowledge base* for that domain.

knowledge engineering Refers to the work of a *knowledge engineer*, and more generally, to the design, development and production of *expert systems*.

Knowledge Index An evening and weekend service offered by the US host *Dialog* for home computer users. It provides access to Dialog's most popular *databases* at cheaper rates.

kph Keystrokes per hour. Unit of *keyboarding* speed.

KPIC Key phrase in context. An

indexing system similar to *KWIC* and *KLIC*, but using phrases instead of letters, or words, as the fundamental units.

KPO *Key punch* operator.

KSR *Keyboard send/receive.*

Kurzweil reading machine An aid for the blind, which converts printed matter into computer data using an *optical character recognition* (OCR) device. The data are then transformed to spoken form via *speech synthesis.*

Kurzweil 4000 A commercial OCR machine. Kurzweil is probably the best-known producer of OCR equipment.

KWAC Keyword and context. An *indexing system* similar to *KWIC.* Titles of documents are *permuted* to bring each significant word to the beginning, in alphabetical order. This *keyword* is followed by subsequent words in the title, and then by that part of the title which came before the significant word.

KWIC *Keyword in context.*

KWOC Keyword out of context. An *indexing system* in which titles are printed in full under as many *keywords* as the indexer considers useful (contrast *keyword in context*).

L

LA Library Association. The UK professional association for librarians.

label A *character*, or group of characters, used to identify an item of data, a *record* or a *file* (see *internal label* and *external label*).

Labordoc A *database* compiled by the International Labour Office in Geneva, covering labour, demography and related topics. It is accessible via *SDC*.

LAN *Local area network.*

language A set of representations and rules by which information is communicated within, and between, computers, or between computers and their users (see *computer language, indexing language, microcomputer language, source language, target language*).

language translator 1. A computer *program* used to translate other programs from one *language* to another, eg *BASIC* to *FORTRAN*. 2. A program which assists in the translation of spoken languages, eg from English to French. 3. A part of the computer which translates *input data* and *instructions* into *machine code*.

lap-held (computer) A *portable* computer, usually small enough to fit into a briefcase, designed for use away from the office.

large scale integration See *LSI*.

LARP Local and remote printing. An expression used in *word processing* to indicate that *print-out* can be obtained either locally (near the user's *terminal*), or at a more distant (ie remote) point.

Laser Laser stands for light amplification by the stimulated emission of radiation. The laser was first developed in the 1960s. It produces a narrow, high-energy light beam, which can be used for a wide range of communication activities (see diagram). Examples are printing (see *electrophotographic printing*), *microform* production and optical scanning (see *optical character recognition* and *optical disc*). The beam can also be used to carry signals along *optical fibres*.

LaserCard A credit-card size device with an optical data stripe which gives it a storage capacity of up to 2 *megabytes* (about 800 pages of text). The optical data stripe is made of high resolution photographic emulsion, a patented material called Drexon. LaserCards are recorded and read by a *Laser* beam.

laser COM COM produced by a laser system.

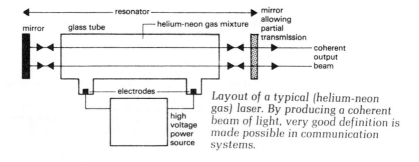

Layout of a typical (helium-neon gas) laser. By producing a coherent beam of light, very good definition is made possible in communication systems.

lasercomp A device (manufactured by Monotype International) which uses *fount*, stored in *digital* form, and a horizontal scanning *raster* (acting on film or photosensitive paper) to record data.

laser electrophotographic printing See *electrophotographic printing*.

laser emulsion storage A *storage* medium based on the use of a *laser* to irradiate a photosensitive surface.

laser line follower An *input device* for graphic information. A *laser* beam follows and traces continuous lines, recording them in *machine-readable* form. The laser line follower offers advantages over other forms of *scanner*, since it eliminates unwanted information, eg marks or dirt on the *hard copy*.

laser platemaker A device which can scan a page with a *laser* at one geographical location, transmit the resultant signals to a remote location, and produce a printing plate there using another laser. This is a form of *facsimile transmission*.

laser printer A very high speed quality printer (see *electrophotographic printing*).

laser scanner The coherence of laser beams enables them to focus on a very small area. Laser scanners can therefore be used for both recording and reading data. This leads to their use for storage devices (see, eg, *laser emulsion storage*), and for the sensing of characters as in *optical character recognition*.

Laser Vision A widely used *videodisc* produced by Philips.

latency A *waiting time* associated with the delay in *accessing* data from a *storage device*.

lateral reversal An image which has been reversed left-to-right.

launch vehicle The rocket used to place a satellite in orbit.

Lawtel A *closed user group* on the *Prestel* (UK interactive *videotex*) service, which provides legal information to a restricted group of users, including details of every legislative activity of central government within hours of publication.

layout In publishing, to describe page design, including all text and graphics.

layout character Synonymous with *format*.

LC Library of Congress, US.

LCCC Library of Congress Computer Catalog.

LCCMARC Library of Congress Current *MARC* file. A *database* giving a catalogue of monographs from 1977. Includes *CIP* data.

LCD *Liquid crystal display.*

LCMARC Library of Congress *MARC* files starting in 1968.

LCR Longitudinal redundancy check. A procedure for checking errors in a computer *program*.

LDRI Low data rate input.

LDX Long distance xerox. A form of communication combining *facsimile transmission* with *xerographic* copying.

leader 1. The first *record* in a *file*, or the first *field* in a record, which is used to identify that particular file or record. 2. The blank piece of paper which precedes the data recorded on a *paper tape*.

LEADERMART Derives, in part, from Lehigh Automatic Device for Efficient Retrieval. A system for automatic *natural language* *searching*. Documents are reduced to noun phrases for searching purposes. English language requests are entered, and those noun phrases which best fit the request are displayed for examination. Documents can also be ranked in order, depending on the extent to which they match the original search statement (see *BROWSER* and *SMART*).

leaders Dots (or dashes) used by the printer to fill in a line so as to lead the reader's eye across the page to data at the end of the line.

leading (pronounced 'ledding') A term (derived from traditional *typesetting*) for the insertion of space between lines of text. The amount of space is usually measured in *points*. In *phototypesetting*, the term is used for the advance of the film after each line is set.

lead-in pages Videotex *routing pages*.

learning curve The growth of individual productivity with experience. For example, operators using *word processors* for the first time will usually become increasingly efficient as their experience of the system grows. The name derives from the practice of plotting productivity gains graphically.

leased line A telecommunications link (most often a telephone line) reserved for the sole use of the leasing customer.

least significant bit The last (ie 'rightmost') *bit* in a *binary number*.

least significant digit The last (ie 'rightmost') digit in a number.

LED display. *Light emitting diode* display (see diagram).

left justify Sometimes used as the equivalent of *flush left* (see justify).

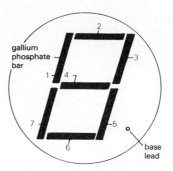

Example of an LED display element. To display, for instance, the numeral 6, terminals 1, 4, 5, 6 and 7 must be energized.

legal retrieval The use of an *information retrieval system* to obtain information on legal matters.

letterpress The main printing process for the last 500 years, but now in decline. Printing is by direct contact between an inked, raised image and the paper. There are three main types of press: plates, flat-bed cylinder (where the paper is wound on a cylinder), and rotary (where the printing plate, itself, is cylindrical).

letter-quality printer Any *printer* that can produce print of the same quality as a typewriter.

letter shift (capital shift) 1. Shifting from lower to upper case when entering text at a *terminal*. 2. In *Murray Code*, a shift from figures to letters.

LEXIS 1. Lexicography Information Service. This is a West German pure *MAT* system offering translation between English, French, German and Russian. It is based on an automated *dictionary*, normally interrogated in *batch* mode, with *COM* and printed output (see *machine-aided translation*). 2. A legal *database* which can be searched *on-line* (see *on-line searching*).

LIBCON/E Library of Congress

English. A *database* covering English-language monograph records derived from the Catalog of the US Library of Congress. It is accessible via SDC.

librarian 1. Person who controls a *library*. 2. A *program* used in maintaining a library (sometimes more explicitly called a librarian program).

librarian program See *librarian* (2.).

library As used in computer terminology, this refers to a collection of tested *programs*, *routines* and *subroutines*. Computer centres often maintain such libraries for internal use and external loan.

library automation The use of computer technology in libraries to replace manual systems for cataloguing, circulation control, etc.

library routine A tested *routine* that is kept in a computer *library*.

LIBRIS A Swedish cooperative *on-line cataloguing* system which incorporates the Swedish National Bibliography.

Libris A US *teleordering* system.

LIFO Last in, first out. Computer jargon referring to a sequence followed in *data processing*.

ligature Two or more characters which are joined together for printing purposes, eg fl.

light conduit An assembly of *optical fibres* used for the transmission of light signals.

light emitting diode A *diode* (electrical *switching* component) which emits light when excited by an electrical current.

light gun Synonymous with *light pen*.

light pen An electronic *stylus*, containing a light sensor, which can be used to specify a position on a *cathode ray tube display* (see diagram). Used for communication between a user and a computer, eg in *computer graphics*, page layout.

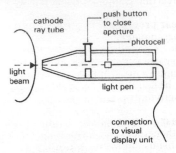

Schematic diagram of a light pen.

light stability The extent to which OCR characters are resistant to changes in apparent colour under varying types and intensities of illumination.

LILO Last in, last out. Computer jargon referring to a sequence followed in *data processing*.

limited distance adapter A *modem* designed to operate over short distances (up to, say, 30 miles).

limited distance modem Synonymous with *limited distance adapter*.

limiter A device used to reduce the power of an electrical signal when it exceeds a specified value.

Lindop Committee A committee established by the UK Government in 1978 to investigate and make recommendations for the safeguarding of information held on computers. The committee's work formed the basis for the *Data Protection Act*.

line 1. Any long narrow mark. 2. A *channel* through which signals can be transmitted. 3. A horizontal row of *characters* on a page, or *display screen*. 4. One scan across a *CRT* (especially in television).

linear predictive coding (LPC) A technique for analysing speech and converting it into *digital code*.

linear program A form of programmed instruction which follows a predetermined sequence of (ever more complex) steps (see *computer-aided instruction*). Should not be confused with *linear programming*.

linear programming A mathematical technique for breaking problems down into a form amenable to *computer* solution.

line-at-a-time printer Synonymous with *line printer*.

line concentration A means of matching a larger number of *input* channels with a smaller number of *output* channels – the latter usually working at a higher speed.

line drawing See *line illustration*.

line drawing display A *cathode ray tube display* on which lines can be drawn. The lines are either *input* directly using a *graphics tablet* or a *light pen*, or indirectly by defining the end points of the lines via a *keyboard*. Once entered, the lines can be extended, rotated or otherwise altered. Line drawing displays therefore provide a valuable tool in *computer-aided design* (see *computer graphics*).

line driver See *bus driver*.

line extender An amplifier in a *CATV* network that compensates for attenuation at a *spur* junction.

line-feed code A *code* which instructs a *printer* to move the *platen* up one *line* (3.).

line finder A device attached to a *platen* which moves it automatically to print on a specified *line* (3.) of a printed form.

line flyback See *flyback*.

line (display) generator A device used in conjunction with a *cathode ray tube* to generate dotted, dashed or continuous lines.

line illustration An illustration made from drawn lines only.

line level 1. The strength of a signal in a communications *line* (2.). 2. A set of *protocols* for data communication.

line load The percentage of a communications *line*'s (2.) total capacity that is in use at a given time.

line misregistration Deviation of a *line* (3.) of *characters* from an imaginary horizontal base line.

line number 1. *Photocomposed galley proofs* often have their lines numbered (as does *computer printout* of text) to facilitate locating the position of corrections. 2. In some *high level languages*, eg *BASIC*, line numbers are used to order and locate each instruction.

line printer A device for printing computer output. The printer contains sets of characters on continuous belts (called print chains) which are driven by the computer. An entire line of characters is printed as paper is fed continuously past the printing head (see diagram).

Line skip Synonymous with *white space skid*.

line speed The rate at which data can be transmitted over a communications channel. It is usually expressed as *bits* per second, or in *bauds*.

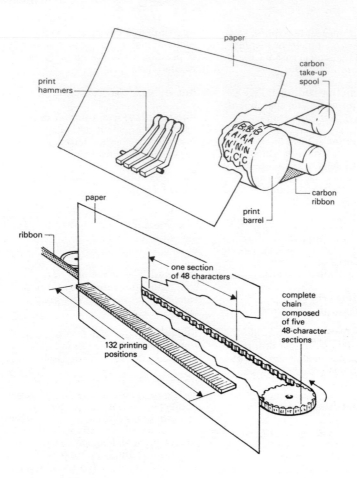

Two examples of line printers: a drum (or barrel) printer (above); and a chain printer (below). With the chain printer, each of 132 hammers can push the paper against the required character at the moment that it is brought into position on the rotating chain. With the drum printer, complete sets of characters are placed around the circumference of a wheel, a number of these wheels being mounted side by side along the drum. All the wheels move independently, allowing an entire line of required characters to be assembled. A signal input then instructs the hammers to strike, printing the whole line.

line status The status of a communication *line* (2.), eg whether it is ready to receive or transmit.

line switching *Switching* where a *circuit* is set up between incoming and outgoing *lines* (2.) (contrast *message switching*). The term is synonymous with circuit switching.

line termination unit Alternative name for a *data set adapter*.

link 1. A means for transmitting signals between two *terminals*. 2. A *routine* which brings together two *programs* for *execution*. 3. Code used to indicate associations between *index terms*.

link control procedure Synonymous with *link protocol*.

link protocol A *protocol* for data transfer over a *channel*.

link (segment) A *segment* within a *hierarchical database* which forms a link between a database *record* and a record on another database.

LIPL Linear Information Programming Language. A *high level language*.

liquid crystal display Liquid crystals do not generate light (unlike LEDs), but can be switched from an opaque to a transparent state. This can provide a *data display* if the liquid crystals are interposed between a light source and the observer.

LIS 1. Library and Information Science (see *information science*). 2. Lockheed Information Systems (see *Lockheed*).

LISA 1. Library and Information Science Abstracts. A UK-based database accessible via *SDC*. 2. An Apple microcomputer with *hardware* and *software* enhancement for automated office

procedures. It has advanced graphics features and *mouse* control.

LISP List processing. A *high level language*, first formulated in the late 1950s. Now widespread, and provides basis for *fifth-generation* languages, eg *LOGO* and *PROLOG*. Also used in *artificial intelligence* and text manipulation. LISP is one of the earliest list processing languages (more than 20 years old). It has developed numerous applications, eg in artificial intelligence, automatic theorem proving and computer programming verification.

LISR Line Information Storage and Retrieval. An information system used by *NASA*, US.

list 1. An ordered set of items of data. 2. An ordered set of *records* within a *file*. 3. The action of printing, or displaying, a list (in either of the above senses) without performing any additional *processing*.

list processing *Processing data* which are arranged in the form of *lists*.

literal 1. A symbol which defines itself, rather than standing for some other entity. For example, an integer is a literal, whereas a term in an algebraic expression is not. 2. In printing, it can mean a single *character* error. 3. A non-variable character *string* displayed on a *screen* or printed on an output document (eg a column heading).

literature search A search through a mass of documents to find those which can satisfy a user's requirements. The material sought usually relates to a particular specified topic, and the search is now increasingly carried out on-line (see *on-line information retrieval*).

lithography A method of printing

from a flat surface of stone or metal. The image areas on the plate are coated with a water-repellant ink, whilst the non-image areas are protected from the ink by a film of water. Modern presses typically use a rubber-covered cylinder to transfer the plate image to paper. This process is therefore called *offset litho*.

liveware Personnel involved in the running of *computers* and computer systems.

load To enter information, or a *program*, into a *computer*.

loader A *program* which is held in *permanent memory* and serves to enable any other program to be loaded into memory.

loading Adding *inductance* to a *transmission line* to reduce amplitude distortion.

loading program Synonymous with *loader*.

loading routine Synonymous with *loader*.

load on call Loading data, or *programs*, into *storage* as, and when, they are required.

load sharing *Distributed processing* technique.

lobe The angular region over which an antenna (or *aerial*) experiences strong reception.

LOCAL Load on call. This usage should not be confused with the normal use of the word 'local', as in *local area network* (see *load*).

local area network A system which links together *computers*, *electronic mail*, *word processors* and other electronic office equipment (see *work station*) to form an inter-office, or inter-site *network*. Such networks

usually also give access to 'external' networks, eg public telephone and *data transmission networks*, *viewdata, information retrieval systems*, etc).

local central office See *local exchange*.

local exchange The *exchange* where individual subscribers' *lines* terminate.

local line The *channel* connecting a subscriber's equipment to the *local exchange*.

local loop See *local line*.

local mode When a *terminal* which normally provides *access* to a *network* is used as a *stand-alone* facility.

local network See *local area network*.

local origination In the context of *cable television*, this refers to television programmes which are produced within the local community.

local printer A printer used for *local printing*.

local printing *Remote printing* using a printer which is connected to the same *controller* as the *terminal* used to enter the print request.

location A *storage* position which can hold one *computer word*. Location is designated by a specific *address*.

Lockheed The world's largest *database host*. It offers *on-line* access to over a hundred databases covering a broad spectrum of subjects.

lock-up The state of a computer when a program has locked it into a procedure from which it cannot escape.

log file A *file* which records all transactions in a system to provide recovery *back-up* and historical records.

logic When used in such terms as 'logic system' or 'logic *chip*', this refers to a system whose components can only take up one of two states. It is often taken to be synonymous with *binary* and *digital*.

logical database A *database* as viewed by its users. This may differ from the actual configuration of the database (see *physical database*).

logical data link In *data communication*, the procedure for the accurate transfer of data over the circuits used in *packet switching* operations.

logical record A *record* which is defined in terms of all its functions, rather than being limited by the need to describe the physical manner in which it is to be stored.

logic bomb An unauthorized alteration to a computer *program* which, when activated, will erase data, programs or *operating systems* carried out with the purpose of sabotaging the computer system (see *Trojan Horse* and *hacking*).

logic card A *circuit board* carrying electronic components which plugs into a computer to give additional facilities.

logic circuit A *circuit* which performs a *logic* function and contains one or more *gates*.

logic unit See *arithmetic and logic unit*.

log in Synonymous with *log on*.

LOGLISP A *programming language*, used in some *artificial intelligence* applications.

LOGO A *high level interactive language* most frequently used in educational applications, usually involving the generation of *turtle graphics*.

logo See *logotype*.

log on/off To initiate, or terminate *on-line* interaction with a computer.

logotype A trademark or similar small diagram.

log tape See *log file*.

long-haul Usually refers to *data transmission* channels over long distances or wide geographical areas.

longitudinal parity check 1. A *parity check* performed upon *strings* of *serial data* held on each *track* of a magnetic *tape*. 2. A *parity check* performed on *serial data* received at a *terminal*.

lookalike clone Computer equipment (*hardware* or *software*) which appears to users to be similar to an already known and familiar piece of equipment.

loop A sequence of instructions within a *program* which are performed repeatedly until some predetermined condition is met. At this point, the computer exits from the loop, and proceeds with the next instruction in the original program. For example, the loop may contain instructions to repeat a series of numerical additions until a certain total is reached. At that point, the computer is instructed to leave the loop, print out the result and stop.

loopback check (or test) Synonymous with *loop checking*.

loop checking A technique for detecting transmission errors: received data are returned to the sending terminal for comparison with the original data.

loop network A *network* in which there is a single path between pairs of *nodes*, with all nodes linked in a closed circuit (for diagram see *network topology*).

loss Synonymous with *attenuation*.

Lotus 123 A *spreadsheet* program.

low activity data processing Carrying out relatively few transactions on a large *database*.

lowercase (characters/letters) Small letters of a *fount*, eg 'a' as opposed to 'A'.

low level language A *programming language* in which each statement in the *source code* is equal to no more than a few statements in *machine language*.

low level protocol A *protocol* concerned with the mechanics of communication within a *network* (compare *high-level protocol*).

low speed storage Storage for which access is so slow that it limits the rate at which data can be processed. This implies that the access speed is slower than the central processor's calculating speed and/or the speed of *peripheral units*.

low speed transmission Refers to systems which operate at less than 2400 *bits* per second.

LPC *Linear predictive coding.*

LPM *Lines per minute.*

L-SAT An *ESA communications satellite* project for *direct transmission satellites* to provide television programmes in Western Europe and to establish the value of *digital* voice links (see *TV-Sat/TDF*).

LSI Large scale integration. An LSI circuit is one whose complexity is such that it would require more than ten thousand *transistors* to duplicate it. However, LSI is often used to refer to the production of a circuit on a single silicon *chip* (see *ULSI* and *VLSI*).

LSI memories *LSI chips* used as *storage devices*. They may be of a variety of different types: *RAM*, *ROM*, *PROM* or *EAROM*.

luminance A measure of brightness: especially applied to television signals.

M

m An abbreviation of milli-. A prefix meaning one thousandth (10^{-3}).

M An abbreviation of *mega-* (signifying one million).

MAC 1. Multiplexed analog components. A colour television system endorsed by the European Broadcasting Union for satellite broadcasting. 2. Machine-aided cognition (see *artificial intelligence*). 3. Multi-access computing (see *multi-access system*).

machine In information technology, 'machine' is often used as a synonym for *computer* (as in, eg machine code, machine language, machine-readable).

machine-aided cognition See *artificial intelligence*.

machine-aided translation (MAT or pure MAT) The problems facing complete language translation by computer (see *machine translation*) are so formidable that no fully-automated machine translation systems have, as yet, been developed. Although any use of computers to assist translation might be described as machine-aided translation, this term is usually reserved for a specific type of system. In this, the computer aids a human translator by providing rapid translations of particular words and/or terms. Such aid is sometimes referred to as pure MAT, as contrasted with pure *MT* and *HAMT* systems.

The relative success of pure MAT, as compared with other fully, or partially, automated translation systems, can be traced to two factors. First, it deals with the aspects of translation which give human translators most difficulty (unaided, they spend over half their working time consulting reference volumes). Second, it deals with those aspects of translation which are most easily automated.

The simplest MAT systems are basically computer-based multilingual lexicons. Translators can use these to determine problematic words and terms, before translating a source text (see, for example, *TEAM* and *LEXIS*). Other systems offer additional facilities. In particular, some allow *text editing* to take place on a *display* screen with a provision for words to be 'looked-up' *on-line* while the text is being processed. Multi-screen, or *split screen*, display facilities provide an additional aid to the translator in such systems as *Target*.

Further variations appear in the way that the lexicons are constructed. Some systems, eg TEAM and LEXIS, use *automated dictionaries* containing separate listings of roots and affixes. This avoids the problem of listing all variants of a given root, with consequent unwieldy growth of the *database*. However, such systems require a high level of expertise on the part of the translator, and can lead to problems of incorrect identification of roots. Other systems, eg *SMART*, therefore use *automated glossaries*, which only contain whole words. Even with these lexicons, a translator may find that some terms cannot be immediately matched with the database. An additional means of access to the lexicon, based on approximate meaning, then becomes necessary. Such access can be provided by an *automated thesaurus*. Automated thesauri do not solve the problems of words which have multiple meanings (see the example discussed under *machine translation*). Many systems, eg Target, TEAM and *Termium*, therefore include a subject classification for entries, so that those meanings of terms which do not relate to the subject matter of the source text can be excluded (see diagram).

MAT systems also have difficulty with terminology in the form of 'phrases', the meanings of which are not clear from their constituent terms. Consider, for example, the phrase 'random-access back projection in computer-assisted instruction'. *Random access* and *computer-assisted instruction* may be included in the lexicon, but a further entry for the complete expression is likely to be needed for satisfactory translation. Such entries are included within some systems, eg Termium, in the form of a *terminology bank*. Flexibility of access is made possible by means of a *permutation index*, which allows an entry to be identified by means of any of its constituent words.

machine code The *code* used in *machine language*.

machine cognition See *artificial intelligence*.

machine cycle The time it takes for a sequence of computer events to be repeated. Also refers to the sequence itself. This consists of two basic steps: a. the instruction phase (I – cycle), when *instructions* are brought from *memory*; b. the execution phase (E – cycle), when the instruction is carried out by the computer.

machine error An error caused by a malfunction of the computer's *hardware*.

machine hearing See *artificial intelligence*.

machine independent language A programming *language* which can be understood by a wide range of computers, eg *high level languages* such as *COBOL* and *FORTRAN*.

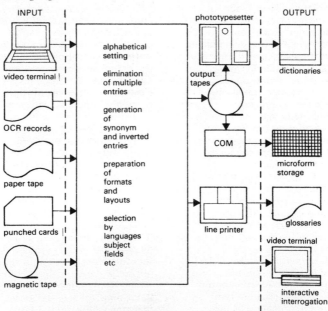

Typical example of a machine-aided translation system: the German TEAM system, which contains within the central computer an automated dictionary and a terminology bank.

machine language The *language* used by a *computer* for communicating internally to its related parts. The language in which the computer performs its arithmetical and editing functions.

machine-orientated language A programming *language* in which each *instruction* has either one, or a limited number, of *machine code* equivalents. Machine-orientated languages therefore require little reprocessing before being 'understood' by a computer. However, they are less easy for users to learn and apply than *high level languages*.

machine-readable Capable of being read by a computer *input device*.

machine searchable Information coded so that a computer, or sorter, can identify the information required.

machine translation Techniques for automated translation of text from one spoken language to another have been sought since the Second World War. Computer technology (with its massive *storage* and *data processing* capabilities) has generally been seen as providing the basis for fully automated translation (ie translation without human intervention). However, a central problem has remained – how to relate the variable meanings of words to their context.
Take, for example, the word 'head'. It can be used as a noun, verb or adjective; it also has different meanings when used in the context of anatomy, numismatology, fluid dynamics, brewing, physical geography, football, analysis of social status, etc. The computer therefore has to recognize grammatical forms (remembering that verbs conjugate and nouns decline in both *source* and *target* languages) and subject contexts. It then has to deal with a further, and yet more difficult problem – that of

recognizing the syntax of a sentence. The difficulties can be illustrated by comparing two simple sentences: a. 'He eats with his knife'; b. 'He eats with his wife'. In English, the preposition 'with', and its apparent place in the sentence, is common to both sentences. However, the human reader discerns that the syntax is different. This clearly has to be recognized by the computer, too, for different syntax may well require different prepositions and constructions in the target language. These problems are such that the ideal of fully-automated machine translation (*pure MT*) seems unrealistic; at least in the immediately foreseeable future. But two types of partially automated translation are currently proving themselves operationally viable: a. *machine-aided translation (pure MAT)* systems. In these systems, translations continue to be made by human beings, but they are assisted by computer-based aids, eg *automated lexicons, automated thesauri* and *terminology banks*; b. *HAMT* systems. In these systems, computers carry out the translation with assistance from human beings, who resolve syntactic and semantic ambiguities.
Pure MT systems are still being developed (see, for example, *SYSTRAN*). At present, they only give satisfactory results when supplemented by pre-input and/or post-output text processing, under the control of a human translator (see *machine-aided translation* and *HAMT*).

Macintosh A *personal computer* manufactured by *Apple* which uses a *WIMP* system. The Macintosh was developed from the *LISA* microcomputer.

macro Abbreviation for *macro code*.

macro assembler An *assembler* for *macro code*.

macro code A *code* which permits

single *words* to generate several *computer instructions.*

macroelement A set of *data* elements handled as a unit.

macro instruction Synonymous with *macro code.*

macro-library A *library* of *routines* held in a mass *storage.*

macro programming The use of *macro code* in writing programs.

macro trace An aid for *debugging* computer *programs.*

MACSYMA An *expert system* used as a mathematical aid.

MAD Michigan Algorithmic Decoder. A *programming language.*

mag An abbreviation of *magnetic.*

magazine A group of up to 100 *teletext* pages.

Magazine Index An American *database* giving coverage of widely read popular literature. Approximately 400 of the most popular magazines in America are indexed. The database is made available via *Lockheed.*

MAGB *Microfilm Association of Great Britain.*

magnetic bubble memory A type of *storage* in which information is encoded onto a thin film of magnetic silicate in the form of bubbles. The presence, or absence, of a bubble in a particular location can be used to denote a binary digit. Detection of bubbles is carried out by means of a special sensor, which emits an electronic pulse as each bubble passes its *read head* (see *storage devices*).

magnetic card A card with a magnetizable surface upon which data can be recorded. (Used

especially with some typewriters.)

magnetic card file A form of *backing storage.* Batches of *magnetic cards* are held in a magazine. When a data *location* on a card is called up, the card is transported at speed past a *read/write head,* giving *direct access* to the data.

magnetic card reader A device which can be used to input information from *magnetic cards* or transfer information from magnetic cards to another type of *storage device.*

magnetic card storage See *magnetic card file.*

magnetic cartridge Synonymous with *magnetic tape cassette.*

magnetic cell A basic *storage* element in magnetic recording.

magnetic character A *character* which has been imprinted on a document using magnetic ink (see *magnetic ink character recognition*).

magnetic code Synonymous with *core storage.*

magnetic delay line A *delay line* whose mode of action depends on the time that magnetic waves take to propagate.

magnetic disc A form of *backing storage.* It consists of circular plates with magnetizable surfaces which possess a number of recording tracks, divided into sectors. Each track and sector is *addressable,* which gives disc storage its *random access* capability. Several *read/write heads* enter and access data on each surface, each head covering a particular area. This provides *direct access* to data with *access times* of the order of 20-100 milliseconds.

magnetic disc drive See *disc unit.*

magnetic disc unit See *disc unit.*

magnetic document sorter-reader See *magnetic ink character sorter.*

magnetic drum A form of *backing storage* giving rapid *direct access* (*access times* of a few milliseconds) and large capacity (in excess of 200,000 *words* for each drum, and several drums can be attached to a *central processor* at one time).
The drum is a cylinder with a magnetizable surface containing a number of recording tracks. The drum is continuously rotated, at speeds up to 7,000 revolutions per second while an array of *read/write heads* enter and access data with transfer rates as high as ten million *bits* per second.

magnetic head Synonymous with *read/write head.*

magnetic film An *internal storage* medium consisting of a very thin (a few millionths of an inch) film of magnetizable material deposited on a plate of non-magnetizable material (usually glass).

magnetic ink See *magnetic ink character recognition.*

magnetic ink character recognition The automatic recognition of *characters* printed with a special ink. The ink contains magnetic particles which can be detected and traced by appropriate

input devices (see diagram). Various standards are used for different purposes.

magnetic ink character sorter A machine which reads *magnetic characters,* and then sorts the documents upon which they appear. (Such machines are extensively used by banks to sort cheques.)

magnetic ink scanner An optical scanner capable of reading characters printed in magnetic ink.

magnetic memory Any *memory* using a magnetized material as the *storage* medium, eg *magnetic discs, drums, tapes.*

magnetic storage media Any magnetically coated device on which data may be written, read or stored.

magnetic stripe system A magnetic stripe is applied to an object, and relevant information (usually about the object) is added. The data on such stripes can be read and updated, as necessary, using a *terminal,* or *wand.*
Magnetic stripes are extensively used in bank credit and *debit card* systems to identify a customer. They are also used to label products for sale in shops, so that details of the product can be recorded at the point and time of sale (an input to *automated stock control*).

(*Left*) *magnetic ink character recognition characters, which are printed in special ink, picked up by input devices according to their shape on the grids seen here.* (*Below*) *typical figures as used on bank cheque.*

⑈459199⑈

magnetic tape Currently, the
commonest form of *backing storage*
(and the cheapest form of magnetic
storage). It consists of reels
(normally 10½ inch diameter) of
plastic tape (the commonest being ½
inch by 2,400 feet) coated with a
magnetic oxide. Data are entered
and accessed by means of *read/write
heads* past which the tape is wound
from one reel to another. *Direct
access* is thus not possible; and all
entries and searches have to be
carried out in sequence. This limits
the possibilities for *file* construction
(see *serial file*), and gives slower
access times than for other magnetic
storage devices (*drums*, *discs*, etc).
Different methods of recording data
on magnetic tape are possible (see
NRZI and *phase encoding*).

magnetic tape cartridge
Synonymous with *magnetic tape
cassette*.

magnetic tape cassette Usually a
standard *audio cassette*, used for
storage in conjunction with a
microcomputer.

magnetic tape drive See *tape drive*.

magnetic thin film storage See
magnetic film.

MAI Machine-aided index (see
automatic indexing).

mailbox service A name for
electronic mail, especially applied to
systems based on interactive
videotex.

mailbox system Refers to any
system in which computer messages
are transferred from one user (or
organization) to the *file* of another,
to await collection. The use of this
term extends beyond *electronic mail*,
to include, for example, the relay of
document requests (made on
completion of an *on-line search*)
from a host's computer to that of a
document fulfilment agency (see

ADRS, *Dialorder* and *electronic
maildrop*).

Mailmerge A *microcomputer
software package* which is used in
conjunction with *word processing*
programs to produce mailing lists.

mainframe Sometimes refers to a
computer's *central processor*, but is
more frequently used to refer to any
large computer, distinguishing it
from a *minicomputer* or
microcomputer.

main index Index displayed on the
initial *routing page* of a *videotex*
system.

main memory Synonymous with
core *memory*.

main storage Synonymous with
core storage.

make-up The preparation of a *page*
for reproduction.

MAMMAX Machine made and
machine-aided index (see *automatic
indexing*).

Management Contents A US
database containing business and
management information. It is
accessible via *BRS*, *Lockheed* and
SDC.

**management information
systems** Systems providing
information for decision making,
usually intended for senior
management. The information may
be internal to an organization, eg
inventory levels, absenteeism,
statistics, or external, eg commodity
prices.

manipulate See *data manipulation*

man-machine interface The actual
device or point of contact used for
human-computer interactions.

manual entry Entering data into a
computer *store* using a *keyboard*.

MAP 1. Microprocessor Application Project, launched by the UK Department of Industry in 1978 with the aim of encouraging UK manufacturing industries to use *microelectronics* and *information technology* in products and processes. 2. Manufacturing Automation Protocol. Pioneered by General Motors, a standard for high performance *local area networks* based on the *Open Systems Interconnection* (OSI) seven-layer model.

map A list of the contents of a *storage device*.

MARC Machine Readable Cataloging. A US Library of Congress system, developed by them and by the British Library, for the creation of *machine-readable bibliographic records.*

MARC (LC) Machine Readable Catalog (Library of Congress). A *database* made available via *BLAISE* and *SDC*.

MARC (S) Machine Readable Cataloging for Serials (see *MARC*).

MARC (UK) See *UKMARC*.

Marecs Marine *communications satellites* under development by ESA (see also *Inmarsat*).

margin-adjust mode A term used in some *word processing* systems. It refers to the facility to scan forthcoming *text* as an aid to justifying margins.

mark reading The reading of marks on a document using a *photoelectric* device.

mark scanning See *mark reading*.

mark sensing See *mark reading*.

mark up The addition of coded instructions to a document to

indicate the format in which it should be printed.

MARVLS *MARC* and *REMARC* Videodisc Library System. The MARC and REMARC records are stored as a *database* on *videodisc*.

mask In *word processing*, a form displayed on the screen with blank areas for the operator to complete.

masked ROM A type of mass-produced non-programmable *ROM*.

mask matching A method used to determine the nature of *characters* during *optical character recognition*.

MASS Multiple access sequential selection. A method of computer *data storage* and retrieval.

massaging Manipulation of *input* material to produce the desired *format*, eg in *word processing*.

mass data An amount of data that is larger than the amount storable in the *central processing unit* of a given computer at any one time.

mass storage Usually refers to *backing storage*.

master Used to describe a basic *record* or *file*, from which other records or files are derived.

master film Synonymous with *master negative film.*

master negative film An original negative, or a duplicate negative, reserved for the special purpose of making copies of *microform* for distribution.

MAT See *machine-aided translation* and *pure MAT*.

math(s) processing The capability, incorporated in some *word processing software*, which allows mathematical computations to be done.

matrix The master from which *type* images are formed in *phototypesetting*.

matrix printer A printer in which each character is composed of a series of dots produced by a stylus (or more than one) which moves across the paper (see diagram).

MATV Master antenna television. An antenna capable of providing television programmes in a similar way to *CATV*, but on a much smaller scale.

MB Megabyte (= a million *bytes*). Used as a measure of storage capacity, eg of a *videodisc*.

McCarthy Online A *news database* which provides the *full-text* of 42 newspapers with special emphasis on UK sources.

MCRS Micrographics Catalog Retrieval System (of the Library of Congress, US).

MDO Marc Development Office (of the US Library of Congress) (see *MARC*).

MDS Multipoint distribution system. A *microwave* transmitter distributes television programmes to subscribers, who possess receiving *antennae* (usually mounted on the roof).

Mead Data Central US company, producing full text *LEXIS* and *NEXIS* databases.

meantime between failure The average length of time for which equipment will operate without developing a fault. Used as a measure of reliability.

mean time to repair The average length of time taken to repair equipment. A guide to *hardware* performance.

measure A printing term referring to the length of a line, eg in *picas*.

media drive *Disc* unit or *tape drive*.

media-resident software *Software* which is not an integral part of a computer system but is, instead, stored on some *medium*, normally a *magnetic disc* (contrast *system-resident*).

Meditel A *closed user group* on the *Prestel* (UK interactive *videotex*) service for medical practitioners and members of allied professions.

medium Any material used to store information, eg *magnetic disc*. The word is often used in the plural – 'media'.

MEDLARS Medical Literature Analysis and Retrieval System. A *database* compiled by the US National Library of Medicine, which has offered a *batch retrospective search* service since the mid-1960s. An *on-line service* has been available since 1973 (see *Medline*).

Medline The *on-line* form of the

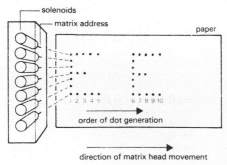

(Dot) matrix printer: the writing head moves from left to right across the paper, each character being built up by 'firing' the needles (of which there are seven) in sequence. Five such firing positions are required to generate a character, so one speaks of a 5 x 7 matrix.

solenoids
matrix address
paper
1 2 3 4 5   6 7 8 9 10
order of dot generation

direction of matrix head movement

MEDLARS database (the largest medical database, produced by the US National Library of Medicine). It is available in the UK via *BLAISE* (and, hence, via *Euronet*).

mega- Prefix signifying one million (10^6). Abbreviated to M.

megabyte One million *bytes* – often used in the context of *hard disc* storage capacity.

Megadoc System A system developed by Philips, which uses *digital optical recording* (DOR) technology to record large numbers of documents on high capacity DOR discs. Can be utilized in an *electronic document delivery system* (such as *Adonis*). The name derives from 'mega (= million) documents' (see *videodisc*).

megaflop Millions of *floating point* operations per second. A measure of computing speed.

MegaStream *Digital data transmission* service offered by *British Telecom*.

memory A device into which *information* can be introduced and stored for extraction by a *computer* when required. *Direct access* is required to the main memory of a computer. Such access must be rapid with *access times* independent both of the location of the information sought, and of the location of the last data elements accessed. *Magnetic core storage* and *thin film memory* satisfy these criteria, with access times of the order of *micro-*, or even *nano-*seconds. However, this storage is expensive (per data unit), and less costly *backing storage* is therefore used for large amounts of data. *Magnetic drums*, card *files* and *discs* can be used to give direct access back-up, with access times of the order of *milliseconds*. *Magnetic tape* offers even cheaper memory capacity, but it does not offer direct

access. Memory is often used as a synonym for storage.

memory capacity The amount of information which a *memory* element, or device, can store. It is also referred to as *storage capacity*.

memory cycle 1. The sequence of operations required to insert data into, or extract data from, memory. 2. The time taken to perform such a sequence of operations.

memory dump See *dump*.

memory map A guide to the location of various elements, eg *operating systems*, language *compiler*, graphics facilities, etc, within a computer's *memory*. Hexadecimal code is normally used to identify memory location (addresses).

memory workspace Synonymous with *working storage*.

menu A list of options, or facilities, from which a computer user can choose. A menu is usually displayed on the *VDU* of a *terminal*; a menu selection is made via the *keyboard*, or *keypad* or on some systems by pointing a light pen at the selected option.

menu-driven Refers to a computer system or *software* which employs *menu* techniques instead of *commands*.

menu selection Making a choice from a *menu*.

MEP *Microelectronics Educational Programme*.

Mercury A privately owned telecommunications network in the UK which acts as a *carrier* for voice and data traffic. Set up by a consortium of Cable and Wireless, British Petroleum and Barclays Bank. It offers digital communications services based on an *optical fibre* network and *microwave* techniques.

merge To combine two or more *files* into a single file.

Merlin A division of *British Telecom*, set up after *deregulation*, to exploit the market for telecommunications and *office automation* equipment.

MESH Medical Subject Headings. A *thesaurus* developed by the US National Library of Medicine, and used with *Medline*.

mesh network A network in which there are two or more paths between any two nodes (for diagram, see *network topology*).

message A group of *words*, fixed or varied in length, which are moved about together as a unit.

message control flag A *flag* which indicates whether the information being transmitted is data or control information.

message header/heading The first *characters* of a message, indicating to whom the message is addressed, the time of transmission, etc.

message routing The selection of a route through a *switching* system.

message switching In telecommunications, the technique of receiving self-contained *messages* (which include the *address* to which they are being transmitted). Such messages are stored until an appropriate outgoing line is available, and then retransmitted. No direct physical connection between outgoing and incoming lines needs to be established (see *switching*).

message switching centre Location in a network where *message switching* takes place.

messaging Refers to a form of electronic communication in which a message is sent directly to its destination, eg *telex* (contrast *store and forward*).

METADEX Metal Abstracts/Alloys Index. These are *databases* compiled by the American Society for Metals and The Metals Society, UK. They are accessible via *ESA-IRS* and *Lockheed*.

metafont A *program* (devised by Knuth) which allows the operator to control the forms of *digitized type* used. The typeface style desired can be specified by an appropriate set of input parameters.

METAPLAN Methods of Extracting Text Automatically Programming Language is a *language* for text retrieval (see *text retrieval systems* and *information retrieval techniques*).

metropolitan area network A *wide area network* operating over a specific urban area.

MF 1. *Microfiche*. 2. *Microfilm*.

MFLOP A million *floating point* operations per second. A measure of *computing power*, particularly in supercomputers.

MHz MegaHertz. Million cycles per second.

MIC Medical Information Centre. A Swedish *host*.

micro- 1. A prefix denoting one millionth (10^{-6}). 2. Often used simply to denote smallness (as in *microfiche* or *microprocessor*). 3. Often used as an abbreviation for microcomputer.

MICRO Multiple indexing and console retrieval operations. An *on-line* system for retrieving, ranking and qualifying document references.

microcard An opaque card on which microcopies are reproduced photographically in rows and columns. It resembles a *microfiche*, but has its images printed positively. In consequence, the images cannot be directly reproduced.

microcassette A small *audio cassette* used for *storage* in conjunction with a microcomputer or word processing system.

microchip See *chip*.

microcircuit Synonymous with integrated circuit (see *chip*).

microcode Synonymous with *micro instructions*.

microcomputer A small (desktop) computer which uses a *microprocessor* as its processing element. Often used loosely to refer to the microprocessor itself.

micro copy A copy of an image, or document, so reduced in size (from its original) that it cannot be read by the unaided human eye (see *microform*, *microfiche*, *microfilm*).

microelectronics The use of integrated circuits in electronic devices.

Microelectronics Education Programme A project sponsored by the UK Department of Education and Science, designed to enhance the teaching of computing in schools.

microelectrostatic copying A system for updating *microform* using an *electrophotographic* technique.

microfiche A type of *microform* in which pages of text and graphics are photographically reduced and then mounted (usually as the negative) on a film. Each film usually has dimensions of 4 inches x 6 inches, and holds a matrix of 7 x 14 page

frames. The fiche can be read a frame at a time using a *microfiche reader*.

microfiche book *Hard copy* text and plates are reduced to *microform* scale, and mounted on standard *microfiche*. The individual microfiches are then bound together in a hard, or soft, cover in such a way that they can be removed for reading. A lengthy book or report is thus reduced to a more convenient size for postage and storage.

microfiche management system A system for the storage and retrieval of information on *microfiche* (see COM and *information retrieval systems*).

microfiche reader An optical device for illuminating *microfiche* and providing an enlarged, readable image (usually projected on to a screen).

microfilm A type of *microform* in which photographically reduced pages are mounted, in sequence, on a roll of film.

Microfilm Association of Great Britain A body whose main aims are to promote the effective use of *microfilm* and raise the standard of microfilm production.

microfilm flow camera An automatic camera for taking microcopies of documents (ie recording documents on *microfilm*).

microfilm reader An optical device for illuminating a *microfilm* and presenting an enlarged, readable image on a screen.

microfilm reader-printer A *microfilm reader* which can produce (*blow back*) full-scale copies of the micro-images on demand.

microfloppy A small *floppy disc*, current sizes being 3½ or 3 inches in diameter. It differs from the 5¼ inch floppy disc in that it is housed in a rigid case which provides better protection from dirt. On some microfloppy discs, the magnetic surface is permanently protected by an automatic shutter which opens orly when the disc is correctly inserted into the *disc drive*.

microfolio A type of microform *jacket*. A number of strips of *microfilm* are placed adjacent to each other, and sheets of acetate film are attached on both sides. This produces a package which is about the same size as a conventional *microfiche*.

microform Film in strips (*microfilm*) or sheets (*microfiche*) or opaque cards (*microcard*) on to which pages of photographically reduced documents are impressed. Some form of special magnifying device is required to read any type of microform.

microform in colour The vast majority of *microforms* are produced in monochrome, but colour *microfiche* and *microfilm* can be produced (usually for colour illustrations).

microform reader-printer A device for reading *microforms* which combines a viewing screen for visual display with a mechanism for producing enlarged print-on-paper copies of the material viewed.

micrographics The technique of reducing documents to *microform*.

microinstructions A single computer instruction representing a simple concept, such as 'add' or 'delete'.

micromainframe A *microcomputer* having the *computing power* of a *mainframe*. Such a computer is predicted for the near future (see *supermicro* and *supermini*).

micron One millionth of a metre $(10^{-6}m)$.

Micronet 800 A *closed user group* for *microcomputer* users available on the *Prestel* (UK interactive *videotex*) service. It is so named because 800 is its initial page number on Prestel. It provides information about new products and computing news, and allows *downloading* of *telesoftware*.

microopaque The opaque card used as a base for a *microcard*.

microperforated (paper) *Continuous stationery* with very fine perforations, so that when separated, the pages have the appearance of cut sheets.

microphotographics See *micrographics*.

microprint A positive *microcopy*, photographically printed on to paper.

microprocessor A *central processor* in which all the elements are contained on a single *chip*. It is often used now as a synonym for *microcomputer*.

Microprocessor Application Project See *MAP*.

microprogram A program written in *microinstructions* to be implemented by *hardware*. It is not normally accessible to the computer user.

MICROPROLOG A version of *PROLOG* designed for microcomputers.

micropublishing The production and distribution of information via *microform*. The information may be original, but, in present practice, has often been previously published in conventional form.

microrecording A copying technique in which the copy is reduced so much in size that a special optical device is needed to read it. The copy may be on film (*microfilm*, *microfiche*), opaque card (*microcard*), or paper (*microprint*).

microrobotics The production of small handling devices (especially small robot arms) controlled by a *microcomputer* (see *robotics*).

microwave Any radio wave with a frequency above 890 megacycles per second.

microwave relay A point-to-point beamed *microwave* transmission consisting of one or more links. Microwave transmission is generally used for data being sent beyond regional *cable networks*, but does not have the scope of intercontinental *communications satellite* systems.

Microwriter A hand-held text *capture* device produced by Microwriter Ltd. It has a *chord* keyboard, small *liquid crystal display* of a few words and an 8K *RAM* memory. It is battery operated and allows text to be *input* almost anywhere.

MIDAS Multimode International Data Acquisition Service. A *network* which allows *on-line searches* to be made from Australia of *databases* held by international *hosts*. The charging system is independent of distance (see *AUSINET*).

MIDI Musical Instrument Digital Interface. A *standard interface* which allows communication between musical keyboards and between computers and musical keyboards, eg for *sampling*.

midicomputers A computer of intermediate size and *computing power*, between a *mainframe* and a *minicomputer*.

Mighty Bee A champion backgammon computer program.

milking machine Device physically

taken to a location and used to extract data from a machine. On return, unloads these data into a central system. For example, a milking machine can be used to extract text from a word processor at a printer's client via a *RS232 interface*, and then unloads these data to a typesetter at the printer.

milli- A prefix meaning one thousandth (10^{-3}).

Mind A pioneering experimental *HAMT* system which translates English into Korean.

minicomputer A computer of intermediate size and *computing power*, between a *mainframe* and a *microcomputer*.

MINICS Minimal Input Cataloguing System. A document cataloguing system.

Minimedline Subset of *Medline* database, eg to provide for local decentralized searching.

Minitel A computer *terminal*, integrating a telephone unit with a small *screen* and *keyboard*, introduced by the French *PTT*, originally as an electronic telephone directory, but now also as a *gateway* to other information sources.

MIPS Millions of instructions per second. A measure of *computing power*, particularly in general purpose *mainframe* computers.

mirroring The rotation of a *computer graphics* display image through 180 degrees.

MIS *Management information systems*.

Missive French national *electronic mail* service. It will link together *telex*, *viewdata terminals* and automatic office *networks*.

Mistel A Finnish *viewdata*
(interactive *videotex*) system.

MITI Ministry of Trade and
Industry in Japan.

MLA Modern Language Association
Bibliography. A standard
philological reference source,
accessible via *Lockheed*.

MLS Machine literature search(ing)
(see *information retrieval systems*).

MMI *Man-machine interface.*

MMS *Microfiche management
system.*

Mnemonic code Instructions
written in concise, easily
remembered symbolic or
abbreviated form, eg SUB for
subtract (see *assembly language*).

Mnemos A *storage device*,
consisting of a 12 inch plastic disc
which can store both reduced
images (similar to a *microfiche*), and
encoded *digital* data which can be
processed by a computer.

MOBL Macro Orientated Business
Language. A *high level language.*

mode A particular method of
operation, especially on a computer,
eg *interactive mode.*

modelling 1. The construction of a
simplified but organized and
meaningful representation of an
actual system or process. 2. The use
of computing equipment to create
numeric models of financial or
planning data.

modem An abbreviation of
modulator-demodulator. A device
for converting a *digital* signal
(generated, for example, by a
computer) into an *analog* signal by
modulation. In this form, the signal
can be transmitted along a standard
telephone line. The received signal
can be reconverted from analog to
digital by the same device.

modern typeface Printers use the
term 'modern' to mean any typeface
which shows a considerable contrast
between the thick and thin strokes
of letters.

modified frequency modulation A
technique for increasing the *storage*
capacity of *magnetic discs* by
modulation of the electronic signal
at a *read/write head.*

modified NTSC *NTSC* television
colour pictures played on *PAL*
standard equipment.

modifier A quantity used to *modify*
the *address* of an *operand.*

modify To alter the *address* of an
operand.

modulation The addition of
information to an *electromagnetic*
signal (the *carrier wave*).
Modulation can take the form of an
adjustment to the carrier wave's
amplitude (*amplitude modulation*),
frequency (*frequency modulation*) or
phase angle (*phase modulation*).

modulator A device that impresses
audio or video signals on to a *carrier
wave.*

module 1. Any self-contained unit
that can be added to (ie plugged
into) an existing system. 2. A
segment of core *storage* containing
20,000 *addressable* locations.

MOLGEN An *expert system* to
assist experimental design in
molecular biology.

Molinya The name of a series of
communications satellites launched
by the Soviet Union. They have not
generally been placed in
geostationary orbits, but in elliptical
orbits which provide maximum
coverage of Soviet territory. In order
to provide continuous
communications coverage, it is
therefore necessary to have a
sequence of satellites following each
other across the sky. In the 1970s,

the Soviet Union began to launch
Molinya satellites into geostationary
orbit. The satellites in the Molinya
series have been intended primarily
for communication within the Soviet
Union (see also *Statsionar*).

monitor 1. *Hardware* or *software*
used to monitor a computer system
to detect deviations from some
prescribed condition. 2. A synonym
for an *operating system*. 3. The box
containing the *VDU* of a computer.

monochrome Single colour, usually
black and white but can be some
other colour (especially with
reference to television).

monospaced characters Letters all
of the same *set width* (as on an
ordinary typewriter). This should be
contrasted with *proportional spaced
characters*.

mortising In *phototypesetting*, this
means removing film with incorrect
text and replacing it by film with
correct text.

MOS Metal oxide semiconductor
field effect transistor. A very small,
low power transistor which
facilitates high packing densities in
integrated circuits (see N MOS and
P MOS).

most significant bit The *bit* at the
extreme left of a *string* comprising a
binary number.

most significant digit The digit at
the extreme left of a *string*
comprising a number.

mother board A large circuit board
into which can be plugged a number
of smaller boards, or circuit
elements.

mouse A small hand-held device
connected to a computer by a thin
cable. Under the mouse is a large
ball which rolls as the mouse is
moved over the surface of a desktop.
The computer senses the movement

of the rolling ball and acts as though
receiving *cursor* movement
instructions from the *keyboard*. On
top of the mouse are several buttons
which are used to indicate the
required action in conjunction with
the *icon*, text or data shown on
screen.

MP/M Multiprogramming control
program for microprocessors. A
multiprogramming version of *CP/M*
for systems with multiple *terminals*.

MPS *Microprocessor system.*

MPU *Microprocessor unit.*

MRDF *Machine-readable data files.*

MSB *Most significant bit.*

MSD *Most significant digit.*

MS-DOS Microsoft Disc Operating
System. A microcomputer *operating
system*. It was developed after, and
is rather more powerful than, *CP/M*,
and is usually found on *16-bit*
machines.

MSI Medium Scale Integration. A
microelectronic circuit which
contains a number of *logic* functions
(see *LSI* and *VLSI*).

MTBF *Mean time between failure.*

MTBM Mean time between
maintenance. A guide to *hardware*
performance.

MTST Magnetic tape selectric
typewriter. A typewriter providing
some editing facilities (see *word
processor*).

MTTR *Mean time to repair.*

multi-access system A system
which allows a number of users to
access a *central processor* in
conversational mode at virtually the
same time.

multi-disc reader Equipment which

can read a variety of *floppy discs* and output on to floppy discs of a different type (or to some other equipment, such as a *phototypesetter*), thus overcoming problems of lack of *compatibility*.

multidrop line A *line* (or *circuit*) which connects several stations.

multifrequency A means of transmitting *serial* data over *analog* systems using a combination of predetermined tones in the voice *band*.

multifunction system A computing system which can carry out a variety of tasks, eg a *word processor* with communication and mathematical capabilities.

multi-layer microfiche The normal 4 inch x 6 inch *microfiche* carries 98 'pages'. A long report or book can therefore require a large number of fiches.
Multi-layer microfiche offers a means for reducing this number. Two-layer microfiche can be made using polarization techniques, and four-layer microfiche using *holography*.

multi-media publishing The communication of more than one data type (eg text, graphics, sound, pictures) as an integrated package.

multiple access The ability of a system to receive messages from, and transmit them to, a number of separate locations.

multiple key retrieval *Information retrieval* using more than one *key* in a *search*.

multiple-pass printing A capability of a *printer* in which the print head passes over each line of type twice in order to produce a *bold face* effect, or to produce *near letter quality* print.

multiplex To transmit two or more

messages simultaneously via the same *channel*. This is achieved either by splitting the transmitted *frequency band* into narrower bands (frequency-division multiplexing), or by allotting the channel to several different inputs successively (time-division multiplexing).

multiplex mode Interleaving *bytes* of data on a *multiplexed channel* when communicating with low speed *input/output devices*.

multiplexor A device which uses and controls several communication channels simultaneously, both sending and receiving messages.

multipoint line See *multidrop line*.

multiprocessing The simultaneous execution of two, or more, computer *programs* on a *multiprocessor*.

multiprocessor A computer with several processors each of which can work independently (ie perform different operations) (contrast *array processor*).

multiprogramming Refers to the handling of more than one task by a single computer.

MultiStream A service offered by *British Telecom* which is designed to provide widespread access to *PSS* services over local direct or *dial-up* lines. The service offers two forms of connection: *MultiStream EPAD* and *MultiStream VPAD*.

MultiStream EPAD Part of *British Telecom's MultiStream* service. It uses a range of sophisticated *error control protocols* over the *dial-up* link between the customer's *terminal* and the *PSS* exchange.

MultiStream VPAD Part of *British Telecom's MultiStream* service which provides *dial-up* access to *PSS* for *viewdata* applications.

multi-strike ribbon *Printer* ribbon,

usually made of inked fabric, which can be used many times.

multi-tasking The process whereby the *CPU* of a computer is shared by many *programs*. While idle in one program (eg while data are being sought from a *disc*) the *idle time* is automatically allocated to the next program. When that program releases the CPU, then the next or the previous program jumps back in, and so on. While the CPU appears to be performing *parallel processing*, it is in fact only processing a single program at any given moment.

multi-user Describes a computer system which allows a number of users to access the system simultaneously on a *time sharing* basis.

multi-user microcomputer (system) A *microcomputer*-based system in which a number of

terminals can access a central *microprocessor* simultaneously. Increasingly, the term is being used to describe any system based on interlinked microcomputers.

multiway wiring A communication cable consisting of a flat ribbon round a multicore cable, often used in very small *local area networks*.

MUPID Multipurpose Universal Programmable Intelligent Decoder. An *intelligent terminal* used on the Austrian interactive *videotex* service.

Murray Code (see *Baudot code*).

MUX Abbreviation for *multiplexor*.

MYCIN An *expert system* used in medical diagnosis and prescription.

Mylar Polyester film used as a base for *magnetic tape*.

N

NAK Negative acknowledgement. A signal indicating to a sender that a previous message, or *data stream*, is unacceptable, and the receiver is ready for a repeat transmission (contrast *ACK*).

NAM *Network access machine.*

NAND *NOT AND*, a *Boolean* operator.

NAND element Synonymous with *NAND gate.*

NAND gate A *gate* that implements the *logic* of a *NAND* function: ie only giving out a signal if a zero signal is received from one of its inputs. A NAND gate with two inputs produces outputs as follows:

Input 1	Input 2	Output
1	1	0
1	0	1
0	1	1
0	0	1

nano- Prefix denoting one thousand millionth (10^{-9}).

narrowband Refers to a *bandwidth* of up to 300 Hz (contrast *voiceband* and *wideband*).

narrowcasting Transmitting information (over a general purpose *network*) or television programmes (over a *CATV* network) intended for a specific, relatively small audience.

NASA The National Aeronautics and Space Administration in the US. One of its activities is to compile a large *database* covering all areas of aeronautics, space science and related technology. Part of the *database* (*IAA*) is publicly available via *ESA-IRS*. The remainder (*NASA STAR*) is only available to accredited users.

NASA STAR *NASA* Scientific and Technical Aerospace Reports. A *database* produced by NASA, and accessible *online* to accredited users.

National Aeronautics and Space Administration See *NASA.*

National Data Processing Service A division of *British Telecom* offering *data processing* and *transmission* services (and consultancy) to commercial customers. Its areas of specialization include *business information systems, Prestel, COM* and *information retrieval systems.*

National Library of Medicine A major centre for medical information in the US. Acts as a *host* and also compiles *databases.*

National Microfilm Association An association in the US whose main aims are to promote the use of *microfilm* and to improve standards of production (see *National Micrographics Association*).

National Micrographics Association A trade association in the US representing producers of *microforms.* It has several committees dealing with standards for such areas as *microfiche* of documents, terminology, *information storage and retrieval*, newspapers on microfiche, reduction ratios, and *COM* format and coding (see *National Microfilm Association*).

National Register of Microform Masters A register of *masters* located at the US Library of Congress (see *microform, COM* and *master negative film*).

NATO Codification System A system established by member

countries of the North Atlantic Treaty Organization to provide a unique identification code for any item of military equipment (see *classification and coding systems*).

natural language Ordinary spoken, or written, language. It is to be contrasted with a *programming* or *machine language*.

natural language system An *information retrieval system* in which the *index terms* are words actually used in the document. Indexing by natural language is generally cheaper than by ascribing index terms from an *authority file* or *thesaurus*.

NBM Non-book materials.

NBS National Bureau of Standards, US.

NBS-SIS *National Bureau of Standards* – Standard Information Services.

NCR National Cash Register. A computer manufacturer.

NCR paper *No carbon required paper*.

NDPS *National Data Processing Service.*

NDRO *Non-destructive read out.*

near letter quality A function of many *dot-matrix printers* which makes use of *multiple-pass printing* in order to produce a typed product of sufficient quality to be used for letters and finished documents.

Nectarring system A communication system which uses existing electrical mains circuits as *data transmission* media. The computer is linked to the standard mains socket by a device called a Nectarring unit which transmits data through the mains by modulating a high frequency *carrier wave*.

needle printer Synonymous with *matrix printer*.

negative An image (usually photographic) with *tones* which reverse those of the original.

negative acknowledgement See *NAK*.

NEPHIS Nested Phrase Indexing System. An automated *permuted* subject indexing system (see *automatic indexing* and *indexing systems*).

nest 1. A *subroutine* embedded within a *program*. 2. A *block* of *data* embedded within a larger body of data.

nested loop A *loop* within a loop.

nested phrase indexing See *NEPHIS*.

Net Book Agreement UK retail price maintenance agreement covering books.

network In general, this term refers to a set of components connected by channels. In the context of information technology, it usually refers to a system of physically dispersed computers interconnected by telecommunications channels, eg Euronet.

network access machine (NAM) A *computer programmed* to help a user interact with a computer *network*, eg a network connecting a series of *host* computers. The NAM generates the specific procedures necessary to gain access, and then allows the information to be sought in a uniform way (ie it performs the necessary translation of commands). The user gains access via a *terminal* to the NAM.

network control program *Software* which controls and monitors communications between users and a *host* in a computer *network*.

network diagram A diagrammatic representation of *network topology*.

network planning A management technique for scheduling and controlling large projects. It is more often called *critical path method* (CPM), or *PERT*.

network topology The geometrical arrangement of *nodes* and pathways in a *network*, usually represented by a *network diagram*.

neutral transmission A method of transmitting *teletypewriter* signals which employs a two-state (on/off) signal (see *polar transmission*).

new information technology The contents of this book. Distinguished from *information technology* only in the sense that the latter may include applications which are in no way related to *electronic* handling.

news database A *database*, produced by a newspaper company or wire service, providing news information. Many news databases provide the *full-text* of daily and weekly newspapers.

Newsnet A US *news database* containing the *full-text* of over 115 newsletters on topics ranging from popular items to technical and business subjects.

Newspapers On Microfilm The published *microfilm* records of the US Library of Congress holdings covering both US and foreign newspapers.

New York Times Information Bank A *database* containing detailed *abstracts* from the New York Times and over sixty other major newspapers and magazines. *Online* and *off-line* search facilities are offered. Full texts of New York Times articles are available to subscribers in *microfiche* form.

NEXIS A US *database* offering full-text of newspapers and agency news items. It can be searched *online*. Similar in concept to the *LEXIS* legal database.

nexus A point in a system at which interconnections occur, eg the meeting point of a number of *channels* in a *network*.

NFAIS The National Federation of Abstracting and Indexing Services, US.

nibble Computer jargon for a block of 4 *bits* (ie half a byte).

NIC Network *Interface* Controller.

NIM Newspapers In Microform (see *microform*).

NISO A body of the American National Standards Institute (*ANSI*).

NIU Network *Interface* Unit.

NLM *National Library of Medicine*.

NLQ *Near letter quality*.

NMA 1. *National Microfilm Association*. 2. *National Micrographics Association*.

N MOS N-channel metal oxide semiconductor. A common form of *transistor* (where 'N' stands for negative). N MOS is more frequently employed than *P MOS*. Electronic circuits based on N MOS are relatively slow, but they are compact and consume little power.

no carbon required paper Paper which is chemically impregnated so that impact on a top sheet produces an image on second and subsequent sheets without the use of interleaved carbon paper.

node Generally refers to a point of convergence in a network; within the context of a switched network (see *switching*) refers to a *switching centre*.

noise 1. Refers, in telecommunications, to unwanted (usually random) electronic signals. 2. Refers, in information storage and retrieval systems, to retrieved documents which do not deal with the required subject (see also *signal-to-noise ratio*).

noise factor In *bibliographic information retrieval*, the fraction of retrieved documents which are not relevant.

noise killer An electrical device used to reduce *interference* from a *transmission*.

non-destructive cursor A *cursor* that can be moved around a display of information on a *VDU* screen, without altering that information.

non-destructive reading *Reading* in which the source data are not destroyed.

non-destructive read out Process in which data are obtained ('read out') from a *file*. The data in the file meanwhile remain unaltered in the computer's *memory* or *backing storage*.

non-impact printing Systems which do not require physical impact for printing, eg *ink jet printing* and *electrostatic printing* (see *impact printing*).

non-volatile memory Computer *memory* which preserves data during a loss of power to the computer, or a shutdown of the system.

NOR *NOT OR*, a *Boolean operator*.

NOR circuit Synonymous with *NOR gate*.

NOR element Synonymous with *NOR gate*.

NOR gate A *gate* that implements the logic of a *NOR* function: ie only giving out a signal (1) if no signals are received at any input. A NOR gate with two inputs produces outputs as follows:

Input 1	Input 2	Output
1	1	0
1	0	0
0	1	0
0	0	1

NORIANE A French *database* which provides information on standards.

NORVIEW A *private videotex system* operated by Northamptonshire County Council.

Notepad *Computer conferencing software* adapted and used for the *BLEND* electronic communication network experiment.

NRMM *National Register of Microform Masters.*

NRZI Non-return to zero indicator. A method of recording binary *digits* on *magnetic tape*. A change in direction of magnetization corresponds to 0 (see *phase encoding*).

NTIA National Telecommunications and Information Agency. An agency of the US Department of Commerce.

NTIS National Technical Information Service. A US service which generates a multi-disciplinary *database* covering technical and scientific reports produced by US Government agencies and their contractors. It is accessible via *BRS*, *CAN/OLE*, *ESA/IRS*, *Lockheed* and *SDC* and supplies copies of reports in microform.

NTSC National Television System Committee. A US body responsible for the specification of the US colour television system. The system is also used in Japan and South America (see also *PAL* and *Secam*).

NUA Network User Address. A type of *password*, unique to each user, which must be entered in order to provide identification before accessing a *host* computer system (see *NUI*).

NUI Network User Identifier. A type of *password*, of 11 or more digits, which is unique to each user, and must be entered at the *keyboard* in order to gain access to a *host* computer system (see *NUA*).

null character A *character* employed either to fill unused time in a *data transmission*, or to provide a space in a *storage device*.

number crunching The large-scale numerical, analytical and statistical computations carried out by large *mainframe* computers.

numerical control The automatic control of machinery (especially of production systems) by means of numerical instructions.

numeric database A non-bibliographic *database* which provides numeric or statistical information (see *databank*).

O

OA *Office automation.*

object code The *machine code* output from a *compiler.*

object language The language into which a *source language* is translated. When the source language is a *high level language,* and the translation is carried out by a *compiler,* the object language is often referred to as object code.

object program A program in *object language.*

oblique In *phototypesetting* refers to the possibility of adding an angle of slant to a *typeface.*

Occam A *high level language,* designed for *artificial intelligence* applications, developed for the *transputer* in order to handle the *parallel processing* and data transfer requirements of its circuitry.

OCP Oxford Concordance Program. Text *concordance software* developed by the Oxford University Computing Service.

OCCS Office of Computer and Communication Systems of the US *National Library of Medicine.*

Oceanic Abstracts A *database* covering oceanography and related topics, eg fisheries and pollution. It is accessible via *ESA/IRS, Lockheed, QL* and *SDC.*

OCI Office of Computer Information. An office of the US Department of Commerce.

OCLC Ohio College Library Center. An *on-line computer network,* mainly in North America, for cataloguing information. It has a variety of library uses, eg *inter-library loan,* and locating

information. Over 3,500 remote computer *terminals* are linked into the system.

OCR *Optical character recognition* (see diagrams).

OCR-A A special typeface used on documents intended to be read by *OCR.* Presents a rather clumsy appearance to the eye (see also *OCR-B* and diagrams).

OCR-B A special typeface used on documents intended to be read by *OCR.* Pleasanter to the eye than *OCR-A.*

octal A number system based on the base 8 (ie it consists of digits 1 to 7).

octal (code) A *code* which operates with a base 8 (compare *binary*).

octet A group of eight binary digits, treated as a single unit.

ODA Office document architecture. A set of standards for exchanging documents in electronic form between different computer systems.

ODB Output to display buffer. An auxiliary *storage* area in a computer. It holds data during their transmission from *output* to a display *device* (see *buffer*).

odd-even check See *parity check.*

OECD Organization for Economic Cooperation and Development. An inter-governmental organization which produces a number of statistical *databases.*

OEM Original equipment manufacturer(s). A term used when procuring compatible equipment for an existing computer system.

office automation The use of computer-based systems to replace conventional manual office operations. Can refer to a range of levels of automation, from the introduction of a single *stand-alone* word processor to the development of a fully *electronic office*.

office information system Any

electronic system which can help perform a variety of office functions, including *word processing*, *information retrieval* and *telecommunications*.

office of the future See *electronic office*.

office of tomorrow See *electronic office*.

Practical application of two different optical character recognition systems, for information on a paperback book. The universal product coded barcode is used to represent both price and ISBN number, these sets of figures also being reproduced in OCR-readable characters above.

```
GB £ NET    +001.50
ISBN 0-600-20346-8
                    00150

9  780600 203469
```

```
0123456789
ABCDEFGHIJKLM
NOPQRSTUVWXYZ
abcdefghijklm
nopqrstuvwxyz
*+-=/ . , : ; " ' _
? ! ( ) < > [ ] % # & @ ^
¤ £ $ ¡ ¡ \
Ä Å Æ IJ Ñ Ö Ø Ü
å æ ij ø ß § ¥
" ( ) ^ ~
            '
{ } m _
```

Examples of OCR-B character set

off-line Not having a direct interaction with the *central processor* of a computer.

off-line print The results of an *online search* which are not printed out at the user's *terminal*, but at the central computer after the user has *logged off*, and are then forwarded by post.

offset litho(graphy) See *lithography*.

OFTEL Office for Telecommunications (UK).

Ohm *SI* unit of electrical resistance.

OIS *Office information system.*

old style A *typeface* design with less contrast than *modern style*.

OLRT *Online real time* operation.

Olympus European satellite planned for launch in autumn 1987.

omission factor In *information retrieval*, the fraction of relevant items in a *file* which are not retrievable in a search.

OMR Optical mark reader. An *optical scanning device* which reads hand or machine-made marks on specially designed forms.

on-demand publishing (system) A system in which documents are printed as and when they are required. Such operations often make use of computerized *composition* systems and *laser printers*.

one element Synonymous with *OR gate*.

one gate Synonymous with *OR gate*.

online Refers, in general, to any use of equipment to interact directly with the *central processor* of a computer.

online cataloguing The creation of a computerized library catalogue. This may be achieved by the use of a *bibliographic utility*.

online editing The manipulation of information stored in a computer using access via a *terminal*.

online information retrieval systems See *information retrieval system* and *online searching*.

online journal See *electronic journal*.

Online public access catalogue A *machine-readable* replacement of the library card catalogue. Library users access the catalogue by means of a *VDU* and *user-friendly software*.

online remote microfiche reader A central bank of *microfiches* is indexed and coded for retrieval. The index can be searched *online*, and a particular fiche requested. A user can select and view any desired frame from a remote terminal, using a *video monitor* and *keyboard*.

online retailer See *host*.

online retrieval See *online searching*.

online searching This describes the activity of using a computer-based *information retrieval system* when there is direct *online access* to the *database(s)* available on the computer (or *computer network*). In online searching, the computer responds to a series of queries from the user. The latter starts by selecting appropriate search terms (ie the indexing terms used for the database) from a dictionary (which can normally be called up online). The computer responds by listing items identified by these search terms and/or presenting more highly focused search options. The search can then be extended until an acceptable number of the most suitable items has been located.

Relevant items can either be printed out at the user's *terminal*, or, if the number of items is too large, *off-line* at the computer, whence they are dispatched to the user. *Bibliographic databases* deliver references and, sometimes, *abstracts*. The full text of documents is currently only provided by a few systems as printout, but some allow a photocopy or *microfiche* to be ordered via the terminal (see diagram).

The entry point to such a retrieval system is typically a *video terminal* or an *online typewriter*. With an on-line typewriter, the systems response is printed on the paper output. With a video terminal, messages are shown on the screen and a printer is used to make a *hard copy* record.

Throughout the 1970s the number and size of databases available on-line has grown. Simultaneously, accessibility has been improved, and the costs of access reduced, by linking computers via *time-shared* telecommunications channels. Access to most databases is normally obtained through information retailers, or *hosts*, the largest of which are currently *Lockheed* and *SDC* (System Development Corporation of Santa

Monica, California) in the US. There are many smaller hosts in Europe, several of which are linked via *Euronet*. (This was established to bring European systems and users closer together, and to protect the European online information market.)

on-screen Used to describe: a. information which is displayed on the surface of a *CRT*. b. The activities and applications which can be carried out with information displayed in this way.

ON-TAP Online Training and Practice. A *database*, accessible via *Lockheed*, which contains extracts from other databases. It is designed to be used as an aid for the training of personnel in the techniques of *on-line searching* (no *off-line* printing facility is offered).

OPAC *Online public access catalogue.*

opaque screen A diffuse reflecting surface for viewing a projected image, eg of a *frame* of *microform*.

open system 1. A system which allows a variety of different computers and *terminals* to work

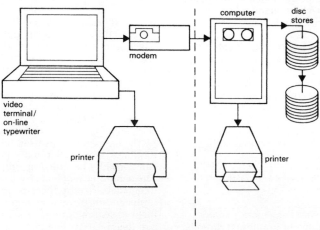

Information flow in an online searching system.

freely together. 2. A system to which access is publicly available.

open system interworking The establishment of links between discrete computer systems and *networks* to create a freely interacting *open system* (2.).

Open Systems Interconnection A standard defined by the *International Standards Organization* (ISO) and the *Comité Consultatif International Télégraphique et Téléphonique,* which is intended to facilitate the exchange of information between computers of all types. The OSI *network architecture* is divided into seven layers: physical, data link, network, transport, session, presentation and application (see diagram). The physical layer involves the transmission of a *raw bit stream*. The data link layer detects transmission errors and converts an unreliable transmission channel into a reliable one. The network layer is responsible for network routes and switches. The transport layer provides *host* to host communication. The session layer is concerned with setting up, controlling and dismantling process-to-process connections. The presentation layer presents the transmitted data in a form recognized by the application. The content of the application layer is left to the users, and standard *protocols* are expected to develop for specific types of application. At each level the sending device believes it is communicating with its corresponding layer in the receiving unit; it accepts messages from the layer immediately above it, adds control information to it and passes it on to the next layer below it. At the receiving end the process is reversed.

A selection of OSI standards will be implemented by European manufacturers from 1987. The UK

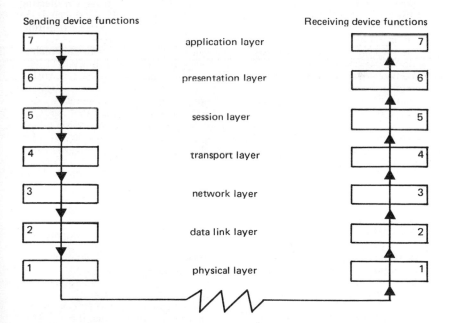

Sending device functions

Receiving device functions

7	application layer	7
6	presentation layer	6
5	session layer	5
4	transport layer	4
3	network layer	3
2	data link layer	2
1	physical layer	1

Open Systems Interconnection.

Department of Industry is attempting to speed up the process by using the *Intercept Strategy* to pinpoint areas in which agreement has almost been reached (see *open system interworking* and *Systems Network Architecture*.)

open wire An electrical conductor supported above the ground surface, eg telephone wires on poles.

operand Any one of the quantities entering into, or arising out of, an operation. In computing, it typically refers to the items, eg data, *addresses*, on which the computer is operating at the time.

operating environment Refers to the way in which users can access the *CPU* in a computer system. In a *real-time* environment the user has one-to-one access to the CPU and to other components of the system. In a *virtual* environment, users share CPU time with other users, although it appears as though they are in continuous direct contact with the CPU.

operating system *Software* contained in a computer which allows it to control the sequencing and processing of *programs*, and so respond correctly to user requests, eg to store a *file* of *data*, to compile and run a *program*.

operational amplifier A device which both amplifies and operates on an input *signal*. It is used in *analog computers*.

operational research The analysis of organizational operations by means of quantitative models which are usually computer-based.

operator 1. A person who operates a *computer*. 2. A *character* which designates the operation to be performed (eg +, ÷).

Opitz Classification System A German classification and coding

system for engineering tools and components. Their shape and significant characteristics are described by a five-digit number, while a second four-digit number gives supplementary information on dimensions, materials, etc (see *classification and coding systems*).

OPM Operations per minute.

OPR Optical *pattern recognition*.

Optel A *private videotex system* operated by the Open University, (UK).

optical cable See *optical fibre*.

optical character reader See *optical reader*.

optical character recognition A technique in which information recorded on *hard copy* is examined by an *optical scanning device*. This *optical reader* converts the scanned information into *digital* form, so that it can be handled subsequently by electronic means. The input *characters* that can be accepted by the scanner are currently limited (see *OCR-A* and *OCR-B*). But the range is expanding rapidly to include handwriting, etc.

optical computer A computer which uses *laser*-generated light instead of electron flow, with optically bi-stable crystals instead of *microcircuits*. Optically bi-stable crystals can be changed from one state, where light is transmitted, to another, where it is not.

optical data disc See *optical disc*.

optical digital disc See *optical disc*.

optical disc A digital data storage device based on *videodisc* technology. The differences between a videodisc and an optical disc concern, first, the way information is encoded, and second, the way the discs are made. Videodiscs have information encoded on a standard video signal designed to be displayed on a television screen; they are produced by a stamping process from a master disc at a central mastering facility. In contrast, optical discs use an alphanumeric *binary* coding system. This means that the digital data stored on the discs can be displayed on a *high resolution CRT* screen. The information is recorded on the disc directly by the user by means of a computer and an optical disc recorder, which operates in a similar way to a hard or floppy *disc drive.* In the same way as *magnetic discs,* the information can be read directly after it has been written on the disc; this is known as a *DRAW* facility. Optical discs offer a high storage capacity – in the region of 4 *gigabytes* on a 12 inch disc. This is equivalent to about one million pages of typed text, or 2,500 average sized text books. A high error rate is one of the potential problems associated with *optical storage* technology. Errors on videodiscs may be noticeable, but they seldom cause problems in receiving the visual image or sound. However, for computer data on optical disc, one or two errors can result in the *corruption* of a whole block of data. For this reason *error detection* and correction techniques are essential. Information may be recorded on optical discs on the user's own equipment. However, currently available discs are non-erasable; once data have been recorded, they cannot be erased or altered. A number of prototype erasable discs have been developed but problems remain to be solved in mass production.

Applications for optical disc include: the storage and retrieval of library records (see *DEMAND*); the storage of documents for *document delivery* (see *EuroDocDel*); and the publication and distribution of large-scale reference works.

optical fibre A very thin flexible fibre of pure glass. It can carry as much as a thousand times the information possible with traditional copper wire. A large number of fibres can be packed together into flexible cable. There are two main light sources used for optical fibres: *lasers* and *light emitting diodes* (LEDs). Lasers have some advantages, especially over long distances. They have narrower spectral width (ie the light they produce varies less in *frequency*), and they have greater 'launch' power into the fibres. However, LEDs tend to last longer, and are more stable over some *bandwidths* (see *fibre optics*; diagram).

optical reader A device which can read data from a card, or document, using optical techniques.

optical scanning device A device which scans text or *graphics* and generates *digital* representations for computer processing (see *optical character recognition*).

optical storage There are three main types of optical storage media: *read-only, write-once,* and *erasable.* Each type may be either *digital* or *analog,* depending on the type of signal for which the medium is designed. Optical technology may be used to record and store text, graphics, sound, digital data, pictures, or any combination of these. Optical devices are written and read by *laser* beam, so there is no surface contact with the recording medium and therefore no wear and tear. Optical storage media are also more robust and less susceptible to dust than *magnetic storage media* (see *videodisc, optical disc, compact disc, CD-ROM, LaserCard*).

optical transmission Use of the visible part of the electromagnetic *spectrum* for communication. Currently, two main methods predominate: a. non-coherent transmission. Typically, a *light emitting diode* (LED) is used which emits light when a current is passed through it. This is observed at the reception point by a suitable photo-detector. This method of transmission is normally used over short distances (a few hundred metres); b. coherent transmission. The transmitting device here is a

laser, which can provide a larger *bandwidth* over longer distances.

optical type fount A *fount* which can be read both by machines and by the human eye.

optoelectronics The use of electrical energy to generate optical energy, or vice versa (see *optical*

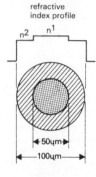

refractive index profile

Rays are trapped within a glass core surrounded by glass of a lower refractive index. Multiple beams travel down the fibre, slightly dispersing the signal as they have differing path lengths.

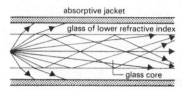

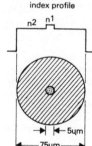

refractive index profile

By using a smaller core of the same type as above, the light is effectively forced to travel purely as axial rays. Low dispersion results, allowing a high bit rate to be transmitted, but a laser is needed to inject sufficient light into the small diameter core.

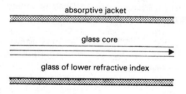

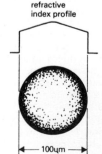

refractive index profile

A refractive index made variable across the cross-section of the glass produces continuous re-focusing of the rays. This allows very high bit rate transmission.

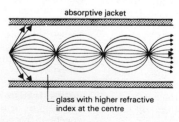

Three types of optical fibre transmission of light.

fibres and *light emitting diodes*).

OR 1. A *Boolean operator*. 2. *Operational research*.

ORACLE The *teletext* system of the British Independent Television Authority in the UK. The name is an acronym for optical reception of announcements by coded line electronics.

ORBDOC A document service operated by *SDC* in the US. A document identified by an *online search* on SDC, or any other document, can be requested by the user online. The system then stores the request in an *electronic mailbox* which can be accessed by the nominated document delivery centre. The centre then services the request, normally sending the document by conventional mail. The former name of the service was *Electronic Maildrop*.

ORBIT Online Real Time, Branch Information. A *computer language* developed by *IBM* and used by *SDC* for its *online databases* (see *SDC* and *online searching*).

Orbital Test Satellite An experimental *communications satellite* program begun by *ESA* in the latter part of the 1970s (see *European Communications Satellite*).

OR circuit Synonymous with *OR gate*.

OR gate A *gate* that implements the *logic* of the *OR* function. An OR gate is used in computer logic to combine *binary* signals in such a way that there is an output signal (1.) if any input channel carries a signal. For the case of two input signals, this leads to the following table:

Input 1	Input 2	Output
1	1	1
1	0	1
0	1	1
0	0	0

ORION Online retrieval of information over a network (see *information retrieval system* and *online searching*).

OS *Operating system.*

OSD *Optical scanning device.*

OSI *Open Systems Interconnection.*

OSI Reference Model A model put forward by *ISO*, which is intended to coordinate the development of standards at all levels of communication (see *Open Systems Interconnection*).

OTP Office of Telecommunications Policy, US.

OTS *Orbital Test Satellite.*

OURANOS A type of *expert system* available for microcomputers, written in *BASIC*.

outage The period during which a system is not operating.

outline processor See *idea processor*.

output Information transmitted by a computer, or its storage devices, to the outside world. It may, for example, be in the form of print-on-paper, *punched cards* or *paper tape*.

output bound A system whose speed of performance is restricted by the capabilities of the *output* system, eg a computer system might be output bound by a slow *printer*.

output device Any device capable of receiving information from a *central processor*. It may be some form of *backing storage*, or a *peripheral unit* which 'translates' information into another medium, eg a *line printer* or *VDU*.

output file A *file* containing data to be *output* from a system. Typically, such a file will constitute a *print file*.

output limited See *output bound.*

overflow 1. Data which cannot be accommodated in the *storage* space provided. 2. Data in excess of the capacity of a *channel.*

overflow routine A sequence of operations required to locate and retrieve (*storage*) *overflow* data.

overhead bit A *bit* included for error checking, or control, purposes.

overlay A technique used to overcome the problems of running a large *program* with a limited amount of *core storage.* Parts of the program (the overlays) are held in *auxiliary storage* and transferred, or overlaid, into core storage as and when they are required.

override function The function, or operator, within a relationship which outweighs other relationships. The *connector* 'NOT' is an example, as in (A AND B) NOT C.

overstrike The substitution of one *character* for another on a *visual display unit.* For example, in *word processing,* the *cursor* may be positioned below the character to be changed, and the desired character substituted via the *keyboard.*

overwrite An explicitly specified change (or to apply such a change) to the values held in a *file* or *database.* Overwrites are required to correct processing errors and to create text conditions.

overwriting The writing of data into a computer *memory,* or to its *auxiliary storage,* in such a way that they displace the data previously held in the *location* to which they are *addressed.*

P

PA Paper advance. The movement of paper through a *printer*.

PABX Private automatic branch exchange (see *private branch exchange*).

PAC 1. Personal analog computer (see *analog* computer and *microcomputer*). 2. Public access catalogue (see *OPAC*).

PACC Product administration and contract control. A concept applied in business *data management systems*.

package A generalized *program*, or set of programs (*software package*), written to cover the requirements of a number of users.

packaged search An *online search*, run by a *database producer* and marketed as a separate service. Packaged searches may be retrospective or may provide a current awareness service. They usually contain a broad selection from one or more databases and may be offered in a variety of formats: *hard copy*, on *floppy disc*, or on *CD-ROM*.

packet A set of *bits* which can be sent over a *network* as a self-contained message (see *packet switched*).

packet assembler/ disassembler See *PAD*.

packet density 1. The number of *logic circuits* per unit area of a *microprocessor*. 2. The number of *bits* that can be stored in a unit length of a *storage medium* recording surface.

packet radio A technique envisaged for communicating with computers using small radio units. These may be either hand-held, or attached to computer *terminals*, and are able to transmit and receive short bursts of data.
The concept was devised by researchers working on *packet switching networks*, but is not limited in its application to such networks.

packet switched (or switching) A method of routing data, or a message, from transmitter to receiver which splits the message into small units or 'packets'. The splitting may be done either at the transmitting *terminal*, or at an *exchange*. Each packet includes the 'address' of the message's destination. Packet switching can then use different routes for the various parts of a message so as to make the most efficient use of the telecommunications network. Packets have to be sorted, monitored and reassembled at the receiving point. There are two main techniques for packet switching: a. the *autonomous* mode where each packet is sent individually within the network according to the routing information attached to it; b. the *virtual link* mode where a path is pre-established within the network for each packet (see diagram).

Packet SwitchStream *Packet switched data transmission network* provided by *British Telecom*. This has public *dial-up nodes* in about 25 towns in the UK, and large users can also have private connections to the network.

PACNET Plymouth Audioconferencing Network. A large-scale trial of *audioconferencing* techniques set up in the UK to establish a permanent *teleconferencing* network.

PAD Packet assembler/

disassembler. A device for attaching *terminals* which do not operate in a packet mode to a *packet switched network*.

paddle A hand-held control unit with a press button (or buttons) mainly used with computer games.

page 1. One side of a sheet of paper in a document (the commonest usage). 2. A section within a *computer memory*. 3. A term used in *viewdata* (interactive *videotex*). It represents an assembly of information in the *database* which can be accessed via its page number.

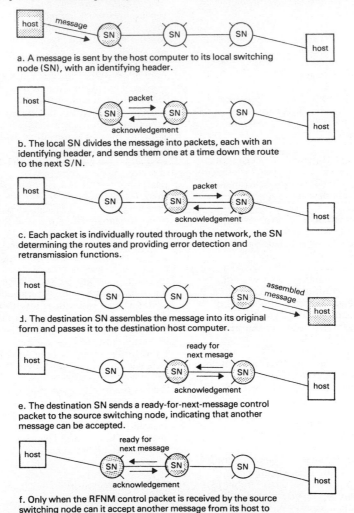

a. A message is sent by the host computer to its local switching node (SN), with an identifying header.

b. The local SN divides the message into packets, each with an identifying header, and sends them one at a time down the route to the next S/N.

c. Each packet is individually routed through the network, the SN determining the routes and providing error detection and retransmission functions.

d. The destination SN assembles the message into its original form and passes it to the destination host computer.

e. The destination SN sends a ready-for-next-message control packet to the source switching node, indicating that another message can be accepted.

f. Only when the RFNM control packet is received by the source switching node can it accept another message from its host to the same destination.

Key:
SN = switching node
RFNM = ready for next message

Data flow in a packet switching network, here ARPANET.

A page may consist of several *frames*.

page header General information about a *page*, presented on its first line.

page-layout package *Software*

which allows the operator to compose and arrange text and *graphics* as pages *on-screen*, in the same format as they would appear in the finished document.

page make-up In printing, the process of laying out text and

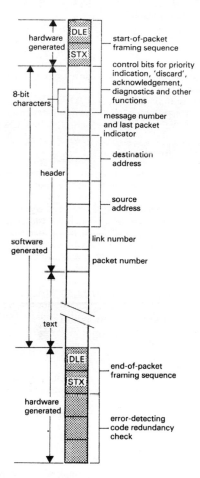

Structural diagram of a typical packet used in a packet switching network; in this case the ARPANET system. The text or data to be transmitted is preceded by a start-of-message signal and by bits for error-detection. This is followed by the header, which contains the destination and source address, the link number and the packet number. This ensures that packets are not lost or, if in error, are correctly transmitted. It is not necessary for the contents of the text to be investigated at any point, and there are usually safeguards against this.

graphics in pages, in the format they will appear in the finished document.

page printer A printer which sets the *character* pattern for a complete page before printing. It may be contrasted with a *line printer*.

page proof A printing term for the trial impression of a document laid out in the page divisions of the final product (see *proof*).

page reader An alphabetical character reader (see *optical character recognition*) which processes documents a page at a time.

page scrolling See *scrolling*.

page view terminal See *graphic display terminal (2.)*.

pagination 1. The (normally sequential) numbering of *pages* in a document. 2. A word processing function used to create and, if desired, number pages.

paging 1. The division of data, or a *program*, into *pages* (ie sub-units). 2. The scanning of text on a *VDU* page by page, rather than by continuous *scrolling*. 3. As in radio paging, eg use of 'bleepers' etc, to inform someone that they are wanted on, for instance, the telephone. 4. The transfer of data between a computer's *auxiliary storage* and *main storage*.

paint To fill in an area of a *computer graphics* display.

PAL Phase Alternate Line. This refers to one of two European standards for colour television broadcasting (the other is *Secam*). It is also used in Australia and South Africa (see *NTSC*).

palantype A *keyboard* which produces phonetic characters for subsequent transcription.

(Transcription may be done automatically by computer.)

PAM *Pulse amplitude modulation.*

pan See *scroll.*

PANDA *Prestel* Advanced *Network* Design *Architecture.*

paper-advance mechanism A device which drives paper through a *printer*. Typically, sprockets in the device engage with holes punched down each side of the paper.

PAPERCHASE An *expert system* which offers self-service *online searching* for users with no experience of *information retrieval.*

paper tape Used as a computer *input/output* medium, normally in reels a thousand feet in length and one inch wide. Information is recorded by means of punched holes: each *character* is registered as a row of holes across the tape. The choice of holes for each character is determined by the particular code being used.

paper tape reader A device which can detect the holes in a *paper tape* and translate them into *machine-readable* form.

parabolic dish An *antenna* whose cross-section is a parabola. Typically used in *satellite communications.*

paragraph assembly A *word processing* term for the compilation of a document from stored sections of text.

parallel bit transmission A data transmission system where the *bits* representing a *character* are transmitted simultaneously.

parallel computer Computer capable of performing more than one task at the same time. The term includes *array processor,* *multiprocessor* and *pipelined* computers.

parallel interface An *interface* which permits *parallel bit transmission* (compare *serial interface*).

parallel processing Computer processing where more than one arithmetic operation is carried out at the same time (rather than sequentially as in most computers). Parallel processing finds particular use in some *pattern recognition* applications.

parallel publishing A technique of publishing in which the information is presented in both electronic and printed form. In some cases, the electronic version appears simultaneously with the printed publication (although it may be in advance when postage delays are taken into account); or there may be some delay in the appearance of the electronic publication (for example, some newspapers impose a 48 hour delay on the electronic publication of their material in *news databases*).

parallel-search storage See *associative storage*.

parallel transmission The simultaneous transmission of information either over distinct channels, or by different *carrier* frequencies over the same channel.

parameter A *variable* to which a specific value is given in order to execute a *program*.

parent page A term used in *viewdata* (interactive *videotex*). A user is led to the *page* with the required information via *routing pages*. The routing page immediately prior to the required page is called the parent page.

parent segment Describes the relative logical position of a *segment* in a *hierarchical database*.

parity A condition in which the number of items is always odd or always even.

parity bit A *binary digit* added to a set of *bits* so that the sum of all the bits is either always odd, or always even.

parity check A method of testing whether the number of ones (or zeros) in a set of *binary digits* is odd or even.

parser *Software* used in *expert systems* which breaks down *natural language* statements into their grammatical components.

partition A section of a *hard disc* allocated to a single user whose access is restricted to it alone.

party line A communication channel which is shared, but without *multiplexing* (ie only one signal can be sent at a time). An example is the use of telephone party lines.

PASCAL Program Appliqué à la Selection et la Compilation Automatique de la Littérature. A very large multidisciplinary *database* compiled by the French Centre National de la Recherche Scientifique. PASCAL is accessible via *ESA-IRS*.

Pascal A *high level computer language*, particularly used for *systems programming*.

pass A complete computer processing run, including *input*, processing and *output*.

passband The *bandwidth* of a given *channel*.

passifier An *online* operation facility which enables a user to specify what to do in the event of a transmission failure: more specifically, the number of times retransmission should be attempted, and the time lapse between attempted retransmissions.

PASSIM President's Advisory Staff on Scientific Information Management, US.

passive An electronic component which cannot generate power, or amplify a signal.

password A group of *characters* which a user inputs to a computer to gain access to the system.

PATOLIS Patent Online Information System. A system which allows *online searching* of Japanese patent information compiled by *JAPATIC*.

PATRICIA Practical algorithm to receive information coded in alphanumeric (see *information retrieval techniques*, *algorithm* and *alphanumeric*).

pattern articulation unit A *microprocessor* which is used to reduce graphic images into *data streams*, and to reconstruct images from such data (see *character recognition*, *pattern recognition* and OCR).

pattern recognition (PR) A general term which can be used to cover recognition of any sort of stimulus, or input, eg visual, tactile, acoustic, chemical, electrical. It is normally used for the computer recognition of patterns (implying a reference to something already known) for the purpose of classification, grouping or identification.
The currently proposed main areas of application are in medical diagnosis, industrial inspection and control, and military systems. PR is essentially an information processing activity, which means that a range of techniques can be used. Those of general interest in information technology include OCR (*optical character recognition*), MICR (magnetic ink character

recognition) and *speech recognition*.

PAU *Pattern articulation unit.*

pause retry A transmission facility which enables a user to specify what to do in the event of a transmission failure: more specifically, the number of times retransmission should be attempted, and the time lapse between attempted retransmissions.

PAX *Private automatic exchange.*

pay cable A *cable television* system with a pay-as-you-view charging structure.

PBX *Private branch exchange.*

PC *Personal computer.*

PC-AT *Personal computer – advanced technology.*

PCB *Printed circuit board.*

PC-DOS An *operating system* designed especially for the *IBM personal computer*. It is very similar to *MS-DOS*.

PCK *Processor controlled keyboard.*

PCM 1. *Pulse code modulation.* 2. Punchcard machine (see *card punch*). 3. *Plug compatible* manufacturer.

PCMI Photo-chromic micro image. An *ultrafiche* with up to 3200 images on an A6 size base. The production process requires a more stringently controlled environment than is necessary for ordinary *microfiche*.

PCS Punched card system (see *punched card*).

PDL Publishers Database Limited. A UK consortium of publishers formed to help exploit their potential for *electronic publishing*.

PDM *Pulse duration modulation.*

peek A term used in *high level languages* to retrieve information from a specified *memory* location (see *poke*).

Pel Picture element (see *pixel*).

P/E News Petroleum/Energy News. A US *database* giving coverage of petroleum and energy business news. It is accessible via *SDC*.

PERA System A classification code for technical components developed by the UK Project Engineering Research Association (see *classification and coding systems*).

Perceval A Belgian *teletext* system.

perfecting Printing so that pages of text are printed on both sides and the paper is ready for folding.

perforated tape See *paper tape*.

perforator Any device that can produce perforated *paper tape*.

Pergamon-Infoline A UK *host* giving access to a number of *databases*, predominantly in the sciences.

perigee The point in an orbit at which a *communications satellite* is nearest the earth's surface.

peripheral See *peripheral unit*.

peripheral interface An *interface* between a computer and its *peripheral units*.

peripheral transfer Moving data between two *peripheral units*.

peripheral (unit) A device under the control of a *central processor*. It may mean an *input device*, an *output device*, or a *storage device*.

permanent file A *file* which remains in the system after termination of the session in which it was created (compare *scratch file*).

permanent memory *Memory* which retains its information when power is cut off. It is to be contrasted with *volatile memory*.

permutation index An *index* which lists all the words in a document's title so that each word appears, in turn, as the first word, followed by the remaining words.

permuted index See *permutation index*.

perpendicular magnetic recording A technique designed to increase the recording density of *magnetic storage media*. Existing media rely on magnetic particles which lie in the plane of the tape or disc. If the particles can be made to stand vertically, then their density on the medium can be increased, and they also have a reduced demagnetizing effect on neighbouring particles.

persistence The length of time for which a fluorescent screen (as used in a *CRT*) retains an image.

personal computer A synonym for *microcomputer*, sometimes used to describe a machine which is more powerful than a *home computer* but less powerful than a *work station*.

personal data A term used in the *Data Protection Act* to denote information held on computer which relates to a living individual who can be identified from that information (see *data subject*).

personal identification number See *PIN*.

PERT Programme evaluation and review technique. A management technique for scheduling and controlling large projects. It is more often called *critical path method* (CPM) or *network planning*.

petal printer Synonymous with *daisy wheel printer.*

PF 1. Page footing. The record of information to be printed at the foot of a page, or pages, in a document. 2. Pulse frequency.

Pf key Programmable function *key*. A key (ie button) on a *keyboard*, the depression of which initiates some pre-programmed activity (eg page forward, return to *menu, database* update).

PGI UNESCO's General Information Programme.

PH Page heading. The record of information to be printed at the head of a page, or pages, in a document.

phase encoding A method of recording *binary* digits on *magnetic tape* in which a '1' and a '0' are represented by different directions of magnetization (see *NRZI*).

phase modulation See *modulation*.

Philips/MCA Discovision A *videodisc* system developed by Philips and MCA. A master disc is created by exposing a surface to the action of a *laser* beam, which is *modulated* by the signals to be recorded. The laser beam creates pits in the surface, and these are reproduced in the copies made subsequently. Playback is achieved by focussing another laser beam on to the pitted surface. The reflected light is monitored and used to reproduce the original video (and audio) signals. The discs, which have about 625 tracks per millimetre, are covered with a protective coating, and the reading laser is focussed on the surface below this. Consequently, the playback is unaffected by dirt, fingerprints, etc. There appears to be little limit to disc life, even when frozen on a single frame. This contrasts with videotape players, where use of a *freeze frame* facility can ultimately damage the tape. It

should be noted that MCA have now changed their name to DVA (Discovision Associates).

phoneme The smallest element of spoken language which distinguishes one utterance from another. For example, the word 'bit' consists of three phonemes – /b/, /i/ and /t/.

phosphor dot The element of a *cathode ray tube* which glows to form a *display*.

photocomposer Often used as a synonym for *phototypesetter*.

photocomposition See *phototypesetting*.

photo-detector Light-sensitive device.

photoelectric detection Detecting and reading marks with a *photoelectric detector*, as in *optical character recognition*.

photoelectric detector A device for detecting the presence of light and measuring its intensity.

photogravure A *gravure* printing process where the image is produced photographically.

photolithography A *lithographic* printing process where the image is formed photographically.

photonics Another term for *fibre optics* (see *optical fibre*).

photo-optic memory Memory which uses an optical storage medium (usually film).

photo-optic typesetter A *phototypesetter* in which the character master is a grid, or disc. Characters are optically projected from this onto a photosensitive surface.

photosensitive printing A general

term for printing methods which depend on radiation, not on temperature-induced effects. These include *electrophotographic printing*, *photo-polymer printing* and some dye-based methods.

photosensor Any light-sensitive device used in conjunction with an optical arrangement for *scanning* images, eg in *facsimile transmission*.

photosetting Used to describe the typesetting of headlines by optical means, but is often employed as a synonym for *phototypesetting*.

phototelegram service *Facsimile transmission* service operated by British Telecom. Graphic material is telegraphed from London worldwide over line circuits and radio links. The receiving office then mails the phototelegram to the final recipient by express, or registered, post.

phototelegraphy The name in Europe for newspicture transmission using *facsimile transmission*.

phototypesetter Any device which makes it possible to set images of *type* on photographic material (see *computer-aided typesetting*) (see diagram).

phototypesetting The production of *type* images on a photographic medium by optical techniques. A machine that can perform this function is called a *phototypesetter* (see *computer-aided typesetting*).

physical database Description of a database in the exact form in which it is stored (see, in contrast, *logical database*).

physical data independence A *data structure* which enables a *physical database* to be changed without altering the user interface (ie the *logical database* and its *information retrieval software*).

Physics Abstracts A *database* compiled by *INSPEC* in the UK, giving extensive bibliographic coverage of the physics literature. It is accessible via most of the major *hosts*.

pica See *point (system)*.

Pi character In *phototypesetting*, a *character* which is not normally stored on a *master grid* or in the computer's *memory*.

pico- A prefix meaning one million millionth (10^{-12}).

picture element Synonymous with *pixel*.

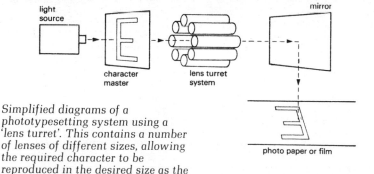

Simplified diagrams of a phototypesetting system using a 'lens turret'. This contains a number of lenses of different sizes, allowing the required character to be reproduced in the desired size as the selection of different lenses alters the magnitude of the image that is exposed on the photosensitive drum.

Picturephone A particular type of *video telephone*. 'Picturephone' is a trade name registered by the US company *AT&T*.

Picturephone Meeting Service *Video teleconferencing* service (*AT&T*).

Picture Prestel A system introduced by *British Telecom* to handle *high resolution* pictures.

piece identification number See *PIN*.

pie processor 1. A computer which performs some preliminary processing of *input data*, prior to them being processed by another, usually larger, computer. 2. A program which performs preliminary processing of *input data* prior to them being incorporated in a more major processing operation.

PIN 1. Personal identification number, ie user *ID*. 2. Piece identification number: a *bar-coded* label. 3. Pergamon-Infoline Number. A number assigned to each *record* in *databases* offered by *Pergamon-Infoline*, which is used for the purpose of *document delivery*.

pinfeed platen A *platen* which moves paper through a printer using 'pins'. These engage in holes along the edges of the paper.

pipelined A type of parallel computer in which several tasks, eg reading data from *memory* and processing earlier data, can be performed simultaneously. This leads to faster operation. Some of the world's largest computers are pipelined. The name refers to the analogy between a flow of operations and a flow of liquids in a pipe.

PIRA Paper, Printing and Packaging Industries Research Association. A UK body which carries out research in all areas suggested by its title (including *electronic publishing*). PIRA compiles a database (also called PIRA) and a second more specialist database, *Electronic Publishing Abstracts*.

piracy The practice of copying or reprinting *copyright* material – books, audio tapes, videotapes, computer software – without permission for subsequent resale.

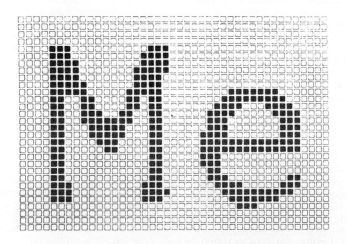

Letters as they would appear on a VDU showing the pattern of pixels.

PIRS Personal information retrieval system. Refers to the storage of information on the *magnetic tapes* or *discs*, of a mini- or microcomputer, using a *software package* to help order and index the information.

pitch Number of characters per inch.

Pittler classification system A system for classifying technical components and describing them in *digital* code (see *classification and coding systems*).

pixel A picture element on a visual display screen (*VDU*).

pixel pattern The matrix used in building the image of a character, or symbol, on a display screen (see diagram).

plasma display A form of *display* which uses a flat panel as a screen. The display device consists of two panels, one in the x-axis and one in the y, each of which is laced with minute conductors. Between the panels is a gas which conducts an electronic plasma at the point where an x and a y current intersect. The plasma display has many advantages over a *cathode ray tube* display: most notably its compact size, good readability and internal *memory* capability.

platen The plate in a printing machine against which paper is held in order to have printed material impressed upon it.

plausible reasoning Equivalent to *inexact reasoning*.

PL/1 Programming Language/1. A *high level language* with a wide range of scientific and business applications.

plotter A print device used to reproduce drawings and graphics on paper. Plotters perform the function of drawing by machine under computer control. A pen (or bank of pens) is carried across the paper and raised or lowered as needed to produce a continuous, smooth image.

PL/M Programming Language for Microcomputers. A *high level language* derived from *PL/1*.

plug board A board into which electrical plugs can be inserted manually to control equipment.

plug compatible Any two devices which will operate from the same socket are said to be plug compatible.

plug-to-plug compatible See *plug compatible*.

PMBX Private manual branch exchange (see *private branch exchange*).

P MOS P-channel metal oxide semiconductor. A common form of *transistor* (where 'P' stands for positive – see *N MOS*).

PNI Pharmaceutical News Index. A US *database* covering journal articles on pharmaceuticals, drugs and cosmetics. PNI is accessible via *BRS*, *Lockheed* and *SDC*.

PO British Post Office: previously GPO (General Post Office).

pocket computer Small *computer*, about the size of a pocket calculator. Its use is usually limited to acting as an electronic diary and address book, with the addition of some *programmable* computations.

POCS Patent Office Classification System, US.

pointer 1. Indicator added to *records* stored on a *direct access storage device* to enable the logical structure of a *file* to be preserved (see *logical database*) irrespective of the physical location of the *data* (see *physical database*). A pointer gives the *address* of the next data element relative to the prescribed logical file structure. Multiple sets of pointers enable many file structures to exist while the constituent data are only stored once. 2. An indicator used in *window* and *mouse* systems. The pointer, usually in the shape of an arrow, is moved around the screen by *software* under the control of the mouse (or *joystick*) in order to 'point to' various options offered by the *menu* on screen.

point of sale See *electronic point of sale*.

point (system) A measurement of length in typography, used in English-speaking countries. One point = 0.351 mm; 12 points = one pica.

point-to-point connection A *dedicated* communication link that joins only two *nodes* in a *network*.

poke A term used in *high level languages*, to deposit information in a specified *memory* location (see *peek*).

polarization The direction of vibration of an *electromagnetic wave*, and, correspondingly, the direction in which a receiving or transmitting *aerial* must be orientated.

polar transmission A method of transmitting *teletypewriter* signals which employs a three-state signal (see *neutral transmission*).

POLIS Parliamentary Online Information System. The *information retrieval system* of the House of Commons Library in the United Kingdom.

polling A means of controlling communication along a series of *lines* by seeing if any of them is waiting to deliver a message.

Pollution Abstracts A US *database* covering pollution, environmental quality, pesticides and related

topics. It is accessible via *BRS, ESA-IRS, Lockheed, QL* and *SDC*.

Polynet A ring *local area network* developed by Logica VTS.

POP-2 A *high level language* used in *artificial intelligence* applications. Derived from *LISP*.

port A place of entry to, or exit from, a *central processor*.

portable 1. With regard to *hardware*, has the general meaning, ie can be carried from place to place. 2. With regard to *software*, refers to the ability to be *run* on a variety of different types of computer.

POS *Point of sale.*

POSH Permuted on subject headings (see *permutation index*).

positive An image (usually photographic) with *tones* which are the same as those of the original.

post To enter data into a record.

Postcode Project A service offered by the UK Post Office which provides advice, assistance and financial aid to companies wishing to make use of the postcode in their computerized address lists.

post coordinate indexing See *indexing*.

post editing Carrying out *editing* on *output*.

poster session An alternative method of information dissemination used at, or instead of, conferences. Participants present their papers in poster form using display stands, and conference delegates are free to wander around and consult those that interest them.

postings 1. In *information retrieval*, the number of records retrieved by a *search*. 2. The number of documents entered for each *index term* in a *bibliographic file.*

postings dictionary A dictionary of *index terms* giving the number of documents entered in a *bibliographic file* under each such term.

post mortem dump A *dump* carried out following a program's *execution,* usually to facilitate *debugging.*

post mortem program Synonymous with *post mortem routine.*

post mortem routine A *routine* used to analyse the functioning of a program following its *execution.*

post mortem time The time it takes for a system to recover following a failure.

post processor 1. A computer which performs a processing operation on *output* from another computer. 2. A program which performs a processing operation on *output* from an earlier and usually

larger processing operation.

power restart A function of some computer systems which is designed to safeguard the system against fluctuations in power supply.

PPS Pulses per second. A unit of signal transmission rate.

pragmatics The way in which a language is used.

precedence Used as a synonym for *priority.*

precedence code A *code* which signifies that the *characters* in the following code (or codes) will have a different meaning from normal.

PRECIS 1. Preserved context index system. A subject *indexing system,* developed for the British National Bibliography, in which initial *strings* of *terms* are organized according to their linguistic function. The computer manipulates the strings so that selected words function in turn as the 'approach' term (ie the term in which the user is primarily

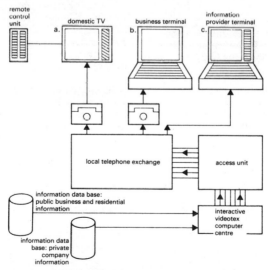

Prestel: this diagram illustrates the three types of user terminal available; (a) a domestic television set with viewdata, (b) a business terminal and (c) an information provider's terminal.

interested). 2. Precoordinate indexing system. A system in which terms are combined at the time of indexing a document. The combination of terms is recorded in the entries (see *indexing*).

precision 1. A measure of exactness (for example, the number of decimal places to which a value is shown). Should not be confused with *accuracy*. 2. In bibliographic *information retrieval systems*, precision means the percentage of all *items* retrieved by a search on a particular topic which actually prove to be relevant to that topic (see *recall*).

precoordinate indexing See *indexing*.

Predicasts Files These contain over three million summaries of information from documents covering a variety of business and industrial statistics. Most of the files are accessible for *online searching* via *Lockheed*.

pre-editing Carrying out *editing* prior to *input*.

Prestel The *viewdata* (interactive *videotex*) system implemented by British Telecom in the UK (see diagram).

Prestel Education Service A special service for schools offered by *Prestel*, the UK *videotex* system, and part-funded by the Department of Industry. The core of the information is provided by the *Microelectronics Education Programme*.

prestore To store data prior to *processing*.

Pricedata A *databank* covering world commodity prices. It is compiled in Italy, and is accessible via the *ESA-IRS host* computer and *Euronet-DIANE*.

primary key A *key* used in the compilation of a database which uniquely identifies an item.

print drum See *drum printer*.

printed circuit board A mass-produced unit consisting of electrical components on a board and interconnected to produce a *circuit*.

printer In new information technology, this refers to an *output device* which converts electronic signals into print-on-paper (see *line printer*, *page printer*, *daisy wheel printer*).

printerfacing The provision of an interface between *microcomputers* and output printing *terminals*.

printer limited When the relatively low speed of the *printer* is the limiting factor in determining the rate at which *data processing* can take place.

printer plotter A printer (usually of the *daisy wheel*, or *matrix* type) which can undertake graphics reproduction in addition to character printing.

printer spacing chart A form used in deciding the format of printed output.

printer's type The range of different *characters* and *typeface* designs available from a printing office.

print file An *output file* which is designed for use by a print *program* to produce *hard copy* output.

print head The part of an *impact printer* which hammers the inked ribbon to the paper.

printout The printed paper *output* (pages, or continuous roll) which a computer produces via a *printer*.

print run 1. The production of

printed copies. 2. The number of printed copies produced.

print wheel A wheel (which can be changed when necessary) used to print characters in some types of *printer* (see, eg, *daisy wheel printer*).

priority Refers to the execution of programs, or the transmission of messages, following some designated order of importance.

PRISM Personal Records Information System for Management. A computerized personal information system used by the civil service in the UK.

privacy See *data protection*.

private automatic exchange (PAX) An exchange for a private telephone service, within an organization, which is not connected to the public telephone network.

private branch exchange (PBX) A *switching* facility (exchange) within an institution which also provides access to the public telephone network. The exchange may be manually operated, in which case it is, strictly, a private manual branch exchange (PMBX), or, it may have an automatic switching facility, and so be classified as a private automatic branch exchange (PABX).

private line A channel with associated equipment provided for the exclusive use of a particular subscriber.

private videotex system An independent *videotex* system run in-house by an organization using *proprietary software* on its own computer and accessible over its own *network* or via public *packet switched* networks. Private videotex systems are used primarily for internal purposes such as stock control, communication or access to corporate *databases*. A number of private systems (such as those run by local authorities in the UK) also provide information to the general public.

privilege Refers to the range of activities and resources to which a user is allowed *access* by a computer's *operating system*. For example, a high level of privilege will allow users to modify information held on the computer, whereas a low level will only allow them to read it.

problem-orientated language A *high level language* developed for convenient expression of particular problems.

procedural language A *programming language* which is structured in terms of the procedures a computer must follow in order to perform a task or solve a problem. Most conventional languages (eg *BASIC, COBOL, FORTRAN*) are procedural.

procedure-orientated language A *high level language* designed for convenient expression of particular procedures.

process colour work The equivalent of four-colour reproduction (ie the use of combinations of red, yellow, blue and black to give a full range of colours).

processing See *data processing*.

processor Synonymous with *central processor*.

processor controlled keyboard Another name for a *key-to-disc* system.

production rules See *rule-based*.

production run Routine execution of a regularly run program.

profile A term used for the range of interests of an individual or group in *SDI*.

program An ordered list of instructions directing a computer, or other *intelligent device*, to perform a desired sequence of *operations*.

program crash A *program* crash occurs when a computer program attempts to execute an impossible instruction, but has no way of recognizing the impossibility and stopping. Well-written programs which are unlikely to crash are referred to as 'crash-proof' or 'robust'.

program flowchart A *flowchart* diagram which describes a computer *program* in terms of a series of steps, and of the relationship between these steps. Standard sets of symbols are used in constructing the flowchart. The most common such set are shown in the diagram.

symbol	represents
	PROCESSING A group of program instructions that perform a processing function within a program.
	INPUT/OUTPUT Any function of an input/output device (making information available for processing, recording processing information, tape positioning, etc.).
	DECISION The decision function is used to document points in a program where a branch to alternate paths is possible based upon variable conditions.
	PROGRAM MODIFICATION An instruction or group of instructions which changes a program sequence.
	PREDEFINED PROCESS This identifies a group of operations not detailed in a particular set of flowcharts.
	TERMINAL The beginning, end, or a point of interruption in a program.
	CONNECTOR An entry from, or an exit to, another part of a program flowchart.
	OFFPAGE CONNECTOR A connector used to designate entry to or exit from a page.
	FLOW DIRECTION The direction of processing or data flow.
	ANNOTATION The addition of descriptive comments or explanatory notes as clarification.

Selection of symbols used in program flowcharts.

program library See *library*.

programmable Capable of storing and *executing* an ordered list of *instructions*.

programmed learning See *computer-aided instruction* and *educational technology*.

programmer A person who writes *programs*.

programming language The language in which coded *instructions* are written for a computer. See *high level language* and *low-level language*.

program specification A description of a *program* which specifies all the information needed to design it in detail. The description normally includes a *program flowchart* (compare *documentation*).

Project Quartet A collaborative research project funded by the British Library and being undertaken by University College London, the Universities of Birmingham and Loughborough, and Hatfield Polytechnic. Their object is to develop an integrated information and communication system, bringing together existing research into computer *networks*, *mass data storage* and *retrieval* – in the form of text, pictures and graphics – and visual display techniques. The system will provide *electronic messaging*, *computer conferencing*, *database* access and *document delivery*, all based around the X.400 standard (see *BLEND*.)

Project Universe Universities expanded ring and satellite experiments. An experiment being carried out by a consortium of UK government departments, industries and universities. It connects members' *ring networks* and *local area networks* (*LANs*), and makes use of the *Orbital Test Satellite* for high *bandwidth* data transmission.

The *programme* contains a variety of experiments including mixed media (eg text, pictures and sound) in *electronic document delivery*.

PROLOG A *high level language* derived from *LISP* which allows programs to be written in terms of the rules governing the solution of problems, and logical relationships relevant to sets of problems. This contrasts with the conventional approach, ie the specification of solution procedures. Through this distinctive feature, PROLOG is found useful for the development of *expert systems*.

PROM Programmable read-only memory (see *ROM* and *blowing*).

prom blowing See *blowing*.

PROMIS Problem Orientated Medical Information System. A very flexible computer-based medical record and hospital information system developed in the US. All data are entered and retrieved electronically, using *terminals* with *touch-sensitive screens*.

prompt A message given to an *operator* (*1.*) by an *operating system*. It usually indicates that particular information is required before a *program* can proceed.

Pronto The trade-name of a five-finger *keyboard*, having eight *keys*: three shift keys and five (one for each finger) character and symbol selection keys. It has the advantage over conventional keyboards of being small and light (potentially portable) and allowing data entry to be performed with one hand (see *chord keyboard*).

proof In printing, a trial impression, obtained after *composition*, which can be used to introduce corrections (see *galley proof* and *page proof*).

proportional spacing In *typesetting*, the horizontal spacing of characters in proportion to their width. This may be contrasted with the constant spacing used on a standard typewriter.

proprietary Describes a system or device developed by a private organization which does not adhere to international standards.

proprietary software Copyright *software* sold on a commercial basis.

prosodic The stress and intonation of spoken language.

Prospector An *expert system* to find commercial minerals from assay data.

protected field An area on a *screen* into which *data* cannot be keyed.

protected location A computer *location* in which data cannot be stored without undergoing some test procedure beforehand.

protection ring See *file protection ring*.

protocol A set of conventions governing the *format* of messages to be exchanged within a communication system.

prototyping The process whereby certain parts of a system are designed and demonstrated with a minimum of development work having to be done. The objective of prototyping is to clarify and agree user requirements by demonstrating the provisional user *interface* and then modifying it according to users' reactions.

PROXI Protection by reflection optics of xerographic images (see *xerography*).

proximity See *word proximity*.

PRR Pulse repetition rate. The number of electronic pulses received in unit time at a specified point in a computer.

PSS 1. *Packet switching* service. 2. *Packet SwitchStream*.

PSTN Public switched telephone network (see *switching*).

PSU Power supply unit.

Psychological Abstracts *Bibliographic database* covering psychology and related subject areas. It is accessible via *BRS, DIMDI, Lockheed* and *SDC*.

PTO Public Telecommunications Operator. Organizations, such as *British Telecom* and *Mercury*, which operate publicly available *telecommunications networks* and supply equipment for connection to them.

PTS F and S Indexes One of the biggest business information *databanks*. It contains information on companies, products and industries, and includes sales figures and profit forecasts. Based in the US, it has international coverage and is accessible via *Lockheed*.

PTS Files Predicasts Terminal System Files (see *Predicasts Files*).

PTT Postal, Telegraph and Telephone Authority.

public data network A *data communications network* usually operated by a *PTT*.

public dial port A *port* through which a user can dial into a public *packet switched network*.

public domain software Non-copyrighted *software* which is available free of charge. Many *programs* of this type are available as *telesoftware*.

published search See *packaged search*.

PUCK Used as a *light pen*, eg with a *graphics tablet*.

pull-down menu A *menu* of commands which does not normally appear on-screen but can be displayed, usually by moving a *pointer* to the top of a screen and pressing on a specific word. The menu appears at this point, as if pulled down like a roller blind.

pulse amplitude modulation A form of *modulation* in which the amplitude of a pulse is adjusted in response to an input signal.

pulse code modulation The most common form of *pulse modulation*. It allows *analog* information to be transmitted in *digital* form. The *amplitude* of an analog signal is sampled, and the sampled value is represented by a binary number. This number is then transmitted as a string of digital pulses.

pulse duration modulation A form of *modulation* in which the duration of a pulse is adjusted in response to an input signal.

pulse modulation A form of modulation in which the characters of a standard pulse are adjusted in response to a standard signal (see *pulse amplitude modulation, pulse code modulation* and *pulse duration modulation*).

pulse width modulation Synonymous with *pulse duration modulation.*

punch 1. To make holes in a *card*, or *paper tape*, so as to enter information. 2. A piece of equipment to make such holes.

punched card See *card.*

punched tape See *paper tape.*

pure machine-aided translation An approach to the design of *machine translation*. The lexicons of two, or more, languages are computerized in order to supply a human translator with *target language* equivalents of *source language* lexical items. Usually only specialized vocabulary is included in an *automated lexicon*, leaving the common core vocabulary to the human translator (see *machine-aided translation* and *machine translation*).

pure machine translation A *machine translation* system in which the computer attempts to do the entire translation itself. Only pre-input and/or post-output text editing by human translators is required. Despite a great deal of research and development, pure machine translation is still in the experimental stage, while *machine-aided translation* has become an operational reality (see *HAMT* and *SYSTRAN*).

pure MAT Pure *machine-aided translation.*

pure MT Pure *machine translation.*

purge To erase *data* from a *file.*

pushbutton dialling The use of pushbuttons instead of a rotary dial for feeding in a sequence of numbers or letters, eg to a telephone. Each number/letter may be identified by its own audio signal.

pushdown list A list of items compiled in such a manner that the last item added stands at the top of the list (see *pushup list*).

pushup list A list of items compiled in such a manner that the last item added goes to the bottom of the list (see *pushdown list*).

PVT Page view terminal (see *graphic display terminal* (2.)).

PW Private wire (see *private line*).

PWM *Pulse width modulation.*

Q

QAM Queued access method.

Q-band Frequency band used in radar (36-46 GHz).

QED A software package for text editing.

QL Quick Law Systems. A Canadian host offering access to databases containing legal information.

QTAM Queued telecommunications access method.

quadding A term used in typesetting. It refers to the insertion of blank space, or to the blank space itself, in a typeset line.

quadruplex transverse scanning See transverse scanning.

quantizing error Distortion brought about by analog to digital conversion. It occurs when analog signals fall between the possible digital values (see analog-to-digital conversion).

Quartet The four institutions taking part in Project Quartet.

Qube US CATV and videotex network (Warner Amex Cable Corp).

Québec-Actualité Canadian database covering items of Canadian and world news drawn from several French-Canadian newspapers. It is accessible via SDC.

query language A high level language, resembling a natural language, which is designed to make online searching easy for inexperienced users.

Quest A computer language used for searching databases via ESA-IRS.

Questel A French host covering a number of French and EEC databases in science, technology and business.

queue The processing of jobs or items (eg data) awaiting action (execution, transmission, etc) on a FIFO principle.

queued access method A data processing method in which the transfer of data between devices is automatically synchronized to eliminate delays.

queued telecommunications access method When the transfer of data between a computer and its peripherals is automatically synchronized via telecommunications channels (see queued access method).

quick access memory Memory with relatively short access time.

QUICKTRAN Quick FORTRAN. A high level language, developed from FORTRAN, designed for use in conversational mode on time sharing systems.

Qwerty keyboard A keyboard which has the keys laid out in the same pattern as that used on ordinary typewriters. The word derives from the letters at the top left of the keyboard.

R

RACE Random access computer equipment (see *random access*).

RAD Rapid access disc (see *magnetic disc* and *access time*).

RADA Random access discrete address. A location in a *RAM* (see *address*).

radio communication Any communication using radio waves (see *spectrum*).

Radio Suisse A Swiss *host* system.

RADIR Random access document indexing and retrieval (see *random access*, *RAM*, and *information retrieval system*).

ragged left An uneven left-hand margin (see *justify*).

ragged right An uneven right-hand margin (see *justify*).

RAM *Random access memory*.

RAM disc A collection of *RAM* chips inside a computer which can *emulate* the action of a *magnetic disc*. RAM discs are much quicker than normal discs but, in general, cannot retain data once the computer is switched off.

RAMIS Random Access Management Information System. An *information retrieval system* which stores management information in *RAM*.

RAMPI Raw Material Price Index. An *online databank*.

R&D Research and development. Designates technical and applied scientific activity, particularly directed towards the development of new products, processes, services or systems.

random access file (organization) A *file* held on *disc* in such a way that the physical location of a given *record* can be calculated by applying an *algorithm* to the record's *key*. Such a file organization is typically used when rapid *access times* are required.

random access memory (RAM) Memory where any location can be read from, or written to, in a *random access* fashion.

random access (storage) *Access* to *storage* where the next *location* from which information is to be obtained is unrelated to the previous location. Normally implies that the *access time* to any location is the same.

random number A number generated, usually by a computer, in such a way that its value cannot be predicted beforehand.

range The gap between highest and lowest values.

ranged left Text which is justified at the left-hand margin only. Used as a synonym for *ragged right* (see *justify*).

rank 1. To arrange in ascending order according to some fixed criterion. 2. The position of a member of a group, following such ranking.

RAPID Random access personnel information system (see *RAMIS*, *RAM* and *information retrieval system*).

RASTAC Random access storage and control (see *RAM*).

RASTAD Random access storage and display (see *RAM* and *display*).

raster A grid on a *terminal* screen

which divides the *display* area into discrete elements (like a map reference system).

raster count The number of positions on a *display* screen which can be defined using its *raster* (ie the product of the number of horizontal and vertical divisions).

raster graphics A form of *computer graphics* which, unlike *vector graphics*, utilizes a full matrix of *pixels*. Each pixel has its own code, and is switched on, or off, according to a guiding *program* (see *raster*).

raster plotter A *plotter* which draws a complete picture on a CRT, including an image both of the object of interest and its background. It is used in *computer graphics* (see *calligraphic plotter* and *raster*).

raster scan The sweeping of the display area of a device, line-by-line, to generate, or read, an image.

raw data Data which have not been processed.

RAX *Remote access.*

Rayleigh fading Variations in *signal* strength encountered in radio-based communications. Radio waves which have travelled along many different paths and have been reflected off stationary and moving objects interfere to produce unpredictable variations in signal strength.

RCA Selectavision See *Selectavision.*

reactive mode When each entry at a *terminal* causes some action to be taken by a *central processor*, but the processor does not necessarily return an immediate response to the terminal. It is to be contrasted with *conversational mode.*

read 1. To copy, usually from one *storage* area to another. 2. To sense

information from some form of recorded medium, eg from a *card* or *magnetic tape*.

READ 1. Real-time electronic access and display (see *real time, access* and *display*). 2. Remote electrical alphanumeric display (see *remote access, alphanumeric* and *display*).

READ code Relative Element Address Designate – a *code* used in *facsimile* machines.

read head See *read/write head*, but may not be able to *write*.

read-only Describes any *storage device* whose contents may be read or copied, but not altered in any way.

read-only memory (ROM) Once information has been entered into this *memory*, it can be read as often as required, but cannot normally be changed. Many currently available *videodiscs* are read-only devices.

readout *Soft copy* output from a computer displayed on the screen of a *VDT*.

read screen A transparent screen through which documents are read in *optical character recognition*.

read/write head An *electromagnetic* device used to read from, or write on, a *magnetic storage device*: similar to a 'pick-up' head on an ordinary audio tape recorder.

read/write memory Information written into a computer *memory* or *storage* area can then be accessed and read. In a read/write memory (or store) this information can be altered at will and read again as often as required. This may be contrasted with *read-only memory*.

read/write storage See *read/write memory*.

read/write videodisc A *rewritable*

videodisc currently under development.

ready A *status word* indicating that a *computer* is waiting for *input* from a *terminal*.

REALCOM Real-time Communications. A system developed by RCA (see *real time*).

real time The computer response occurs at the same rate as the data input. Most control systems, eg an automatic pilot on an airplane, operate in real time, as do *online search* systems.

reasonableness check A quick check for gross error.

reasoning with uncertainty See *inexact reasoning*.

recall In bibliographic *information retrieval systems*, recall is the ratio of all items actually retrieved by a search to the total number of items searched for. It is usually expressed as a percentage (see *precision*).

receive only Refers to a communications *terminal* which can only receive messages.

recognition logic The *software* in an *OCR* reader which allows it to translate printed text into *digital* form.

recognition unit A device for interpreting the electrical signals received when *scanning* a document in order to capture text in *machine-readable* form. It matches the 'read' character against its own store of characters in order to 'recognize' it for conversion into computer code (see *optical character recognition*).

RECOL Retrieval Command Language. A *computer language* used for the interrogation of *databases* within an *information retrieval system* (see *query language* and *search language*).

record A unit, or set of data, forming the basic element of a *file*.

recordable videodisc system Commercial *videodiscs* are produced by a central mastering process and cannot record information, but only play back pre-recorded material. Research is underway on developing a videodisc on which information can be recorded, erased and re-recorded. A number of prototypes exist. One uses a tellurium alloy which changes state under *laser* light. Another uses magneto-optical techniques, in which the laser signals are recorded in a magnetic field.

record gap See *inter-block gap*.

recording density Synonymous with *packing density*.

record locking Mechanism used in *local area networks* and *multi-user* systems which prevents two users from writing to the same *record* at the same time.

record separator A *character* indicating the boundary between two *records* in a *file*, or transmission.

recovery system A computer *program* which records the progress of computer *processing* activities, to allow reconstruction of a *run in* the event of a computer *crash*.

recursion Synonymous with *iteration*.

Reduced Instruction Set Chip A *processor* which uses fewer instructions than the standard set found in conventional processors. This makes RISC processors both smaller and faster.

reduction rates In *micrographics*, this refers to the ratio between the scale of the original material and the scale of the *microform* image.

redundancy 1. The proportion of information in a message which can be eliminated without the message losing its essential meaning. 2. Provision of a back-up system which can be automatically activated if the primary system breaks down.

redundancy check A method of checking for the presence of errors in data. It depends on the use of more bits than are required to represent the information concerned. The check is usually carried out automatically (see, eg, *parity check*).

redundant code *Bits* added to *data* for error checking purposes.

refereed A document which has been subjected to evaluation by experts and passed as suitable for publication.

reference See *citation.*

reference database A *database* which does not hold the full information required by the user, but indicates the source of the information (see *bibliographic database, catalogue database, software database*).

referral database A *database* containing details and addresses of organizations, projects, etc (see *directory database*).

reformat To change the arrangement of data using appropriate *software* (see *format*).

refresh The process of reactivating information. This is required, for instance, with a *VDU* display. Material appearing on the screen is generated by the action of cathode rays on phosphor dots. The phosphors light up, but then immediately begin to fade until reactivated. Refreshing tends to create flicker (see *storage tube*).

refresh rate The rate at which a display screen is refreshed (see *refresh*). A minimum refresh rate of 50 *Hz* (cycles per second) is recommended for comfortable viewing.

regenerative memory *Memory* which needs to be *refreshed*: otherwise the contents disappear.

register 1. A computer *storage* device which holds data, *addresses* or instructions on a temporary basis. For example, if a series of numbers is being added, the intermediate totals can be accumulated in a register as they are produced. 2. Obtaining the correct position relative to each other of two or more printings on the same sheet.

relational database A *database* in which the relations between the *items* it contains are formally stated.

relational operator A symbol used to compare two values, eg $<$; $>$; =,

relay 1. An electromagnetic switch. 2. A point-to-point reception and retransmission system.

Relay A US *communications satellite* launched in the 1970s.

relay centre Synonymous with *message switching centre.*

REMARC Retrospective Machine Readable Cataloguing. A *database* produced by Carrollton Press of *machine-readable bibliographic* records, in the *MARC* format, which do not appear in the *LCMARC* database.

remark A comment inserted in a program to assist the user. It is ignored by the computer.

remote access The use of a *computer* from a *terminal* at a geographically distant point. The terminal and computer may be connected via either cables, or broadcast transmission.

remote batch processing The sending of *data* and *programs* in *batches* to a *central processor*.

remote batch terminal *Terminal* used for *remote batch processing*.

remote job entry (RJE) Entry of data, or operating instructions, into a computer from a *remote terminal* (see *job*).

remote printing The production of *hard copy output* from a *printer* situated in a geographically distant location from the *processor* which provides the printer's electronic *input*.

remote terminal A *terminal* which is in a geographically distant location from the *processor* which it is accessing.

REMSTAR Remote electronic microfilm storage transmission and retrieval (see *COM*).

reorg Short for reorganization. A process by which the physical storage of *data* is reorganized, whilst retaining the same logical structure for the data. Reorgs are required to optimize processing efficiency.

repaint In *computer graphics*, to redraw, or update, a display image.

repeater 1. A device for restoring signals, which have been distorted through *attenuation*, to their original shape and transmission level. 2. A device whereby currents received over one *circuit* are automatically repeated over another circuit, or circuits.

reperforator An automatic *paper tape* punch.

repetitive letter Synonymous with *form letter*.

repertoire 1. Generally, the range of operations that can be performed by a system. 2. More specifically, in

relation to a computer, the range of *machine code* instructions that it can execute.

report generator Part of a *database management program* which organizes and prints out search results according to a pre-specified format.

report program A program designed to print out an analysis of a data file.

report program generator A *general purpose program* that can generate *report programs* to meet a user's specified requirements.

rerun Repeat execution of a program.

rerun point A point in a program from which it is possible to rerun following an *execution* failure.

rerun time Synonymous with *system(s) recovery time*.

rescue dump A *dump* on to *backing storage* performed to enable operations to be restarted quickly, with minimal *rerun*, in the event of a failure.

reserved word Corresponds to a *command* in the computer language, and so cannot be used as a name in a program.

resident software *Software* held permanently in *memory* (usually in *ROM*).

resistor Electronic component.

resolution The fineness of detail that can be distinguished in an image. (Often expressed in terms of number of distinguishable lines per unit length scanned.)

resolution factor In *information retrieval*, the fraction of the total number of *records* in a *file* which are retrieved during a particular *search*.

resource sharing See *shared resource.*

response frame This is a *viewdata* (interactive *videotex*) term. It refers to a *frame* which expects a response from the user. The response is communicated to the *information provider*. Response frames are used for *telebanking* and *teleshopping.*

response time The time interval between an event and the system's response to the event. For example, in computers it might be the time between the pressing of the last key when inputting at a *terminal*, and the terminal's display of the first character of the response.

retrieval See *information retrieval systems* and *information retrieval techniques.*

retrieval centre The name sometimes given to the installation running the *host computer* in a *viewdata* (interactive *videotex*) network.

retrospective conversion The conversion of a library's card catalogue into *machine-readable* form.

retrospective searching An end-user makes a *search request* to a *database* in the form of a call for all items published on a specific topic since a specified date. The user's search request is converted into *search terms*, and then translated into *machine-readable* language. All items in the database which have been indexed under these terms are identified in the course of a single run. The search may be made either *interactively*, or as part of a *batch.* Retrospective batch searching is cheaper than *online searching* for the user, but has less flexibility (see *information retrieval systems*).

reveal The instruction, and facility, for the presentation of text on a *videotex* display.

reverse channel capability Having a *background channel* facility.

reversible videodisc system Synonymous with *recordable videodisc system.*

reverse interrupt Use of a *backward channel* by a receiving station to request that a transmission be prematurely terminated.

reverse leading Movement of the film (or paper) in a *phototypesetter* in the opposite direction to normal operation.

reverse video A *VDU* facility which presents *alphanumerics* as black characters on white, instead of white on black.

revise Any proof produced after corrections have been made.

rewind Return a *magnetic tape* to its beginning.

rewritable videodisc A *videodisc*, the contents of which can be erased and overwritten. Such discs are under development, but are not yet on the market.

Rewtel A UK network for microcomputers run by the magazine Radio and Electronics World (ie REW).

REX Real time executive routine. A computer *routine* which is to be executed in *real time.*

RF 1. Radio *frequency* (see *spectrum*). 2. A type of *output* signal used for computer *displays.* RF produces a generally poor grade of image on a normal television.

RF modulator Radio frequency modulator. A device used to *modulate* the *frequency* of a *carrier signal.* It is frequently used to convert the *output* signal from a *microcomputer* into a form which can be displayed on a normal television screen.

RGB (signal) Red, Green, Blue. A computer or video *display* signal sent directly to the *cathode ray tube* of a display device, bypassing any TV circuitry present and thus producing a clearer image. An RGB signal provides a better display than *composite video* which in turn is of higher quality than *RF*.

RICASIP Research Information Center and Advisory Service on Information Processing. A body, whose aims are indicated by its title, jointly sponsored by the National Science Foundation and the National Bureau of Standards in the US.

right justify Sometimes used as the equivalent of *flush right*.

rigid disc See *hard disc*.

Ring A *data structure* in which *pointers* join items to form a complete loop, ie the last item in a chain is connected by a pointer to the first (see *file protection ring*).

ring code Used for Pharmadokumentationring, which comprises a group of European pharmaceutical companies who have collaborated in indexing material for *chemical structure retrieval*.

Ringdoc A UK *bibliographic database* covering pharmaceuticals. It is accessible via *Pergamon-Infoline* and *SDC*.

ring network A network in which computers are interconnected within a ring, (ie a *loop network*) with messages passed around the ring in *packets*. Each node passes on all packets it receives to the next node, while retaining copies of any packets which bear its own *address*.

RISC *Reduced Instruction Set Chip*.

rivers An undesirable alignment of spaces in a text.

RJE *Remote job entry*.

RO Receive only – equipment which can receive, but not transmit.

robot A machine capable of automatically performing some type of activity which is normally controlled by human beings. Most existing robots carry out simple repetitive tasks, most commonly in an industrial setting, as on an automatic production line. Robots are often linked to a *numerical control*, or *computer numerical control* system (see *artificial intelligence*).

robotics The application of *artificial intelligence* techniques to the design and production of *robots*.

role indicator In *information retrieval*, a code assigned to a word, eg a *descriptor* or *keyword*, which indicates the role, eg part of speech, which the word plays in the text where it occurs.

rolling ball The sequential display of *teletext page headers* as they are received.

ROM *Read-only memory*.

Roman Commonest form of *typeface*.

root In a *hierarchical database*, the *segment* which contains the highest level *key*.

round-robin A technique used in *time sharing* systems which shares a CPU's time equally between tasks of equal *priority* (see *time slicing*).

routine A sequence of operations for a computer to perform.

routing 1. The assignment of the communications channel by which a message can reach its destination. 2. The pattern of movement between *screen* displays within an *online* system.

routing indicator An *address*, or group of *characters*, at the beginning of a message which indicate its final destination.

routing page This is a *viewdata* (interactive *videotex*) term. A *page* whose function is to indicate a choice of other pages.

RPG Report Program Generator. A *high level language* used in drawing up business reports.

RPM Revolutions per minute.

RRP Reader and reader-printer. A device for viewing *microforms* and producing *hard copy* from the microform as required.

RS *Record separator*.

RS232 A 'recommended standard' of the *EIA*, for an *interface* between *data terminals* and communication equipment; it is not commonly used in *microcomputer networks*. The RS232 prescribes voltage levels for various *channels*, but has not standardized *pin* allocations.

RT 1. Real time. 2. Related term: a cross-reference in a *thesaurus*. 3. Remote terminal. A *terminal* with *remote access*.

RTECS Registry of Toxic Effects of Chemical Substances. A *database* compiled by the US National Institute for Occupational Safety and Health.

RTU Remote terminal unit. A computer *terminal* with *remote access*.

rubber banding In *computer graphics*, a technique for displaying a line with one end fixed on the screen, and the other moving in response to the movements of a *light pen* or *stylus*.

rule-based Used to describe *expert systems* in which knowledge is represented as a series of production rules. Production rules are of the 'IF condition THEN action' type, eg 'IF unit is too hot THEN switch off'.

ruler In *word processing*, graduated line drawn across the top, or bottom, of a *VDU* display, used to indicate and set tabulation and margin positions.

run One execution of a computer *routine*, *program* or *suite* of programs.

running head A line of *characters* at the top of each page of a document which provides information concerning the document, eg author, title, chapter.

run length coding A method of collectively coding a number of identical items so as to reduce the total number of *codes* required.

Runner An alternative name for the *Committee Support System*.

RW *Read/write*.

R/W memory (or storage) *Read/write memory (or storage)*.

S

s Second. *SI* unit of time.

S Siemen. *SI* unit of conductance.

SAGE An *expert system shell* produced by SPL International.

SALINET Satellite Library Information Network. A *satellite communication* system used to provide library services to remote parts of Canada.

SAM *Serial access memory.*

sampling The capturing of an audio signal (ie sound) over a certain period of time. The signal is then *digitized* and may be manipulated and replayed. The quality of sampling depends on the length of time covered by the sample and the speed of digitization.

Samson A Dutch *host* offering *databases* via *Euronet-DIANE*. Specializes in maritime information.

sans serif A *typeface* without *serifs*.

Saponet South African *packet switching* network.

Satcom A series of *communications satellites* owned by RCA for communication in the US.

Satellite Business Systems Established by *COMSAT* General (a subsidiary of *COMSAT*), with *IBM* as the dominant partner, to offer *satellite communication* channels within the US. One of its intentions is to provide a US *electronic mail* service.

satellite communication Communication via satellites offers advantages over both radio and cable transmission. The main problems with ground-based radio transmission are: interference between different transmissions; atmospheric *attenuation*; and the propagation of radio waves in straight lines. Satellites help overcome these problems because: a. the *antenna* beam covers only a limited area of the earth's surface; b. attenuation is reduced since the radio waves pass at a relatively steep angle through the atmosphere; c. the altitude of the satellite means that the radio waves are little affected by topographical obstacles. As compared with international communication via cables, satellite links are more flexible and cheaper (currently a third or less per channel) (see diagram).

Most communications satellites are placed in a *geostationary orbit*, since then ground-based antennae can be permanently turned to the same point in the sky. Such an orbit has the disadvantage that the satellite is fairly low in the sky for receivers in high northern and southern latitudes. More importantly, the number of satellites that can be placed in a geostationary orbit is ultimately limited, along with the *frequencies* at which they can receive and retransmit signals. For this reason, successive *World Administrative Radio Conferences* (*WARCs*) have tried, with moderate success, to impose international regulations on the use of communications satellites.

Satellites are already in use for telephone, data, radio and television transmissions. Frequencies in the *gigahertz* range are employed, normally with antennae of ten metres, or more, diameter. Plans are currently in hand to increase the power of satellite transmissions, and so decrease the size of the ground-based antennae required. This might permit the introduction of home-based antennae, for example, to

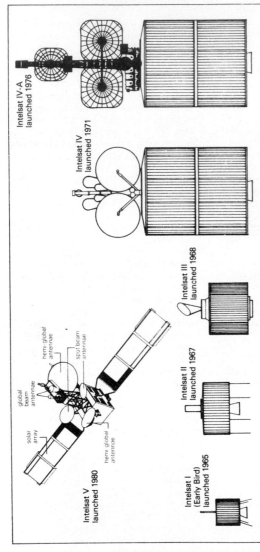

The range of Intelsat communications satellites. Intelsat I had a capacity of 240 telephone circuits or one TV channel and was intended purely for point-to-point communications between Western Europe and North America. Intelsat II had the same capacity but could be accessed by more than just two earth stations. Intelsat III offered 1500 circuits or four TV channels; Intelsat IV no fewer than 4000 circuits or twelve TV channels. It had not only multiple access but also simultaneous transmission capabilities. Intelsat IV-A provides 6000 circuits and two TV channels, or twenty TV channels if devoted entirely to that medium. Intelsat V (above left) is of radically different shape to its predecessors and is capable of carrying 12000 circuits and two colour TV channels, this being made possible by using two frequency bands (6/4 GHz and 14/11 GHz). It is the largest commercial satellite currently in operation.

receive television transmissions directly (so competing with *cable television*). At present the *space segment* consists primarily of a *transponder* which amplifies and retransmits the incoming signal (usually with frequency conversion). *Switching* activities are controlled by the *ground-based segment*. Much the largest satellite communication system is *Intelsat* (which has the US body, *COMSAT*, as its major shareholder). Individual US firms have also placed communications satellites in orbit, eg *Satcom* and *Westar*, and a marine version of Intelsat (called *Inmarsat*) has been sent up. *ESA* and the Soviet Union have already established major programmes in this field. The former has experimented with *OTS*, which is planned to lead on to an operational series of *ECSs*. The Soviet Union has launched a large number of *Molinya* communications satellites (which are not geostationary), and now plans to launch a series of *Statsionar* geostationary satellites. Most of these satellites can be used for any type of communications traffic, though they may, for organizational reasons, be dedicated to one type of transmission only.

satellite computer A smaller ancillary computer used to relieve a central, larger computer of relatively simple, but time-consuming operations.

SATNET A *resource sharing* computer *network* using links which provide access to *ARPANET*.

SatStream An international *digital data transmission* service planned by *British Telecom* for introduction in the late 1980s. It will use the *SwitchStream network* in the UK, and beam messages via two satellites run by *ESA* and the French telecommunications administration.

SBS *Satellite Business Systems*.

scan In information technology, this means to examine material, eg a page of text, the data present typically being converted into *machine-readable* form (see, eg, *optical character recognition*).

scan area The area scanned by an *OCR* operator.

scanner A device for examining printed characters, or *graphics*, and representing them by electrical signals. Used especially for devices which produce a *digital* output which can be input to a computer.

SCANNET Scandinavian Network. A Swedish *host* and *computer network*.

scanning The sequential examination, or exposure, of a set of *characters*, or of an image (see *facsimile transmission* and *optical character recognition*).

scanning device A general term for a *scanner*, but also has the specific meaning of an attachment to a *microform reader*. It allows the user to bring any section of the microform to a position in which it can be most easily read (see *rapid scan system*).

schema The logical structure of a *database*.

SCI *Science Citation Index*.

Science Citation Index Reference work published by the Institute for Scientific Information, which deals with science and technology (see *citation indexing*).

SCIM Selected Categories in Microfiche. An *SDM* service operated by the US *National Technical Information Service*.

SCI Search The *database* of the *SCI*, produced by the Institute of Scientific Information in the US.

Online searching of the database can be made via *Lockheed* and *DIMDI*.

scissor To remove selected parts of an image on a *computer graphics* display.

scratch To erase an area of *storage*.

scratch file A *file* which is destroyed upon termination of the task in which it is created (compare *permanent file*).

scratch pad memory A small high-speed *DASD* used as a *working storage*.

screen 1. A surface (especially of a *CRT*) where information can be displayed. 2. The method of forming dots in *half-tone* illustrations.

screen buffer A *buffer* used to store data displayed on the screen of a *VDU*.

screen editor *Software* that can be used to edit text displayed on a screen.

screenload The maximum number of *characters* that can appear on a *screen* at one time.

screen typing system An advanced electronic typewriter with extra components added on – a *disc drive* or cassette unit to increase *memory* capacity, and a full-size *screen* display. Such systems offer many of the facilities of *dedicated word processors*.

scroll Movement of text up and down, or across, a *VDU* so that the user can view areas of text adjacent to that displayed on the screen. It is used, for example, on some *word processors* where the screen will not hold all the contents of an A4 page. Scrolling across a VDU is sometimes referred to as 'panning'.

SDA *Source data acquisition*.

SDC System Development Corporation. One of the largest database *hosts* in the world, it offers *online* access to over 50 *databases* covering a wide range of topics.

SDI *Selective dissemination of information*.

SDILINE Selective Dissemination of Information Online. A *current awareness service* giving access to the most recent records added to the *Medline database*. It is accessible via *BLAISE* or *NLM*.

SDLC Synchronous Data Link Control. A *protocol* used by *IBM* for the communication of data.

SDM Selective Dissemination on Microfiche. A service which provides subscribers with copies of documents, in *microfiche*, in their (pre-specified) areas of interest.

search A systematic examination of information in a *database*. The aim is to identify *items* which satisfy particular pre-set criteria (see *information retrieval system* and *on-line searching*).

search and replace A *word processing* facility in which every occurrence of a specified *string* of text, held in *storage*, is replaced by a second specified string of text. Thus, for example, one might automatically alter a range of American spellings to English spellings.

search language Term used to describe any language used in the search of a *database* (see *information retrieval system* and *techniques*, and *online searching*). Also called a *command language* or *query language*.

search results The *records* or information retrieved as a result of a *search* of a *database* (see *hit*).

search statement A set of *search*

terms formulated into an enquiry which is put by the user to the *host* computer in an *online search* (see *search strategy*).

search strategy The array of terms, and the relationship between terms, used in defining a user's requirements during a *search* (see *information retrieval techniques* and *online searching*).

search terms Words, or groups of words (often *keywords*), used in *online searching* when specifying a request for information. Search terms correspond to the headings under which items in a *database* are indexed.

search time The amount of time required to locate a particular *item*, or *field* of *data*, in a store.

Secam The name stems from the French: 'Séquential à Mémoire'. It is a colour television system used in France, the USSR and Eastern Europe, together with some African and Middle Eastern countries. Unlike the *PAL* and *NTSC* systems, where the two colour-difference signals are transmitted simultaneously, in Secam they are transmitted alternately.

secondary index An index which identifies the *keys* or physical location of all *records* having a particular value for the specified (ie indexed) *field*.

secondary storage Synonymous with *backing storage*.

sector The smallest unit of *memory* on a *magnetic disc* or *drum* which can be separately *addressed*. The term is also sometimes used to refer to a *block* of data occupying such a unit (see *soft sectoring* and *hard sectoring*).

security See *data security*.

segment 1. Self-contained portion

of a *program*. 2. A portion of a message held in a *buffer*. 3. A set of related *fields* held as a group within a *database*.

segmented record A *record* comprised of a *concatenation* of subrecords.

Selectavision A *videodisc* system developed by RCA. Grooves are produced in a master disc using a piezoelectric *stylus*. Piezoelectric crystals convert electrical signals into mechanical motion, and vice versa. The resultant disc has about 400 grooves per millimetre, and it is used to provide plastic copies.

Selected research in microfiche A *selective dissemination of information* service which not only provides references to new documents, but also delivers these documents on *microfiche*.

selective calling Occurs when a transmitting station can specify which of a number of stations on the same *line* is to receive a particular message.

selective dissemination of information A general term for the provision of a *current awareness service* based on a *bibliographic database*. A subscriber to the service provides a profile of his/her interests (a *user interest profile*), which is translated into *machine-readable* form, stored on *magnetic tape*, and then matched at regular intervals against new additions to the *database*. Any additions matching the subscriber's interest profile are printed out and supplied to the subscriber (see *Group SDI*).

Selective Dissemination on Microfiche See *SDM*.

selective sort A *routine* that extracts items from a list, one at a time, according to a *ranking algorithm*. As each item is selected, it is deposited in rank order in a second list, and the sort continues until the first list is empty (compare *bubble sort*).

self-checking code Synonymous with *error detecting code*.

self correcting code Synonymous with *error correcting code*.

self-test A function of some *hardware* in which the equipment automatically performs a number of internal operations when it is first switched on in order to ensure that it is working correctly.

semantic network A method for representing knowledge in an *expert system* as a network of associated concepts, using facts as the nodes linked by arcs representing the relationships of the facts.

semantics The study of meaning in a language.

SEMCOR Semantic Correlation. A computer-aided *indexing system* (see *automatic indexing*).

semiconductor Any substance which conducts electricity easily when the voltage across it is above a certain value, but not when it falls below that value. Semi-conducting materials form the basis of *transistors*.

semiconductor laser A small *laser* made from semiconducting material, eg gallium arsenide. They can be used to emit beams of light down *optical fibres* for telecommunications purposes.

semi micro xerography See *SMX*.

sentinel Sometimes used as a synonym for *flag*.

separated graphics A set of *videotex* characters which do not fully occupy the space available to them (compare with *contiguous graphics*).

sequential access A computer term meaning that access to *memory* follows a prescribed order.

sequential file A *file* in which *records* are sequenced in ascending *key* order (see *serial file*).

SERCNET The UK Science and Engineering Research Council *packet switched* data transmission *network*. Now subsumed in the *Joint Academic Network*.

serial To handle items, or actions, sequentially.

serial access memory *Memory* in which data are entered in sequence. This leads to sequential *processing* of the data (see *serial processing*).

serial bit transmission A *data* transmission system in which the bits representing a *character* are transmitted consecutively.

serial file A *file* in which *records* are sequenced one after another, but in no particular order (see *sequential file*).

serial interface An *interface* for *serial bit transmission*.

serial printer A computer *printer* which prints one character at a time along a line (rather than a whole line together). An example is the *daisy wheel printer*.

serial processing Processing items in a data *file* in the order in which they are *stored*.

serial storage *Storage* in which *words* appear in sequence. This means that *access time* will include a waiting time.

serial transmission A method of transmitting information in which the data are transmitted in sequence (see *parallel transmission*).

serif A typeface in which the

ascending and descending parts of the characters have small extensions.

SERLINE Serials Online. The catalogue of journal titles received by the US *National Library of Medicine*, which can be made available *online*.

server In a *local area network*, the central unit which provides facilities for the other members of the network, eg *file server*, communications server. A file server provides access to centrally held files of information. A communications server provides access to central communications facilities, such as *electronic mail*, *telex* and *teletex* (see *shared resource*).

service bureau A facility, usually commercial, which allows a computer user to lease time on a *central processor* and appropriate *peripherals* to run his/her *programs*.

set width Measures the width of a piece of type.

sexy Computer jargon used to describe an item of *hardware* or *software* which represents *state-of-the-art* technology.

SGML Standard Generalized Markup Language. An *ISO* Draft International Standard for *generic coding*.

shared logic A computer system in which *logic* (or *intelligence*) is shared between items of *hardware*, eg some *word processing* systems which operate under central control.

shared resource Refers to a system in which the units make common use of a particular facility, eg *storage*, *printer*. Includes *shared logic*, shared storage, and cluster systems. Frequently occurs in *word processing*.

sheet microfilm A sheet of film containing frames of microphotographs in a rectangular pattern.

shelf life The length of time a document, or device, will remain of value to users.

shell *Software* used in an *expert system* to provide a general set of rules which can be applied to different kinds of knowledge data in order to derive conclusions (see *domain independent*).

SHF Super high frequency (between 3,000 and 30,000 *MHz*).

shift Movement of characters to the left, or right, by a prescribed number of places.

shift down modem A *modem* which produces a change from a higher to a lower *bit rate*.

SHL Studio to head end link.

SI Système International. A metric system of measurement units, based on the metre (length), gramme (weight), second (time) and ampere (electrical current). SI units are currently superseding the *British Imperial System* (in the UK) and the US *customary system* (in the US).

sideband A *band* of frequencies above, and below, an associated *carrier wave* frequency.

SIGLE System for Information on Grey Literature in Europe. A project sponsored by the Commission of the European Communities to improve the detection, identification, collection and delivery of 'grey' literature. Grey literature broadly refers to material not formally published, although sometimes made widely available. (The main form is technical reports.) The initial project aims to set up an *online bibliographic database* to be made available through *Euronet DIANE*.

signal The expression of information in the form of electrical disturbances. Also the act of transmitting such disturbances.

signal converter In a CATV system, converts UHF signals to VHF transmissions at the head end. A signal converter can, however, be applied to other types of device, eg one that performs analog to digital conversion, and vice versa.

signal-to-noise ratio Ratio of the power of a signal to the noise in a communications channel. The higher the ratio, the easier the signal is to detect.

sign bit A bit which indicates whether a binary number is positive or negative.

silicon chip A wafer of silicon providing a semi-conductor base for a number of electrical circuits (see chip).

Silicon Glen An area of southern Scotland where many computer and semiconductor manufacturers are located.

Silicon Valley An area south of San Francisco where many computer and semiconductor manufacturers are located.

simplex When transmission can only be carried out in one direction.

simulation The use of a computer program to represent a physical system or process.

sine wave The type of wave associated with a periodic oscillation.

single address message A message to be delivered to only one destination.

single operation A channel or terminal which can only transmit in one direction at a time.

sink The point where the data leave a network.

sinusoidal Having the form of a sine wave.

SIR Selective information retrieval (see information retrieval system).

SISAC Serials Industry Systems Advisory Committee. US Committee looking at standards for numbering articles, etc within serials.

SITA Société Internationale de Télécommunications Aéronautiques: an international network for airline reservations and flight information.

SIXPAC board Circuit board which supports six serial ports rather than the more common '4 + 2' – four serial and two parallel – boards.

skew To be incorrectly aligned, eg a skew picture in facsimile transmission.

skew character A form of incorrect registration in optical character recognition.

skew failure When a document in machine-readable form cannot be read because it is not aligned properly in the reading device.

skip To ignore instructions in a program.

skipping As for skip, and also advancing paper through a printer without printing upon it.

slab In computing, a part of a word.

slanted abstract An abstract which emphasizes a particular aspect of a document, in order to cater for the interests of a particular user group.

slave A device which operates under the control of another device. Especially a device driven by a computer's output.

slave tube A *CRT* connected to another *CRT* in such a way that each gives an identical display.

slice See *wafer*.

slice architecture *Integrated circuit architecture* for a *microprocessor* composed of silicon *waves*, each of which may itself carry a smaller microprocessor (see, for example, *bit-slice microprocessing*).

sloped Roman See *oblique*.

slow rate Signal response rate.

slow-scan (video) A device which compresses the *bandwidth* of a video *signal* so that it can be transmitted over a telephone line. The speed of transmission is too slow to allow moving images to be transmitted.

SLSI Super large scale integration. Similar to *ULSI*, but normally refers to *microprocessors* with the equivalent of over 100,000 *transistors* per *chip* (see *LSI*, *VLSI* and *ULSI*).

small cap(ital)s Capital letters of a similar size to ordinary *lower case* letters.

Smalltalk A programming language (from Xerox) used in *artificial intelligence* and systems development in microcomputers.

SMART 1. System for the Mechanical Analysis and Retrieval of Text. (An occasional variant is Salton's Magical Automatic Retrieval Technique.) A system designed for the *interactive* search of full text documents. A user *inputs* *search words* and groups of words (phrases, etc). SMART analyses the text and produces lists of documents ranked in terms of the relative frequency with which the search words and phrases appear in each document (see *information retrieval techniques*, *natural language*

searching). 2. A *Pure MAT* system which uses an *automated glossary* to provide translation between Arabic, English, French, German and Spanish. It has an exceptionally large *database* covering engineering and military technology (see *pure MAT* and *machine-aided translation*).

SmartCard A credit-card size device with an embedded, programmable *microprocessor*, which is used for *EFT*, security or identification purposes, and to store personal information. SmartCards are used in conjunction with some *videotex* systems, with the cards providing a security key and a self-billing mechanism.

smart terminal A *terminal* which has some *data processing* capability of its own, but not as much as an *intelligent terminal*.

Smectic A *LCD* technology in which molecules are induced with memory. This gives very high quality resolution and overcomes the problem of slow *refresh rate*.

SMX Semi-micro-xerography. A method of *xerographic* reproduction. It produces copies of documents which can then be input in *micrographic* form, via a special *reader*, to a computer.

S/N *Signal-to-noise ratio.*

SNA *Systems Network Architecture.*

snake Another name for *logic bomb*.

sniffing An error *detecting and correcting method* in computing.

SNOBOL A *high level language* designed for the *processing of character strings*.

SNR *Signal-to-noise ratio.*

Social Science Citation Index
Reference work published by
the Institute for Scientific
Information which references
publications within the social
sciences (see *citation indexing*).

SOCIAL SCISEARCH Social
Science Citation Index Search. The
Social Science Citation Index on
machine-readable files, which can be
searched via *BRS* or *Lockheed*.

Sociological Abstracts A
bibliographic database covering
sociology and related fields. It is
accessible via *BRS* and *Lockheed*.

SOFT A *software database*
produced by Online Inc, which gives
details of over 2,000 *software
packages* suitable for
microcomputers.

soft copy 1. Computer *output*
displayed on a *VDU*. 2. Computer
output in some medium which
cannot be directly read by the
unaided eye, eg *floppy disc, COM*.

soft key A *key* which, when
depressed, triggers *software*
specified by the user.

soft keyboard A display
resembling the layout of a *keyboard*
is presented on a *terminal* screen. A
light pen is then used to enter
characters in *machine-readable* form
by pointing the pen at each required
character in turn.

soft sectoring The identification of
sector boundaries on a *magnetic disc*
by using recorded information.
Contrast with *hard sectoring*.

software The instructions,
programs, or *suite* of programs
which are used to direct the
operations of a computer, or other
hardware.

software database A *database* of
information about computer
programs. The information provided

typically includes: name of producer;
description of product; *operating
system* the program is written for;
installation information; *hardware
requirements*; cost; reviews.

software documentation
Instructions on how to use a
software package.

software emulation *Software* that
enables a computer to execute a
program written in the *machine code*
of another computer.

software engineering The design,
development and production of
computer *software*.

software house A commercial
organization which specializes in
writing *software* (computer
programs) for clients.

software licence The terms and
conditions of use of a *software
package* issued by the vendor at the
time of purchase.

software package See *package*.

software tools Computer *programs*
that can write other programs.

solid state device A device using
solid state technology.

solid state technology Technology
based on the electronic properties of
solid materials, eg *transistors* and
integrated circuits.

SOLINET South-eastern Library
Network. A network joining over
200 libraries in the SE United
States. It allows them to share *data
processing* facilities and access to
bibliographic information and
resources.

SOM Start of message. A *character*,
or group of characters, transmitted
to indicate that a new message
immediately follows.

SOP *Standard operating procedure*.

sort 1. Any print *character*. 2. To arrange items of information into a sequence according to some rule. Such a rule normally directs that items having characteristics in common should be brought together in the sequence. To make this possible each item is allocated a descriptor which designates its specific characteristics.

sort key The *field* of a *record* that is used by a sort routine to determine where the record should be positioned.

Source, The A US interactive *videotex* system which is accessible via *microcomputers* (thus avoiding the regulatory restrictions covering use of television-based videotex). It is supplied by the Telecomputing Corporation of America.

source 1. A point of entry for data in a network. 2. A device which emits a signal. 3. One of the terminals of an *FET*. 4. An abbreviation for *source code*.

source code The code in which a programmer writes, ie prior to the program being compiled.

source data acquisition The direct entry of data into a computer at the point where the data originates, eg at a 'point-of-sale' where a cash register is combined with a *terminal* connected to a computer.

source database A *database* which provides the complete information sought, without the need to refer elsewhere (see *numeric database, full-text database, text-numeric database*).

source document An original document from which *data* are prepared in a form acceptable to a computer.

source language A term used especially in *machine translation, machine-aided translation* and

HAMT. It refers to the language from which translation is to be made (see *target language*).

source program A program in *source code*.

SPA Scratch Pad Area. A storage area associated with a *screen* of output data.

space division multiplexing *Multiplexing* via a group of more than one physical transmission path.

space segment A term in *satellite communication*, referring to the space part of the enterprise, as opposed to the earth, or ground, part. Thus, space segment costs are those of the satellite and its launching, as distinct from those of the ground stations, etc.

SPAG Standards Promotion and Applications Group. A consortium of European computer and telecommunications vendors set up to promote the *OSI* standard for interconnection between computer equipment.

sparse array An *array* in which a high proportion of entries are zeros.

Speakeasy A *high level language* designed to have as many commands as possible in 'plain English'.

special character A character that is neither a letter, nor a numeral, nor a blank, eg # or $.

specificity Indexing of a document is deemed specific if the index terms used are coextensive with the concept to be indexed, and are described precisely. As the degree of matching between indexing and concept lessens, the indexing loses specificity. As a simple example, if the concept to be indexed is 'rat', then 'mammal', 'rodent', 'rat' are terms of increasing specificity.

specific coding Synonymous with *absolute coding.*

spectrum In information technology, this refers to the range of *electromagnetic frequencies* available for use in telecommunications. By no means all the available frequencies are currently employed (see diagram). Most of the range at present in use is shown in the diagram, which also indicates the names commonly adopted for each band of frequencies. Note that the scale is logarithmic, not linear (ie the frequency changes by a factor of ten at constant intervals along the

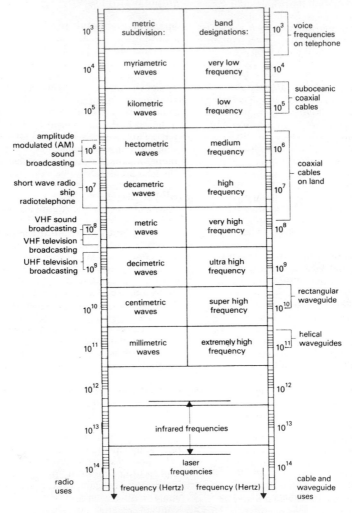

The range of frequencies of the electromagnetic spectrum, illustrating the telecommunications usage of the different wavebands.

scale). Thus the named frequency bands, which occupy roughly equal intervals across the page, are of very different size in terms of the range of frequencies that they occupy (their *bandwidth*). A bandwidth at 'high frequency' is much larger than that at 'medium frequency', which is higher than that at 'low frequency'. The *information-carrying capacity* of a communication channel is roughly proportional to its bandwidth: so the higher bands on the diagram have a much greater capacity.

Transmission in each band of frequencies has its own particular characteristics and problems. The diagram indicates the main uses for each of the bands, both for radio and cable transmission.

Instead of frequency, the electromagnetic spectrum can also be described in terms of the range of wavelengths of the electromagnetic waves. Wavelength is inversely proportional to frequency (ie the higher a wave's frequency, the shorter its wavelength).

speech recognition In the context of information technology, speech recognition means the identification of human speech by electronic means. The basis of speech recognition is the matching of the wave patterns of the speaker with patterns stored in the computer's memory. This is a difficult task, principally because of the complex acoustic wave patterns associated with the human voice. Any particular sound consists of a mixture of many waves with different *frequencies* and *amplitudes*. In addition, the pattern of the sound is only stable for a short time (about ten milliseconds), so that the frequencies and amplitudes continually vary. The sequence of patterns also depends on where in a word the sound appears, and on what sounds precede and follow it. Finally, different people speak differently, and even individual speech varies

with time and emotional state.

At present, devices for recognizing speech are effective only within narrow limits. They vary both in the number of words they recognize (their vocabulary) and in cost. The most sophisticated can recognize some connected speech (that is, strings of words). Simpler models only recognize one word at a time – they operate in 'discrete word mode'. Currently, a good vocabulary consists of a few hundred words.

The basic steps of speech recognition are as follows. First, some means is used to determine the amplitude spectrum of the incoming voice signal. This is referred to as 'feature extraction', or 'preprocessing', and it can be performed in several ways. The most common is by direct measurement of the spectrum amplitude using a series of *filters*. Another popular technique is *linear predictive coding*, in which the speech signal is represented by the parameters of a filter whose spectrum best fits that of the signal. Features extracted in this way, averaged over perhaps ten milliseconds, are then sampled say 50 times per second. At this point, or before, the data are *digitized*. Next, the input features are processed to determine the beginnings and ends of sounds, so that the input and reference pattern can be 'time-aligned'. (A technique known as *dynamic programming* is often used here.) This is one of the most difficult tasks in speech recognition. Beginnings and ends of words (ie word detection) are normally defined by changes in speech energy. The features within the word are then split into 'time slices' for comparison with the reference data. The reference word differing least from the input is the recognized word.

The important performance criteria for speech recognizers are error rate, speaker independence, vocabulary size and ability to recognize connected speech. To some extent these criteria are linked. Speaker-dependent machines (the majority) have to be 'trained': the speaker inputs a series of reference words to the memory, which are stored for later matching. These give some degree of speaker-independence, but the error rate for new speakers is often much higher. The larger the vocabulary to be handled, the greater the possibility of error. For current machines it runs at a few per cent.

The main use of the limited speech recognition machines presently available is in the industrial and military worlds. Here, a limited vocabulary set is sufficient for routine operation, eg warehousing, inspection, where the ability to convey information to a computer by voice, whilst simultaneously performing other tasks, is an advantage. Applications considered for the consumer market include voice-controlled television, ovens and wristwatches.

The effect on information in the office could be extremely significant. Automatic dictation machines are now forecast by the end of the century. Given a good enough vocabulary, these could replace most office keyboarding operations. For simpler tasks, voice operation will come in a good deal earlier. Communication with a computer (ie where the computer replies or initiates a conversation) also requires *speech synthesis*. This is easier, and so is currently more advanced than speech recognition.

speech synthesis The production of speech using artificial means. The synthesis of recognizable speech is simpler than the corresponding task of *speech recognition*, although to make human speech sounds is difficult enough.

Two important methods of speech synthesis are: a. waveform digitization. This uses the human voice to generate words which are then stored in the computer. The words are spoken into a microphone

and the *waveform* of the speech is digitized (ie it is sampled at frequent intervals to produce numbers proportional to the *amplitude* of the wave form). The numbers are stored in *bits*. Speech is synthesized by a *program* which calls up the separate words, puts them together, and then reconverts them to sound (using a *digital/analog converter*).

b. *formant* synthesis simulates electronically the sounds of the human voice, rather than using an actual human voice. This is done by generating simple *frequencies* and then modifying them, eg through *filters*, to simulate the complex sounds of a voice.

Speech synthesis has found several applications, eg in toys, and in translation. It is used as an aid to the blind in its developed form, by using *optical character recognition* to scan text, and then reading the text aloud using speech synthesis, eg the *Kurzweil* reading machine.

speech synthesis data capture A method of using speech as direct *input* (see *voice input*).

spelling check program *Software*, used in conjunction with, or as part of, *word processing* programs, which checks the spelling of words in textual documents. The program works by comparing each word with one in a *dictionary* stored in its *memory*. If the program cannot find a match for any word, it *flags* the word *on-screen*. The operator can then make the alterations. Spelling checking routines are usually used to proof read documents.

Spidel A French *host* (Société pour Informatique) which is linked to Euronet DIANE.

spike A surge of mains electrical power which can adversely affect the operation of a computer system.

SPIN Searchable Physics Information Notes. A *bibliographic database* derived from the publications of the American Institute of Physics. It can be searched via *Lockheed*.

split catalogue A *catalogue* with multiple entries. For example, a *bibliographic database* might contain entries by subject, by author, by year of publication and by title.

split keyword A *word processing* configuration in which *keyboarding* and editing are performed on one system, while documents are inspected and printed on another.

split screen The use of a single screen to display separate sets of images. For example, a page of text may be shown in one section of a screen and the record of an *interactive* dialogue with a computer system in another.

SPOOL Simultaneous peripheral operation online. The *real time* operation of a computer from *online* terminals.

spooler *Software* which allows input and output devices to be shared by a large number of users in an orderly fashion and without interference. Spoolers may also control *input* or *output* sequences in accord with a *pre-programmed* specification of priorities.

spooling The use of *spoolers* to achieve effective use of *input/output* devices.

spreadsheet Computer *software*, in widespread use on *microcomputers*, intended to aid financial planning and forecasting. *Spreadsheets* provide a range of numerical and analytical tools and can normally present results in graphical form.

sprocket feed Synonymous with *tractor feed*.

SPS 1. *String process system*. 2. *Symbolic program system*.

SPSS Statistical Package for the Social Sciences. *Mainframe* computer *software* which carries out statistical analysis.

SPSS/PC A *microcomputer* version of *SPSS*.

spur A junction in a cable *network*.

squeezeout ink Method of printing to aid *optical character recognition*. The outline of each *character* is printed darker than its centre.

SRIM *Selected research in microfiche*.

SSA *Segment* search argument: used in a program which reads *hierarchical databases*.

SSC *Station selection code*.

SSCI *Social Science Citation Index*.

SSIE Current Research A *database* produced by the Smithsonian Science Information Exchange. It offers multidisciplinary *current awareness services* via *Lockheed* and *SDC*.

SSTV Slow Scan Television.

stack A *pushdown* list.

STAIRS Storage and Information Retrieval Systems. *IBM software* for *information retrieval*.

stand-alone (capability) The ability of a piece of equipment to operate independently of any other equipment. For example, a *work station* that can operate independently is often called a 'stand-alone system'.

stand-alone system See *stand-alone*.

stand-alone word processor See *word processing* and *stand-alone*.

standard document In *automatic*

letter writing, the document to which supplementary information is added to produce the final letter.

standard operating procedure A regular, or common, mode of operation, eg of a computer.

standards The systems and procedures applied to computer operations. Standards cover methods and techniques as well as technical specifications for *hardware*, *software*, *interfaces*, *protocols*, etc.

standard subroutine A *subroutine*, available to users of a computer, which is designed to solve a well-established problem, or set of problems.

standing data Relatively static, generally tabular data which are held on a *file* available to more than one *applications program*. A company might, for example, hold tables of product names against product codes, or tax rates against income levels, on its standing data files.

star network A *network* of terminal *nodes* connected to a central node, but not connected directly to each other, eg *LAN* based on a *PABX* with a number of cables radiating out from a central exchange (for diagram see *network topology*).

start bit A *bit* used in *asynchronous transmission* which indicates the start of a character.

start of header (character) In data communications, a *control character* at the start of a *header*.

start of text (character) A *control character* used in a transmission to indicate that all headings, eg time of transmission, name of sender and receiver, have been completed, and that the beginning of the message proper follows.

start stop envelope A *packet* or string of data elements used in *asynchronous* communications. It consists of a *start bit*, the *binary* data and a *stop bit*.

'state of the art' (technology) Technology which is the most up-to-date available.

static RAM *RAM* in which up to one *byte* can be stored at an *address* for as long as power is supplied to a device (contrast *dynamic RAM*).

static video See *still video*.

station 1. A *terminal* or *data processing* facility connected to the computer which the user is using. 2. A *machine location*.

station selection code A computer *code* used to indicate that access is required via a particular *station* (*1.*).

statistical word association See *word/character frequency techniques*.

Statsionar A series of *communications satellites* launched by the Soviet Union into *geostationary orbit*. Though intended to provide the same sort of coverage as *Intelsat*, the system is mainly used at present to transmit radio and television programmes to the Soviet Union (see *Molinya*).

STATUS *Information retrieval* software developed by the UK Atomic Energy Authority.

status lines In *word processing*, information displayed to indicate to the operator factors relating to layout, eg spacing, and progress of work, eg line currently being typed.

status polling *Polling* by a central computer seeking to determine the status of *intelligent peripherals*.

status word 1. A word communicated by the *computer* to

the user to indicate what sort of information should be *input* next, eg *data*, instructions. Examples of such words are 'ready' and 'error'. 2. A word which communicates information about the condition of a *peripheral unit*, eg a warning of some type of malfunction.

STD Subscriber trunk dialling. Direct dialling to a distant location by a telephone subscriber.

stereofiche A form of *microfiche* which allows graphic material to be viewed in three dimensions. The system involves the use of a polarizing stereo box and special viewing glasses in conjunction with a standard *microfiche reader*.

STI Scientific and technical information.

still frame See *freeze frame*.

still video A *telecommunications* technique whereby a telephone is linked to a screen and calls are accompanied, or interspersed, by static images, eg of the caller, or a document. Provision of static images allows a lower *bit rate* than is required for making pictures and/or higher *resolution*.

stop bit A *bit* used in *asynchronous transmission* which indicates the end of a character.

stop code In *word processing*, an instruction to the *printer* to stop, eg in order to change the *fount*.

stop element Synonymous with *stop bit*.

stop list In *automatic indexing*, a list of words which the computer is instructed not to use as indexing terms. An index is normally based on substantive terms, so the computer is usually instructed to place words such as 'and', 'but', etc, on the stop list.

storage 1. A *storage device*, or the medium on which information is stored. 2. The process of storing information.

storage capacity The amount of information which a *storage device* can accommodate. Sometimes also called *memory capacity* (see *memory* and *backing storage*).

storage device A device used as *backing storage* for information, eg *magnetic tape* or *magnetic disc*.

storage tube A *CRT* used in some *VDUs* which requires no *refreshing* of the image. Images on such a tube can only be altered by clearing the screen.

store and forward Refers to a form of electronic communications, eg *electronic mail*, in which a message is not sent directly to its destination but is stored in a computer *file*. Only a notification of the existence of the message is sent. The message itself is transmitted when the recipient calls for it (contrast *messaging*).

STR Synchronous transmitter-receiver.

string 1. A group of *items* which are arranged in sequence according to a set of rules. 2. A set of consecutive *characters* in a *memory*.

string length The number of items in a *string*.

string process system A *software package* designed for the manipulation of *strings* of *characters*.

string search *String* of terms, with or without *connectors*, which may be used to *search* a database (see *information retrieval techniques*).

stringy floppy Magnetic *storage*, consisting of a continuous loop *tape* cartridge.

stroke A mark used to form characters in *optical character recognition* (see *key stroke*).

stroke centreline A line used to designate the midpoint of characters in *optical character recognition*.

stroke edge Imaginary lines equidistant from the *stroke centre line* in *optical character recognition*.

stroke edge irregularity Deviation of the edge of a *character* from its *stroke edge* in *optical character recognition*.

structured language A computer *language* which allows the construction of easily understood and modifiable programs.

structured programming Writing computer programs in a manner consistent with standard procedures; eg for breaking down tasks into program *segments* and working with particular forms of *data structure*. Such programming affects clarity and consistency, and thus aids *debugging* and modification.

studio to head end link In a *CATV network*, a fixed *microwave relay* that transmits signals from a television studio on the system's *head end* (see the diagram for *cable television*).

stunt box A device which performs such functions as *line feed*, carriage return, etc, in a *teleprinter*.

STW The initials stand (in transliterated Chinese) for Experimental Communications Satellite. A planned series of Chinese *communications satellites* in *geostationary orbit*.

STX Start of text character. A *control character* which indicates the end of a heading, or introductory message, and the beginning of the actual text.

stylus 1. Synonym for *light pen*. 2. Device used in conjunction with a *graphics tablet* to *input* and manipulate graphical information (see *graphics tablet* and *computer graphics*). 3. Pick-up from a disc, eg *videodisc*.

subprogram See *subroutine*.

subroutine A part of a *program* (*routine*) which can be called into operation when required.

subscript A *character* that lies below the normal *baseline*, eg X_2.

subset A modulation/demodulation device used as a communications link (see *modem*).

substitute character A *control character* put in to replace a *character* which cannot be recognized or represented.

substitution table A layout chart for a *keyboard*. It is used in *word processing* to show which standard *character* keys can also be used as *special character* keys.

suite (of programs) A number of interrelated *programs* which can be run consecutively as a single *job*.

sun ontage A period during which the operation of a *satellite communication system* is adversely affected by the position of the sun.

supercomputer The fastest and largest computers available today, some capable of working at many *megaflops*. Examples are *Cray-1*, Iltrac IV and Cyber 205.

superconductivity A property possessed by some metals, which, at temperatures very close to absolute zero, can sustain current flow almost indefinitely, even when disconnected from the current supply. Research is currently underway into the use of superconductivity in producing new types of *semiconductor* (see *cryogenics*).

superfiche *Microfiche* with a reduction between 50x to 90x. Between 190 and 400 images can be placed on an A6 sheet. It is one of the forms in which *computer output microform* (COM) can be produced.

supergroup Five communication channels occupying adjacent *bands*, used for simultaneous *modulation*.

super high frequency See *SHF*.

super large scale integration See *SLSI*.

supermicro A *microcomputer* which is almost as powerful as the average, conventional *minicomputer*. A supermicro will usually support *multi-user* applications.

supermini A *minicomputer* which is almost as powerful as a conventional *mainframe*. The traditional microcomputer/ minicomputer/mainframe distinctions are now breaking down, so that *supermicros* can have many of the facilities of a minicomputer, and superminis can have many of the *functions* of a mainframe.

superscript A *character* that lies above the normal baseline, eg X^2.

super twist nematic Variation of *twisted nematic* with better visual characteristics. Displays are limited to yellow and blue.

suppress To prevent printing.

suppressed carrier transmission The transmission of a *modulated* wave in which the *carrier signal* is suppressed, thus reducing the power of the signal.

surrogate In *searching* a *bibliographic database*, a surrogate is a term which can be manipulated as a substitute for a document. It can be a number, an index term, an author, a journal page, etc.

suspend key A *key* which, when depressed, can place the current operation in the background and can *queue* jobs indefinitely while new work is carried out.

SVR Super video recorder. A format for *video cassettes* developed by Grundig.

SWALCAP South West Academic Libraries Cooperative Automation Project (UK). A cooperative project established to give members access to *online cataloguing* services.

SWAMI Software-aided multifont input. *Software for OCR* systems.

SWIFT Society for Worldwide Interbank Financial Telecommunications. A *network* and network operator.

swim Undesired movement of *graphics* displayed on a *VDU*.

switching In telecommunications, the means of interconnecting users. Most switching is still carried out by telephone exchanges, but other types of switching exist for special purposes, eg for distributing computer data (see *circuit switching*, *message switching* and *packet switching*).

switching centre A location where multiple *circuits* terminate and incoming messages can be transferred to the appropriate outgoing circuit.

SwitchStream One A *packet switched data transmission network* operated by *British Telecom*, widely used for high speed data communication. Part of the *Packet SwitchStream* service.

SwitchStream Two A *packet switched data transmission network* operated by *British Telecom* as part of the *Packet SwitchStream* service. It is used for a variety of purposes, including remote order processing, credit verification and *online information retrieval*.

syllable In computing, a string of *characters* or part of a *word*.

symbolic address The form an *address* takes in a *source language*, when it is represented by a *label* chosen by the *programmer*.

symbolic code Synonymous with *symbolic instruction*.

symbolic instruction An instruction in *source language*.

symbolic language A *programming language* which can incorporate the use of *symbolic addresses*.

symbolic name A *label* used in *symbolic programming* to represent *data*, a *peripheral*, *instructions*, etc.

symbolic programming Writing a language in *source language*.

symbolic program system A computer system that accepts *symbolic language*(s).

SYNC Refers to the synchronizing pulses used to provide a stable reference frame for television pictures.

synchronizing signal A signal which accompanies the transmission of data. The signal can be sent by the station transmitting the data, or from a separate source. In either case, its role is to ensure that the data are transmitted and received in synchronizm with a clock (see *baseband*).

synchronous With a constant time between successive events, eg in the transmission of *bits* or *characters*.

syndetic 1. Interconnections within

a system. 2. Cross-referencing in an *index* or *catalog* of documents.

synergy A term, borrowed from biology and applied to *information technology*, meaning the process of separate parts acting together so that their combined effect is much greater than the sum of the effects of each part alone.

synopsis See *synoptic*, which is often used as an equivalent.

synoptic A synoptic is a concise publication in a journal which presents the key ideas and results of a full-length article. It includes an *abstract*, diagrams, references, etc, and is refereed in the normal manner. The full-length article is either also published, elsewhere or subsequently, or it is made available from a repository. It has been suggested that a synoptic, rather than an abstract or full-text document, may be the best method of providing information on a *database* intended for *information retrieval*.

synoptic journal A journal which publishes *synoptics* rather than full-length articles.

syntax error A mistake in the formulation of an instruction to a computer.

system An organized set of components (human beings, equipment, etc) which interact in a regulated fashion.

Système International See *SI*.

system(s) recovery time The period a computer system spends recovering from a failure.

system-resident Usually applied to *software* to indicate the instructions and data which form an integral part of the computer system (contrast *media-resident software*).

systems analysis A technique for analysing systems, and determining the scope for improved efficiency through the introduction of computers and *new information technology.*

systems flowchart A *flowchart* diagram which represents the relationship between 'events' in a *data processing* system, and hence describes the flows of data through, and within, the system. There are various standard sets of symbols used in systems flowcharting. One of the most commonly used is shown below. Supplementary program flowchart symbols are often used (see the diagram accompanying the *program flowchart* entry).

Systems Network Architecture Standards introduced by *IBM* to provide an integrated set

of solutions to the problems affecting *networks.* The basic structure is very similar to that of *OSI,* but there are important conceptual differences. SNA is based on the principle of a *mainframe host* controlling the network, whereas OSI allows for distributed control, where linked systems (*microcomputers* or much larger systems) can exchange data without having to pass through a network host (see diagram). OSI has international support, particularly from standards organizations and suppliers. SNA has reached a more advanced state of development and has a large user base.

systems software See *operating systems.*

System X A computerized digital telephone switching system developed by *British Telecom.*

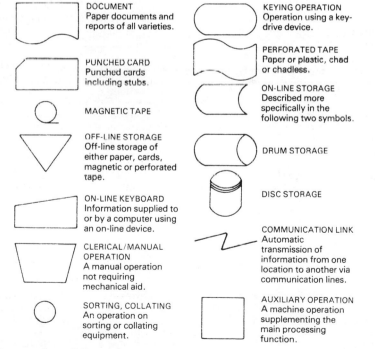

DOCUMENT
Paper documents and reports of all varieties.

PUNCHED CARD
Punched cards including stubs.

MAGNETIC TAPE

OFF-LINE STORAGE
Off-line storage of either paper, cards, magnetic or perforated tape.

ON-LINE KEYBOARD
Information supplied to or by a computer using an on-line device.

CLERICAL/MANUAL OPERATION
A manual operation not requiring mechanical aid.

SORTING, COLLATING
An operation on sorting or collating equipment.

KEYING OPERATION
Operation using a key-drive device.

PERFORATED TAPE
Paper or plastic, chad or chadless.

ON-LINE STORAGE
Described more specifically in the following two symbols.

DRUM STORAGE

DISC STORAGE

COMMUNICATION LINK
Automatic transmission of information from one location to another via communication lines.

AUXILIARY OPERATION
A machine operation supplementing the main processing function.

Selection of symbols used in systems flowcharts

System X exchanges handle both voice *and data* over a single line; *data transmission* speeds are increased and signal reliability improved over existing services. Digital telephone exchanges are the first stage in British Telecom's preparations for *ISDN*; by 1989 they aim to have provided over 75% of the business community with access to System X.

SYSTRAN The name derives from a compounding of the words 'Transatlantic System'. It is a *pure*

MT (ie fully automated) translation system providing translations between English, French, Russian and Spanish. Initially developed in the US and used by US Government agencies, it has been adopted and developed world-wide. In particular, the European Commission has carried out considerable work on the system.

However, extensive practical use of SYSTRAN has not yet occurred, due to the fundamental problems besetting pure MT (see *machine translation*).

OSI			*SNA*	
7	Application		End user	7
6	Presentation		Presentation services	6
5	Session		{ Data flow control	5
			{ Transmission control	4
4	Transport }			
3	Network }		Path control	3
2	Data link		Datalink control (SDLC)	2
1	Physical		Physical control	1

The relation of OSI layers to Systems Network Architecture.

T

tablet See *graphics tablet.*

tab memory A word processing facility for storing details of tabulation settings.

TACS Total Access Communication System. UK standards for operating frequency, channel spacing and user registration for *cellular networks.*

tactile keyboard A *keyboard* display which is laid out on a flat surface. A *character* is registered by touching its *key* location lightly with a finger.

tag Synonymous with *flag.*

tail A *flag* indicating the end of a *list.*

tailoring The process of modifying a *software package* in order to meet specific user requirements.

tape See *paper tape* and *magnetic tape.*

tape comparator A device which automatically compares two supposedly identical *punched tapes,* row by row, and stops when there is a discrepancy.

tape deck Synonymous with *tape drive.*

tape drive A device for winding and unwinding reels of *tape.* Applies especially to *magnetic tape* on a computer.

tape limited When the relatively low speed of the *tape* unit is the limiting factor in determining the rate at which *data processing* takes place.

tape punch A piece of equipment for punching holes in *paper tape.*

The information to be punched is normally input from a *keyboard.*

tape reader Can apply to any piece of equipment which *reads* tape, though applied originally to *paper tape.*

tape streamer A *storage device* consisting of *magnetic tape* mounted in a high speed drive. Tape streamers are used for security *back-up* usually for data stored on a *hard disc.*

tape transport Synonymous with *tape drive.*

tape verifier A device which compares a previously *punched tape* with a second manual punching of the data, *character* by character, or row by row.

Target A pure *MAT* system which uses a *terminology bank* to translate scientific and technical documents in English, French, German and Spanish. The system can be operated *on-line* in conjunction with *text editing* facilities.

target language 1. Synonymous with *object language.* 2. A term used in *machine translation,* machine-aided translation and *HAMT* to refer to the language into which a document is to be translated (see *source language*).

target program Synonymous with *object program.*

tariff The rate at which charges are made for use of facilities provided by a *common carrier.*

TASI *Time assignment speech interpolation.*

TAT8 Transatlantic telephone cable. A *fibre optic* link due to start operation in 1988.

TAXADVISOR An *expert system* used in tax advising.

TCM Terminal to computer multiplexor (see *terminal, computer* and *multiplexor*).

TDM Time division multiplexing (see *multiplexing*).

TDMA *Time division multiple access.*

teaching machine Normally refers to a machine which performs *computer-aided instruction* (see *educational technology*).

TEAM Terminology, Evaluation and Acquisition Method. A German *pure MAT* system based on an *automated dictionary* and a *terminology bank*. It offers *online* interrogation of its *databases*, giving *target language* equivalents for any *input* terms, in eight major European languages. In addition, it is able to produce a variety of *off-line* translation aids and services (see *machine-aided translation*).

technische kommunikation The German term for *information technology*.

TeD See *Teldec*.

TED Tenders Electronic Daily. An *ECHO database* which contains notices of invitations to tender for public work and public supply contracts in over 80 countries. Requests for searches may be made via *telex*, and the database may be searched in six different languages.

Teldec Form of *videodisc* developed by Telefunken and Decca.

telebanking The use of *videotex* for making transactions, transferring money and paying for goods or services.

telebooking The use of *videotex* for booking tickets, making reservations and making travel arrangements. Telebooking is widely used by travel agents.

telebroking The use of *videotex* for dealing in stocks and shares.

Telecenter A simplified version of *EIES*.

Telecom-1 French *communications satellite*.

Telecom Australia The Australian *telecommunications* agency.

Telecom Gold *Electronic mail* system offered by *British Telecom* in the UK. Based on *Dialcom*.

telecommunications The transmission and reception of *data* in the form of electromagnetic *signals*, using broadcast radio or transmission lines. However, it is often used for almost any transmission of signals.

teleconferencing A general term for any conferencing system employing telecommunications links as an integral part of the system. There are three main types – *computer conferencing, video–conferencing* and *audioconferencing*. Hybrid configurations are also possible. Teleconferencing may be accompanied by other facilities, such as *electronic document delivery*, to enhance its effectiveness.

telecopier A device for *facsimile transmission*.

Teledata A Norwegian *viewdata* (interactive *videotex*) system.

telefax The linking of photocopying machines for the transmission of images.

Telefax The name of French and West German *facsimile transmission* services.

Telefax 201 A Dutch *facsimile transmission* service.

Teleglobe Canada Government corporation handling Canada's overseas telecommunications.

telegraph A method of transmitting electrical signals, using simple on-off conventions to provide the code.

telegroup A number of isolated individuals who are joined by *teleconferencing*.

teleinformatics A term used to refer to data transfer via telecommunication systems.

Telemail A US *electronic mail* service.

telematics Information technology and its applications. Derived from the French 'télématique'.

télématique The French term for information technology.

telemetry The remote measurement of physical quantities, eg electrical quantities, fluid flows.

Telenet A US *packet switched* telecommunications network.

teleordering A system which automates the way in which booksellers order from publishers. Taking the UK system as an example, participating bookshops and publishers each have a small intelligent terminal. During the day, the bookshop terminal is used to collect and store orders. Books are uniquely identified via their International Standard Book Number (*ISBN*). The terminal applies procedures to the orders, and checks that no necessary data are missing. At the end of the working day, the terminal is switched to standby. During the night, using public telecommunications (telephone) lines at cheap rates, a central *minicomputer* system automatically dials the terminal at each bookseller in turn. The terminal responds with details of the collected orders to the central minicomputer, which stores them on *magnetic tape*. The tape is then transferred to a *mainframe computer* for further processing. The data from the orders are matched with the publishers' information and orders are put in a format suitable for each publisher. The minicomputer system then returns a confirmation (or error indication) for every order to each bookshop terminal. These data are stored in the terminal memory until the next day, when they can be printed out. At the same time, the minicomputer sends a file of orders for relevant books to the terminal of each participating publisher. Publishers not participating in the system receive their orders by post. This ordering system is currently limited to booksellers and book suppliers (publishers, wholesalers and distributors) in the UK. The diagram shows the main features of the system. Other countries have teleordering systems at various stages of development. For example, in the US there is a system, called *ACCESS*, developed by a wholesaler, Ingram, in conjunction with Software Sciences Limited (who designed the UK system). A library supplier (Baker and Taylor) has produced systems called *LIBRIS* and *Batab*; whilst the Bowker Company had instituted a *Computer Acquisition System* (CAS), based on 'American Books in Print' as the database. Another library supplier (Brodart) has introduced a teleordering service for the New York area. In West Germany, teleordering was introduced in the mid-1970s by two large wholesalers with incompatible systems: *BESSY* (Bestell-System) from KNO (Koch, Neff, Oetinger/Köhler Volckmar) and the Litos TBA (Telefonischer Bestell-Abruf) of Libri (Lingenbrink). Denmark also has a well-established system called *Bookseller Data* (ABD).

Telepack   A US *telecommunications* service offering combined voice and data *channels*.

telephone data set   A unit used to connect a data *terminal* to a telephone circuit (see *modem*).

telephone frequency   Synonymous with *voice band*.

telephotography   The name in the US for the transmission of news pictures using *facsimile transmission*.

teleport   A centre of high technology serviced by *state-of-the-art telecommunications*.

teleprinter   A device resembling a

The British teleordering system, used by booksellers to place orders with publishers and other suppliers, showing the data flow. Below is a schematic diagram of one of the system's terminals.

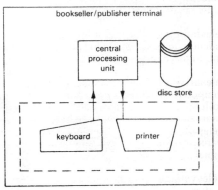

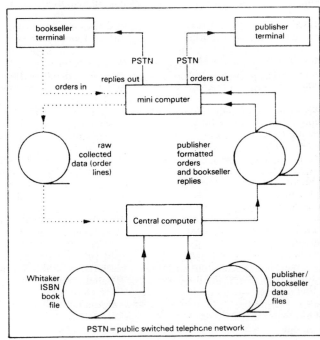

typewriter which is connected to a telegraphic circuit. It can be used to transmit, or receive, and print out data.

teleprocessing *Data processing* and transmission using computers and telecommunication *channels*.

Telesat Canadian *communications satellite.*

Teleset A Finnish *viewdata* (interactive *videotex*) system.

teleshopping The use of interactive *videotex* to select goods for purchase and to place orders.

telesoftware The transmission of computer *software* using *videotex*, both broadcast (*teletext*) and interactive (via the telephone line). Telesoftware has also been transmitted using coded radio signals.

Télésystème A French *host* system.

Teletekst 1. A Dutch *teletext* system. 2. A Belgian *teletext* system.

Télétel The brand name of the French *Antiope-Titan videotex* system.

teletex The *CCITT* name for a system which transmits data between *terminals*. Its ultimate purpose is to link *word processors* via the public telephone network. It represents a combination of *text editing* with high speed telex-related equipment.
If manufacturers produce word processors which conform to teletex standards, current problems of *incompatibility* between word processors could be overcome. Teletex will then not be dependent on a single *dedicated network* in the way that telex is.

teletext See broadcast *videotex*.

teletype grade A level of circuit suitable for *telegraphic communication.*

teletypesetting A system for remote *typesetting* first used before the Second World War. The typesetter is controlled by *punched paper tape* input, either directly, or over a communications link.

teletypewriter Normally called a *teleprinter.*

telex Stands for *Teletypewriter* Exchange service. A worldwide *telegraphic* service, established by *Western Union*, which permits interconnection between *teleprinters*. Operators use *terminals* to produce *paper tape*, which is then fed into a reader for transmission over a *dedicated network*.
The telex system is relatively old and slow. However, it is so well established that it will take some time to replace. It is likely to be superseded by *teletex*, or some related communication system.

Telidon A Canadian *viewdata* (interactive *videotex*) system.

temporary storage In computer *programs*, this refers to *storage locations* reserved for intermediate results.

tera- A prefix denoting one million million (10^{12}).

term Used in information work for a label attached to a group of items in a *record* such that the items can be retrieved via that label.

terminal 1. A device for sending and/or receiving data over a communications channel. It usually has both a keyboard and a *VDU*. The term is sometimes used to describe a single *work station*, eg of a word processor, whether or not it possesses a communications capability. 2. A point of connection for an electrical device or electronic component.

terminal emulator program
Software which allows a *microcomputer* to act as a *terminal*, usually for the purpose of communication with a large *mainframe* computer.

terminal junkies Slang for computer (or microcomputer) operators who become addicted to working on computers, to the detriment of their health.

terminal transparency The ability, in a telecommunications network, to allow incompatible terminals to communicate by automatic *code conversion* and line control conversion.

terminator In *data communications* denotes a *tag* which indicates the end of a message (see *header*).

terminology bank A computer-based glossary of terms which provides translations for each entry. It is used in *machine-aided translation* systems, such as *Termium*, *Target* and *Eurodicautom*.

Termium A Canadian pure *MAT* system which uses a *terminology bank* with a *permutation index* (allowing access to expressions via any significant word they contain). Termium is the largest and oldest terminology bank in the world, and offers *online machine-aided translation* in English and French throughout Canada.

ternary A system in which there is a choice of three states.

Tex A *suite* of *routines* (devised by Knuth) to enable technical text (including mathematics) to be input at an ordinary computer *terminal*.

text capture Synonymous with *data capture*.

text database management system *Software* which combines *word processing* functions with a *database management system*. Blocks of text created via the word processing facility are assigned one or more *keywords* and stored in a *database*; they can then be retrieved either by keyword or by searching for a *string* of characters. It is thus possible to draw together into one document many different kinds of textual material (see *outline processor*).

text editing The editing of text on a computer. It may be carried out on any form of computer, from a *mainframe* with appropriate *software* to a dedicated *word processor*.

Textline A news and business information database, containing, for example, text from European and American newspapers.

Textnet A translation service offered via *electronic mail* by *Telecom Gold*. The user specifies the language required and is offered a list of suitable translators. Translated texts can be transmitted via Telecom Gold for *phototypesetting*.

text-numeric database A *database* which provides both textual and statistical information. Such databases are usually specialized and concentrated in the scientific and business fields.

text processing The computer editing and subsequent production of textual material. It is often used as a synonym for *word processing* and for text management (including systems for storing and retrieving text). The distinction in usage from *word processing* lies primarily in the amount of data handled: working with very large quantities of text is usually referred to as 'text handling'.

text processing system A

computerized system designed to *edit* and manipulate text, which is then output in a specified medium and *format*.

text reader-processor A device which combines a text-reading capability (usually by *optical character recognition*) with a *data processing* facility (usually a *microprocessor*). Data can thus be *read* and processed into a form suitable either for a particular use, or for transmission to a particular piece of equipment.

text retrieval system A computerized system which allows the retrieval of documents included in its *database*(s) by selecting words, word groups and sequences in the documents themselves (see *information retrieval system* and *information retrieval techniques*).

text structure input A method of *input* for *online searching* of a *database* containing details of chemical structures. It resembles *graphic structure input*, except that the description of a chemical structure is given by the user using commands selected from a *menu* (see *chemical structure retrieval*).

text transfer device See *data transfer device*.

Text TV A Swedish *teletext* system.

thermal printing A method of printing using paper coated with heat-reactive dyes that darken at temperatures between 100°C and 150°C. A matrix of small elements, in good thermal contact with the paper, is selectively heated to form individual characters.

thermography Thermography is used in conjunction with *letterpress* printing. Slow-drying ink is used and, after printing, the paper is dusted with a resinous powder. Heat is then applied and the ink fuses and

swells giving an embossed appearance.

thesaurus A structured collection of terms which is used to index documents. It was originally used to control *post-coordinate* systems, but can also provide a subject headings list.
A thesaurus typically provides control of synonyms, and indicates how a particular *index term* is related to others in the *indexing language*. This capability can help define terms when carrying out a *search* during *information retrieval*.

thimble printer A type of *printer* used in some *word processing* systems. The name derives from the shape of the *fount*.

thin film (memory) See *magnetic film*.

thin window display A (limited) form of electronic display; typically containing up to 96 characters, and often a single line only. It is used in some *word processing* devices.

third normal form The product of a transformation process used to combine groups of data prior to the development of a database structure.

third party database A database accessible to a *videotex* system, but not held on the retrieval centre's computer. Instead, it normally resides on the *IP*'s computer and is accessible via a *gateway*.

Thomson-CSF optical videodisc A *videodisc* system developed by Thomson-CSF. The approach taken is basically similar to that of *Philips/MCA Discovision*, but the discs are thinner and more flexible. They are also therefore transparent: both sides can be read without turning the disc over, simply by altering the focus of the reading *laser* (see *videodisc*).

thread A group of *beads* strung

together for testing purposes.

threshold weight In a *search strategy* using *weighted terms*, the total weight above which a record should be identified as relevant.

throughput The amount of work processed during a specified time period.

Tic Tac A French *viewdata* (interactive *videotex*) system.

TIDA A Spanish *data communications* network.

tie line A private communications channel (usually leased from a *common carrier*) connecting two, or more, *private branch exchanges*. Sometimes also called a tie trunk.

tie trunk See *tie line*.

time assignment speech interpolation A technique for sharing transmission capacity on *voice grade channels*: the pauses in user's speech are used to carry data traffic.

time coded page One of a group of *teletext* pages bearing the same page number, and carrying information which continues from page to page. The pages are displayed in sequence, with page changes taking place at set intervals.

time derived channel A channel made available by *time division multiplexing*.

time division multiple access A technique for dividing a stream of signals between *terminals* in a network by allocating time slots.

time division multiplexing See *multiplexing*.

time out 1. In computing systems a preset time after which a *terminal* automatically *logs off* if no instructions are *input*. 2. In

telecommunications, the time between sending out a signal, and the reception at the sender's station of an acknowledgement of receipt.

time sharing Simultaneous *real time* use of a computer by a number of users. It is made possible by ultra-high-speed *switching* of *processing* time.

time slicing The sharing of a *CPU*'s time to give the appearance of simultaneous processing of a range of tasks.

TinMan A *database management system* developed by Information Management and Engineering (UK).

TIP TOP Tape input/tape output. Describes a system which uses *magnetic tape* as both *input* and *output* medium.

TITAN A French *viewdata* (interactive *videotex*) system.

TIU Telex interface unit. A device which can be attached to *microcomputers* or *word processors* to enable them to be used as *telex* terminals.

TNF See *third normal form*.

token A distinguishable unit in a set of *characters*.

token bus A *bus* network *architecture* which works on the basis that each *node* awaits the arrival of a *token* from the nearest upstream node, which indicates that it may send information to the downstream node. Only one token is allowed on the system at a time (see *token passing*).

token passing A method of network control used in *ring* and *broadcast networks*, whereby a *node* which holds a 'token *packet*' is permitted to transmit a large message package, or pass the token on to the next node.

token ring A *ring network* which operates on the basis that each *node* awaits the arrival of a *token* from the nearest upstream node, which indicates that it is allowed to send information to the downstream node. Only a single token is present on the ring at any one time (see *token passing*).

toll 1. A charge for linking to a *network* of telephone lines beyond a prescribed boundary. 2. US name for UK *trunk*.

toll office A US exchange which controls the switching of *toll* calls (see *trunk exchange*).

toll switching trunk A line connecting a toll office to a local exchange. (The US name for UK *trunk junction*.)

tone The relative shades of dark and light in an image (see *tone illustration* and *half-tone*).

tone illustration An illustration in which there is a continuous variation in *tone*, as in an ordinary photograph (contrast *half-tone*).

Topic Teletext Output of Price Information by Computer. The electronic information system of the London Stock Exchange. *Pages* can be retrieved from the Exchange's own *database*, EPIC, and displayed, in colour, on *terminals*. Price rises are marked in blue and falls in red, allowing the experienced user to scan the screen very rapidly to determine how a particular sector of the market is faring. Topic can be accessed outside London via leased *British Telecom* lines.

top down method A technique used in *structured programming*, whereby each successive step in the process adds more refinement until a working *program* is attained.

touchscreen A computer *screen* which is sensitive to touch. This effect is most commonly achieved by building a number of *infrared* transmitters and receptors into the screen surround. The pointing finger (or pencil) interrupts one or more beams in the x- and y-axes. The *software* relates these coordinates to what is displayed on-screen and responds as programmed. Touchscreens allow the user to point at, for example, a *menu* on-screen in order to select a choice of action or process. The technique has also been applied to limited data entry. (For related devices, see *soft keyboard*, *tactile keyboard*, *light pen* and *WIMP*.)

touch-sensitive Describes a switch, button or key which operates by physical contact and requires no mechanical movement (see *tactile keyboard*, *full-travel keyboard*).

TOXBACK Toxicology Information Back-up. In the *BLAISE* implementation of *TOXLINE*, most of the *National Library of Medicine* files are searchable *online*. For the remaining files, TOXBACK offers a back-up service: a query can be entered *online*, but the search is processed over-night.

TOXLINE Toxicology Information Online. A *database* produced by the US *National Library of Medicine* covering toxicology, environmental pollutants, drug chemistry, pharmacology, etc. It is accessible via *BLAISE*, *DIMDI* and *NLM*.

TPI Tracks per inch. A measure of the recording density on a *floppy disc*.

track A path along which a sequence of signals can be impressed on a recording medium. For example, a *magnetic tape* can have several tracks in parallel.

trackball Similar to a *mouse*, but held in the palm of the hand, where movements transmit positioned information to the computer, thus enabling the movement of text, graphics or a cursor on the screen. Also used in arcade video game machines.

TRACKER An *expert system* developed by *British Telecom* for use in diagnosing faults in the power supply of electronic *PABXs*.

tracker ball See *trackball*.

tractor feed A method for advancing paper through a printer. Spiked wheels rotate on the feeding mechanism, and the spikes engage in holes on the edge of the paper.

Tradanet A *value added service* currently under development for transmitting orders, invoices, statistics and other documents in the retail trade.

traffic The messages which pass through a communications system.

trailer A *record* at the end of a *file*.

trail printer A *printer* shared between *work stations*.

transaction Any event which requires that a *record* be *processed*, eg updating a *file*.

transactional videotex The use of interactive *videotex* to effect transactions, eg place orders, make bookings.

transaction file A *file* of *transaction records*.

transaction record A *record* which provides *input* to a *program*, instigating update of a *master file* or *database*.

transborder data flow The flow of data (numerical, bibliographical, factual) across national boundaries. A term mainly used in connection with the problems of *data protection*, *copyright*, etc.

transceiver A *terminal* which can both transmit and receive information.

transcribe To copy data from one *storage medium* to another, with, or without, some form of translation.

Transdoc A French *electronic document delivery* project set up as part of the *DOCDEL* programme, which upgrades the *CDST* document delivery service of *CNRS*. The *full-text* documents are held on *optical disc* and fully automated *microfiche*.

transducer At the most general level, a device for converting energy from one form to another. In information technology, it is an *input*, or *output*, device designed to convert signals from one *medium* to another. For example, a loudspeaker is a transducer which converts electrical signals into acoustic signals.

transfer file A *file* which carries *data* from one processing stage to another; typically an *output file* from one system which is used as a *transaction file* by another system.

transfer operation The movement of data from one *storage* area, or *medium*, to another.

transfer rate The speed at which data can be transferred from one *peripheral device* to another, or from a *CPU* to a peripheral.

transistor The name derives from *transfer* of electricity across a *resistor*. An electronic device made of semiconducting material which can be used to amplify or switch signals (see *semiconductor*).

translate Has a particular significance in computer *displays*: it means to adjust the position of an image on the screen.

transliteration A representation of the characters of one alphabet by those of another, usually corresponding approximately in sound.

translucent screen Synonymous with *opaque screen.*

transmission The electrical, or electromagnetic, transfer of energy. In information technology, it usually refers to the transfer of data signals from one point to another.

transmission loss A decrease in *signal* power during *transmission.* (Note that it does not mean the loss of a transmission.)

transmitter A device that transmits a signal (see *transmission*).

transnational data flow See *transborder data flow.*

Transpac French *packet switching* telecommunications network.

transparent 1. Refers to any computer activity that goes on unseen by the operator. 2. Refers to the combination of data and *word processing software* into a single program.

transponder A device which both receives and transmits data. A received signal can be amplified and retransmitted at a different frequency. *Communications satellites* usually have more than one transponder. Retransmission must take place at a different frequency, since otherwise the powerful retransmitted signal will interfere with the weak, incoming signal.

transportable A lightweight machine – *microcomputer* or *word processor* – which is compact enough to be carried. A number of machines described as '*portable*' are really too heavy to be accurately described as such, hence the term transportable, or 'luggable'.

transputer A powerful *32-bit processor* on a ¼ inch square *chip.* It also has inbuilt 4K *bytes* of *RAM.*

transverse scanning A form of scanning in which the head moves across, rather than along, the recording tape. In particular, it is a technique used in some *video tape recorders.*

tree-and-branch-network Usually consists of *trunk line coaxial cables* which transmit signals from a central location to peripheral locations served by branch lines.

tree structure Usually refers to an index which operates in a series of steps progressing from general headings to particular topics. Typically the user is presented with a series of *menus.*

triad A group of three *characters* or three *bits*, forming part of a message or *record.*

TRIAL Technique for retrieving information from abstracts of literature. A system for the manipulation of *bibliographic data* in the form of *abstracts.*

tribit Three consecutive *bits.*

Trojan Horse A *program* inserted by an unauthorized user in a computer system with the purpose of copying, misusing or destroying confidential data.

truncation 1. In *information retrieval*, removing a portion of a word so that the remainder can be used as a *search term* representing all words containing the word stem. For example, 'PREVENT –' would be taken to represent PREVENT, PREVENTABLE, PREVENTION, PREVENTATIVE, PREVENTATIVENESS, etc. 2. To drop *least significant digits* so as to effect *compaction.*

trunk A telecommunications

channel which carries signals between *switching* centres, often over long distances.

trunk exchange A UK exchange which controls the switching of *trunk* calls (see *toll office*).

trunk junction A line connecting a *trunk exchange* to a local exchange. (The UK name for US *toll switching trunk*.)

truth table A form of *Boolean operation table* in which the two possible values for each *operand* and result are 'true' or 'false' (see *Boolean algebra* and *Boolean operation table*).

TS *Time sharing.*

TSI *Test structure input.*

TSS 1. Time shared system. 2. Time sharing system (see *time sharing*).

TTL Transistor-transistor logic. A technology for constructing *integrated circuits* from *transistors* formed on a single slice of silicon. Lends itself to the production of circuits with a high operating speed, but is unsuited to the most complex types of circuit.

TTS 1. *Teletypesetting.* 2. Teletypesetting code. A development of *Baudot code.*

TTY *Teletypewriter.*

tube Refers, in origin, to the *cathode ray tube*, but is often used nowadays as a synonym for *screen*. Used in the US, formerly, as the equivalent term for the UK 'valve'.

Tulsa A *database* produced by the University of Tulsa (based on Petroleum Abstracts) and made available via *SDC*.

turnaround document A document produced by a computer which, after some intermediate action, is subsequently used for *computer input* purposes.

turn-around time 1. The time required to reverse the direction of a transmission. 2. The time between submitting a *job* to a computer and getting back the results.

turnkey system 1. A complete computerized system installed by a single supplier, who takes total responsibility for the production, installation and operation of all the *hardware* and *software*. 2. A system in which the user does not need to know any programming or *operating system* commands, eg loading programs. When turned on, the system goes into a pre-programmed activity, eg *word processing* or *information retrieval.*

turnwheel A *control device* similar in operation to a *joystick*, but without the attached stick.

turtle Either a wheeled robot, or an image on a screen, the movements of which are under computer control.

turtle graphics *Computer graphics input* facility which allows one to 'draw' by means of instructions given to a *cursor* (the '*turtle*').

TV-SAT/TDF A Franco-German *communications satellite* project set up in 1980. The plans are for a *direct transmission satellite* to provide television programmes in Western Europe. TV-SAT refers to the German component, and TDF to the French component (see *L-SAT*).

TVT Television typewriter. A device for displaying data on a television screen.

twisted nematic *LCD* technology in which a liquid crystal is sandwiched between two layers of polarized glass. Offers relatively poor resolution and viewing angle, and slow *refresh rate*.

twisted pair wiring Probably the commonest transmission media currently in use. Used to connect telephones to a local exchange. Relatively cheap; has the advantage of already being installed in most buildings; but susceptible to noise and interference (see *coaxial cable*).

two-way cable An *interactive* cable system.

two wire circuit See *two wire connection*.

two wire connection A connection which uses a pair of wires to provide both transmission and reception of data in *full* or *half duplex* mode, depending on the system's design.

TWX Teletypewriter Exchange Service. A public *switched teletypewriter* service offered by *AT&T* in the US and Canada.

TX *Telex.*

Tyme-gram A US *electronic mail* service operated by Tymshare Inc.

Tymnet A US *packet switched* telecommunications network operated by Tymshare Inc.

typamatic key A (*keyboard*) *key* that when depressed for any period greater than a specified short time (usually about two seconds) repeats the keying of the relevant character (or 'blank') until the key is released.

typeface 1. The design, or style, of *characters* produced by a particular *printer*. 2. The printing surface of a piece of type which bears the character to be printed.

type fount (font) A complete collection of *characters* of a particular size and design (see *fount*).

typo Typographical error, or other *keyboarding* error.

typographic quality Synonymous with *graphic arts quality.*

U

UA *User area.*

UART Universal asynchronous receiver transmitter. A *chip* which allows for conversion of *serial bit streams* to *parallel* bit streams, and vice versa, for *asynchronous* devices.

UCS *Universal character set.*

UCSD University of California at San Diego. UCSD is the name of a popular *operating system* for microcomputers.

UDC 1. *Universal decimal classification.* 2. *Update centre.*

UHF Ultra high frequency: from 300 to 3,000 MHz (compare *VHF*).

UKITO An acronym for the United Kingdom Information Technology Organization. A group of British companies involved in the application of information technology.

UKMARC United Kingdom Machine Readable Cataloguing. The British Library Bibliographic Services Division's *MARC database*, containing records of books published in the UK since 1950.

UKOLUG United Kingdom Online *User Group.*

ULA Uncommitted Logic Array. One of a new generation of *processors* which set up pathways through the circuits as and when they are required.
Conventional *chips* require each component to be connected with every other component with which it may ever need to communicate (see *GAM*).

ULSI Ultra large scale integration. Similar to *VLSI*, but, while VLSI

refers to *microprocessors* composed of several tens of thousands of *transistors*, ULSI refers to microprocessors with approximately 100,000 transistors (see *LSI*, *VLSI*, and *SLSI*).

Ulticard A development of the *SmartCard*. A credit-card sized device powered by battery and containing a *microprocessor* memory *chip*, conventional magnetic stripe, touch-sensitive *keyboard* and a display *screen*.

ultrafiche A *microfiche* with such small images that 3,000 pages can be mounted on one 4-inch x 6-inch fiche.

Ultra LSI Another way of writing *ULSI*.

ultrasonic Sound with a *frequency* too high to be heard by the human ear (above 20 *kilocycles* per second).

ultrasonics Technology involving the use of *ultrasonic* waves.

ultraviolet Electromagnetic radiation in the range between visible light and x-rays: of the order of 10^{15}-10^{16} cycles per second (see *spectrum*).

U-matic A form of *video cassette* developed by Sony.

umbrella information providers In *viewdata*, an *information provider* who provides services to other information providers.

UMF Ultra microfiche: also called *ultrafiche*.

UMI Ultra microfiche (see *ultrafiche*).

unbundling The separation of charges for *hardware* and *software* in the buying and selling of computers and software.

uncontrolled language See *information retrieval techniques.*

underflow The production of a result from an arithmetic operation, the value of which is too small for the range of number representation being used by the system.

UNESCO United Nations Educational, Scientific and Cultural Organization.

unipolar A *transistor* formed from only one type of *semiconductor*: ie 'N type' or 'P type' (see *C MOS, N MOS* and *P MOS*).

union catalogue A catalogue of all the documents in a given category held by a group of libraries together with information on their location.

Unisat UK *communications satellite.*

UNISIST 1. United Nations Information System in Science and Technology. A UNESCO programme, designed to bring about a world information network. Mainly a coordinating body. One product of relevance to information technology is the *International Serials Data System* (ISDS). 2. Universal System for Information in Science and Technology. A classification system.

UNISTAR User Network for Information Storage Transfer, Acquisition and Retrieval (see *information retrieval system*).

unit buffer terminal A *terminal* with no communications *buffer.*

uniterm indexing A system of *indexing* which uses a single term to describe documents. These single terms (uniterms) are then used to

retrieve documents (see *information retrieval systems*).

universal character set A facility on a *printer* which permits any standard *typeface* to be chosen when printing a document.

universal decimal classification A *decimal classification system* developed by *FID.*

Universal Postal Union A United Nations agency responsible for promoting international cooperation between national postal services.

universal product code Each product, eg in a retail store, is described by a *code* in the form of a series of bars of varying widths. This is usually physically attached to the product.
The code can be read by an *optical scanner* at the point and time of purchase. The information can then be used to produce an automatic receipt and to record transactions. This aids the retailer with stock control, compilation of sales figures, etc (see *bar-code*). (For an alternative, see *magnetic stripe systems*.)

universe See *project universe.*

Unix A general purpose, *multi-user interactive* computer *operating system*, developed by Bell Laboratories. It is written in C-*language.*

unjustified Text which has an irregular right-hand margin.

unprotected field 1. A *data field* to which one can *write*. 2. An area of a *VDU* display that can be modified.

up Has a specific meaning in the context of computer systems. Such a system is described as 'up' when it is operating, and 'down' when it is not.

UPC *Universal product code.*

updatable microfiche By combining micro-imaging processes (see *microform*) with *photocopying*, it is possible to produce a specially coated *microfiche* to which images can be added as and when required.

updatable optical disc See *erasable optical disc.*

update To amend the *records* in a *file*, usually to take account of new information.

update centre A term used in *viewdata* systems to describe a *host* computer centre which receives the updates to a *database* from an *information provider* and distributes copies to other hosts in the network.

upgrade, upgradeable To enhance or improve a piece of equipment by adding on further units or devices; capable of being improved in this way.

uplink The *earth station*, and its transmitted signals, to a *communications satellite.*

upload Transfer of data or programs from a microcomputer to a *mainframe* (see *download*).

upper case Capital letters of a fount, eg 'A' as opposed to 'a'.

UPS Uninterrupted power supply. A protection against breakdowns and blackouts.

upstream Flow of communication in a *CATV* system away from a subscriber's home, and towards the *head end.*

uptime The time during which a computer system is 'up' (ie operating). Uptime is often expressed as a percentage, and this is used as an index of reliability; eg '99.5 per cent uptime' – an indication of a reliable system.

UPU *Universal Postal Union.*

upwards compatibility Describes the situation when a *program* written for one computer can also be run on a second computer, though a program written for the second computer will not run on the first (see *compatibility*).

URL User Requirements Language. A *high level language.*

USART Universal synchronous/ asynchronous receiver/transmitter. A chip which can receive and transmit *serial* data in the form of *synchronous* or *asynchronous* signals.

USASCII United States of America Standard Code for Information Interchange (see *ASCII*).

USDA/CRIS US Department of Agriculture/Current Research Information System. The USDA compiles a *database* on current agriculture-related research projects and makes it accessible via *Lockheed.*

user area The area on a *magnetic disc* in which a user's semi-permanent *data*, or *programs*, can be stored.

user-friendly A system with which relatively untrained users can interact easily. This normally implies the use of a *high level language*, and often of graphical representation.

user group A group of users of a *host* system, or of a specific *software package*, who share information about the system or *program*. A user group may also influence manufacturers or suppliers by acting as a pressure group.

user interest profile A definition of the information needs of an individual expressed as a series of *index terms* (see, eg, *selective dissemination of information*).

Userkit A device for improving and simplifying access to *online information retrieval systems*. The Userkit enables *search statements* to be prepared before going *online*, thus saving time, and also gives access to international systems using stored *host* addresses, *passwords* and *log-on* sequences. The Userkit is a box, containing a *microprocessor*, which plugs in between the user's *terminal* and the *modem* (see *online searching*).

USITA United States Independent Telephone Association. A US-based organization, but having members (independent telephone companies) in many countries. It deals with common problems, technical standards and regulatory matters.

USPO United States Post Office.

USRT Universal synchronous receiver/transmitter. A *chip* which can receive and transmit *serial* data in the form of *synchronous* signals.

utility programs Usually considered to be part of a computer's *systems software*, these *programs* are designed to manipulate data in a manner which is not dependent on the content of specific *files*. They are used for such routine operations as sorting and dumping data.

utility routines See *utility programs*.

UTLAS University of Toronto Library Association System. A *bibliographic utility* provided by the University of Toronto.

UV *Ultraviolet*.

V

V Volt: *SI* unit of electrical force.

VAB Voice answer back. A pre-recorded voice response used in conjunction with a telephone-type *terminal* connected to a computer.

VACC *Value added common carrier.*

validation A check that data have been *input* correctly.

validity The extent to which repeated applications of a process obtain the same result.

value added common carrier A *common carrier* which does not itself establish telecommunications links, but which leases links from other carriers. It can thus create a computer-controlled network offering specific telecommunications services.

value added network A communications service using *common carrier* networks for transmission and providing added services, such as *store and forward* message switching.

value added service See *value added common carrier.*

VAN *Value added network.*

variable Part of a computer *program*, the value of which can be changed during the execution of the program.

variable block A *block*, the size of which is not fixed. Such a block varies within certain limits, according to requirements.

variable field See *field.*

variplotter A high-precision graphic recording device (see *plotter*).

VBI *Vertical blanking interval.*

VCC Video Compact Cassette. A *video cassette recorder* developed by Philips.

VCR 1. *Vertical redundancy check.* 2. A *video cassette* system, developed by Philips, now replaced by V2000 format. The initials are also used more generally as an abbreviation for *video cassette (recorder).*

VDI 1. Visual display input. 2. Video display input. The *input* at a *VDU.*

VDT 1. Visual display terminal. Originally this meant an *online* display, but it is often used as a synonym for a *VDU.* 2. Less frequently, the initials may stand for video display terminal.

VDU Visual display unit. A device equipped with a *cathode ray tube* for the visual display of information. Usually connected to a *keyboard* for inputting and editing information (see *VDT*).

vector graphics A form of *computer graphics* utilizing *line drawing displays.* Lines are entered on a display screen and then manipulated using a *keyboard* or *light pen.* Vector graphics are extensively used in *computer-aided design* (contrast *raster graphics*).

Velotype A *keyboard* design which minimizes hand movement and maximizes keying speed.

vendor Synonymous with *host.*

Venn diagram A diagram showing the relationship between sets of items: more particularly, the nature of their overlap. For example, the Venn diagram below shows the nature of overlap between different types of terminology. 1. Computer terminology. 2. Library terminology. 3. Telecommunications terminology. 4. New information technology. John Venn, after whom the diagram is named, was a 19th century logician (see also *Boolean algebra*).

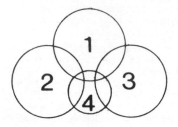

verification The checking of *coded* data against original source data to detect errors.

Vertical blanking interval The unused lines in each frame of a television signal – can be used, for example, in *teletext*.

vertical justification The adjustment of line length and inter-line spacing on a printed document, so that the text fits into a specified page length, or length of column.

vertical raster count The number of vertical divisions in a *raster* (see *raster count*).

vertical redundancy check A form of *parity check*.

vertical scrolling See *scroll*.

vertical wraparound A *wraparound* facility, from the last character space in a column, to the first character space in a new column.

very high frequency See *VHF*.

very high level language A programming language capable of reducing the size of programs by a factor of 10-100 over conventional

high level languages (such as *BASIC, COBOL* and *FORTRAN*). While simplifying programming, very high level languages are less efficient in terms of use of computer processing power. However, with developments in hardware technology leading to dramatic decreases in the cost of processing power, very high level languages are becoming increasingly valuable.

very large scale integration See *VLSI*.

vestigial side band A *modulated* transmission technique. One *sideband*, the *carrier wave* and only a portion of the other sideband are transmitted along a *channel*.

VHD *Video High Density.*

VHF Very high frequency: from 30 to 300 MHz (compare *UHF*).

VHS Video Home System. A *video cassette* system developed by JVC.

Viatel Australian *viewdata* (interactive *videotex*) system.

video A general term implying a visual display. Sometimes used as a synonym for a *VDU*.

video bandwidth The maximum rate at which dots of illumination, eg *phosphor dots*, can be displayed on a screen.

video camera A camera which records images on *magnetic tape* for playback, eg on a *video tape recorder*.

video cassette journal Subscribers periodically receive a *video cassette* and accompanying booklet. The cassette can be played by using a *video tape recorder* attached to a television set. Costs are kept down by the subscriber returning the cassette for reprogramming prior to the next 'issue' of the journal.

video cassette (recorder) A device for visual recording (especially of television programmes) on to *magnetic tape* contained in a plastic housing (see *video tape recorder*).

videoconferencing A form of *teleconferencing* where participants see, as well as hear, other participants at remote locations. *Video telephones* can be used for a limited form of videoconferencing over the *public switched telephone network*. However, most such systems will be on *leased lines*, or lines that can carry full-quality television pictures. Most existing systems operate between cities, eg by the provision of suitable studios in the major centres, either for public hire or for private use. A typical arrangement is shown in the diagram.

videodisc A disc, typically made of plastic, containing recorded visual and sound information designed for playback on a television screen. Videodiscs are *read-only*, non-erasable storage devices, produced by a stamping or moulding process. They can be used for storage of pictures and sound, sound only, for *digital* storage of data, or for all these categories in combination. They are mainly used as a means of distributing standard material.

There are two types of videodisc: capacitance and optical. Capacitance discs use a stylus in a similar manner to gramophone records. In capacitive systems the electrical signal to be read from the disc is determined by its ability to store electricity at each point. RCA's CED (capacitance electronic disc) system was a mechanical system produced primarily for the entertainment market. The CED did not prove successful, and RCA have now withdrawn from videodisc player manufacture. JVC make a grooveless system (video high density, VHD). The stylus does not have to follow a groove, so *random access* of any track is possible by skimming across the surface of the disc.

Optical videodiscs have now replaced capacitance systems. Optical videodisc systems use neon-helium laser beams both to write and read information on the disc. Information is stored as microscopic pits or indentations below the surface of the discs, arranged in 54,000 circular tracks. A separate video frame is recorded on each track, so each side of the disc holds 54,000 frames. The disc has a protective acrylic coating, so it is not easily damaged, and there is no wear when the disc is played. To record for the *NTSC* (North American) television standard with

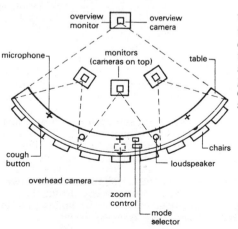

overview monitor
overview camera
microphone
monitors (cameras on top)
table
cough button
overhead camera
zoom control
chairs
loudspeaker
mode selector

Videoconferencing layout, allowing transmission between distant conference areas using ordinary television facilities. The 'mode selector' has a 'normal mode' position in which cameras switch automatically to the person speaking.

525 scanning lines and 30 frames per second, a disc speed of 1,000 revolutions per minute is used. For the *PAL* (European) system with 625 scanning lines and 25 frames per second, the disc speed is about 1,500 revolutions per minute. Playing time is about 30 minutes a side. Players provide *freeze-frame* or slow motion facilities.

The most widely-used videodisc is the Philips *LaserVision* system. It has a capacity of 55,000 frames per side and access times of 5–7 seconds. It can play backwards, forwards, at variable speeds, and can stop on any frame. It stores *analog* information, two sound channels and can encode *digital* information.

Videodiscs were originally developed for the home entertainment market, as a competitor for *video cassette recorders*. As such, they offer three main advantages: a. the materials from which they are made are cheaper than those for video cassettes or conventional film; b. the disc itself is light and compact and is easily stored and transported; c. many (although not all) discs offer random access to various parts of the discs (in contrast to tapes in video cassettes). A disadvantage is that currently available discs are non-erasable and read-only: they cannot record information, but can only play back pre-recorded material. A number of prototype *recordable videodiscs* have been produced but, as yet, these are not commercially available.

The videodisc need not be used solely for the storage of sound and pictures. It has the capacity to store large amounts of text, or a mixture of text, sound, graphics and moving pictures. This, together with its capacity for *random access*, has meant that the videodisc is now being used less for entertainment and more for the purposes of education and information storage, retrieval and transfer.

Videodiscs can be used to store information in digital form. In this case, the capacity of a single side is approximately 10^{10} *bits*, or roughly 1 million pages of 1,250 characters, which is vastly more text than if the disc is used in a direct, television-compatible way. An index for each frame indicates whether digital or video information is being carried on that frame, and the disc output can be directed to a video monitor, or to a computer for subsequent output. The videodisc thus has considerable application as a storage and retrieval device, as well as a *full-text* store and publishing medium, by virtue of its cheap storage capacity, easy access, and ability to mix text and graphics. Videodiscs are also capable of providing *interactive* applications, and these are being used for educational purposes. Three levels of interaction are possible. At the simplest, frame numbers or chapter stops are used to branch to specific sequences on the disc, turn instructions on or off, and use single frame advance to view answers to questions. At the next level, small *programs* are stored on the discs which are executed by the videodisc player, providing limited automatic branching and simple analysis of answers. At the most advanced level, the disc is controlled by a program on a *microcomputer*. Computer-generated text can be imposed on the video images, and it is then possible to provide annotations, simple graphics or captions. Full alphanumeric, touch or speech *input* can be used (see *interactive videodisc*).

videogram A pre-recorded *video tape*, or *video cassette*.

Video High Density A *videodisc* system developed by JVC. Like *Selectavision* of RCA, this is a *capacitive* system. A *laser* is used to record the signals on a glass master disc. The discs produced from this do not have grooves: the *stylus* is guided along the appropriate track by a special signal.

videomatics A term proposed to describe the convergence of *video* and *information technologies*.

videomicrographic system A *computer-assisted retrieval* system. Unlike conventional CAR systems, the retrieved *microform* image is not displayed on an adjacent microform reader, but is scanned by a video camera and then transmitted to the user's computer *terminal*. Some systems use *local area network* links to transfer data to different buildings on the same site, and *satellite communications* to transfer data over longer distances.

Video Patsearch A UK service (offered by Pergamon) for searching US patents. The index to, and text of, patents is held on computer *files*, whilst the *graphics* are recorded on *videodiscs*. The files can be searched from a user's *terminal*, and both text and graphics can be accessed (see *online searching*).

videophone A telephone system which simultaneously transmits images (usually of the two people speaking).

video recorder See *video tape recorder*.

video standards For television, see *MAC, NTSC, PAL* and *Secam*. For *video tape recorders*, see *VHS* and *Beta*.

VideoStream A *videoconferencing* system offered by *British Telecom*.

video tape recorder A device which, when connected to a television set, can be used to record both sound and pictures on *magnetic tape*. This tape is normally enclosed in a cartridge (a *video cassette*). Video tape recorders can also be used to 'play back' these tapes, whether they have been prepared in this way (ie from a television broadcast or transmission), or in some other way, eg using a *video camera*. Also called a *video recorder* and *video cassette recorder*.

Videotel An Italian *viewdata* (interactive *videotex*) service.

video telephone A telephone which also transmits and, depending on the system, receives an image on a screen (see *videoconferencing*).

videotex Videotex is a generic term referring to any electronic system that makes computer-based information available via *VDUs*, or appropriately adapted television sets, to a dispersed and reasonably numerous audience. Videotex systems can be divided into two main categories.
a. broadcast videotex: where information is carried from the computer to the receiver by radio

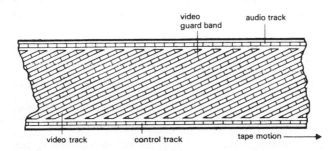

Typical track layout of videotape.

waves. The role of the user in this type of system is generally restricted to the choice of one from a limited number of *pages* for display on a screen, using a simple push-button selection device. For example, the two systems of this type in operation in the UK – *Ceefax* and *ORACLE* – broadcast (without charge to the viewer) frequently updated information on such topics as weather forecasts, sports results, etc. This information is 'piggy-backed' on existing television transmissions, which limits the number of pages available to a few hundred.

b. interactive videotex: where the information is carried from the computer to the receiver by cable (usually telephone lines). Use of cables instead of broadcast videotex generates two advantages. The amount of information available is limited by the capabilities of the computer, rather than by the mode of transmission. Thus, the UK form of interactive videotex – called *Prestel* – already has over a quarter of a million pages accessible. Instead of passively receiving information, users can interact individually with the computer. In making Prestel available, the British *PTT* acts as a *common carrier*. The material to be transmitted is fed in by independent *information providers*, who hope to cover their costs by charging users for consulting pages. The approach varies from country to country. For example, one of the main current developments in France is the government-backed distribution of VDUs to telephone users to replace their print-on-paper telephone directories (see *Electronic Directory Service*). Apart from such public videotex systems, private systems are also appearing; they are usually aimed at restricted audiences in the business sector. A number of UK local authorities have also set up their own systems (see *private videotex system*).

Owing to the large number of pages on offer, *information retrieval*

techniques are necessarily more complex for cable-based transmission, than for radio transmission. Optimum methods by which inexperienced users can track down the information they need are still being investigated. Some videotex services offer the enhancement of limited *keyword* searching. This takes them a step nearer the conventional *online* information retrieval systems. Similarly, the presentation of material on the screen (and especially *graphics*) is becoming more sophisticated. These developments are important for the future growth of interactive capabilities of videotex. Planned or existing user interaction includes carrying out numerical calculations, playing games, consulting sales catalogues and ordering goods online, recording votes in local referenda and exchanging messages with other subscribers to the network (a form of *electronic mail*). One problem with videotex is the different generic names that have been applied to it. Thus 'interactive videotex' is often called 'viewdata', whilst 'broadcast videotex' may be referred to as 'teletext'. The latter term must not be confused with *teletex*.

Videotext 1. A West German *teletext* system. The term is sometimes used as a synonym for *videotex*. 2. A Swiss *teletext* system.

video typing system See *screen typing system*.

vidicon (tube) The basic element of a video camera (normally only black and white).

Viditel A Dutch *viewdata* (interactive *videotex*) system.

Vidon A Canadian *viewdata* (interactive *videotex*) system.

viewdata An alternative term for interactive *videotex*.

Viewdata The Hong Kong interactive *videotex* service.

ViewShare A *videotex*-based *value added service* operated by BL (British Leyland) Systems.

Viewtel A US *viewdata* (interactive *videotex*) system developed in Columbus, Ohio. Sometimes referred to as *Channel 2000*.

Viewtel 202 A UK *viewdata* (interactive *videotex*) system.

Viewtron A US *viewdata* (interactive *videotex*) system, now discontinued.

virgin medium A *storage medium* with no data recorded on it.

virtual Pertaining to conceptual, rather than physical, existence.

virtual address A convenient *address* given in a *program*, which is not the same as the *absolute address* in which the relevant data are to be stored.

virtual circuit Also called 'virtual call' or 'virtual link'. In *packet switching*, virtual circuits are routes established between the origin and destination of a call. These routes are followed by the *packets* in turn. In contrast to *circuit switching*, a fixed circuit does not need to be reserved for the whole duration of the call.

virtual link See *virtual circuit*.

virtual machine In a *multi-user* system, the notional range of *hardware* and *software* which appears to the user to be under his/her personal control. In fact, these resources are shared by all the system's users.

virtual memory See *virtual storage*.

virtual microcomputer system A system which uses low cost *dumb terminals* to access a *remote microprocessor* which, in turn, acts as a microcomputer and uses the wide range of *software* available to micros. The remote processors are

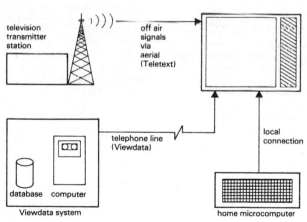

Diagram of the two basic videotex receiving systems. Interactive videotex receives information by cable, whereas broadcast videotex receives it by radio waves. Videotex also covers the reception of local signals from a home microcomputer. For a fuller illustration of interactive videotex, see Prestel.

centrally maintained in 'racks', and system usage and disc space are controlled by management software. The system allows for centralized maintenance, software control and upgrading.

virtual storage The linking of the main *memory* of a computer with external *storage* in such a way that they can function as one memory of larger capacity.

virtual telecommunications access method *Data communications software* which controls the flow of messages between a *host* computer and *remote terminals*.

Visc An early *videodisc* system, which employed a *stylus*.

viscose film Film which is rendered photosensitive by impregnation with a light-sensitive dye. It is sometimes used for *microforms*.

Visicalc The best known of *spreadsheet* programs for microcomputers.

Visiclone Slang for *spreadsheet* programs similar to *Visicalc*.

Visicom An *electronic mail* service specifically designed for the deaf.

visual display unit See *VDU*.

Visual Services Trial An experimental service offered by *British Telecom* in which *videoconferencing* systems are provided to selected UK firms.

VLF Very low frequency: a frequency below 30,000 *Hz* (see *spectrum*).

VLP Video Long Player. A Philips/MCA videodisc system.

VLSI *Very large scale integration*. Electronic circuits constructed on a single *chip* with a complexity

equivalent to over ten thousand transistors and up to a hundred thousand transistors (see *LSI, ULSI* and *SLSI*).

VME Virtual Machine Environment. An *ICL operating system* using *virtual storage*.

vocoder A device for *speech synthesis* which transmits sufficient information for the voice to be synthesized, without attempting to preserve the original voice waveform. It aims at semantic clarity, but not at copying the voice. This means that the sounds produced will not necessarily resemble the voice of the original speaker.

Vodaphone A *cellular radio* network operated by Racal.

voder Abbreviated form of *vocoder*.

VOGAD Voice operated gain-adjustment device. A device which reduces fluctuations in the level of reproduced speech, so improving the *signal-to-noise ratio*.

voice activation The operation of any device that can be trained to respond to the human voice.

voice and data See *Integrated Services Digital Network*.

voice answerback A system in which a computer gives responses (to a user's commands) in the form of pre-recorded voice messages.

voice band The *bandwidth* covering normal speech: 300-3,000 Hz.

voice grade channel A channel suitable for transmission of speech. It must therefore cover a range of sound frequencies from 300-3,400 Hz (cycles per second).

voice input See *direct voice input*.

voice mail See *voice message system*.

voice message system An electronic system for transmitting and storing voice messages, which can be accessed later by the person to whom they are addressed.

voice notes A facility for *terminal* users who cannot, or will not, type to add voice messages to a computerized text. A user can inspect a document on a *VDU* and append audible messages ('voice notes') to it via a microphone plugged into the terminal.

voice output Computer *output* in the form of a spoken voice (see *speech synthesis*).

voice recognition See *speech recognition*.

voice synthesis See *speech synthesis*.

voice unit A measure of the average *amplitude* of an electrical signal which represents speech. Also called a *volume* unit.

volatile memory Memory which loses its *information* when power is cut off. It is to be contrasted with *permanent* memory.

volatility The proportion of records in a *file* that are added or deleted in a *run*.

volume unit Synonymous with *voice unit*.

Von Neumann Named after its original designer, this refers to the *architecture* of the conventional computer, characterized by a single computing element incorporating *processor*, communications and *memory*, and sequential, centralized control of computation.

Votes A *database* which presents the voting records of members of the US Congress on bills, resolutions, treaties etc. It is updated twice monthly, and is accessible via *SDC*.

voxel A three-dimensional *pixel*.

VPS Video Printing System. A technique developed by the Japanese company DaiNippon, which captures images transmitted as *video* signals and turns them into transparencies or colour prints. The system is often used by newspapers.

V series recommendations A series of *CCITT* recommendations covering *analog data transmission*, as specified below:

V.1 Covers equivalence between *binary notation* symbols and the significant conditions of two condition code.

V.2 Covers power levels for *data transmission* over telephone lines.

V.3 Covers International Alphabet No 5 for transmission of data and messages.

V.4 Covers the general structure of signals of International Alphabet No 5 for data and message transmission over public telephone networks.

V.5 Covers standardization of data signalling rates *for synchronous data transmission* in the general switched telephone network.

V.6 Covers standardization of data signalling rates for *synchronous data transmission* on leased telephone-type circuits.

V.10 Covers electrical characteristics for unbalanced double-current interchange circuits for general use with *integrated circuit* equipment in the field of *data communications*.

V.11 Covers electrical characteristics for balanced double-current interchange circuits for general use with *integrated circuit* equipment in the field of *data communications*.

V.13 Covers *answerback* unit simulators.

V.15 Covers use of *acoustic coupling* for *data transmission*.

V.16 Covers medical *analog data transmission modems*.

V.19 Covers *modems* for *parallel data transmission* using telephone signalling frequencies.

V.20 Covers *parallel data transmission modems* standardized for universal use in the general switched telephone network.

V.21 Covers *modems* which operate at speeds up to 300 *baud*.

V.22 Covers *modems* which operate at speeds of 1,200 *baud*.

V.23 Covers 600/1,200 *baud modems* standardized for use in the general switched telephone network.

V.24 Covers the *interface* between a *terminal* and a *modem* for *serial data transmission*.

V.25 Covers automatic calling and answering on the general switched telephone network.

V.26 Covers 2,400 *bit/s modems* standardized for use on four-wire leased circuits.

V.26bis Covers 2,400/1,200 *bit/s modems* standardized for use in the general switched telephone network.

V.27 Covers 4,800 *bit/s modems* standardized for use on leased circuits.

V.27bis Covers 4,800 *bit/s modems* with automatic equalizer standardized for use on leased circuits.

V.27ter Covers 4,800/2,400 *bit/s modems* standardized for use in the general switched telephone network.

V.28 Covers electrical characteristics for unbalanced double-current interchange circuits.

V.29 Covers 9,600 *bit/s modems* for use on leased circuits.

V.30 Covers *parallel data transmission* systems for universal use on the general switched telephone network.

V.31 Covers electrical characteristics for single-current interchange circuits controlled by contact closure.

V.35 Covers *data transmission* at 48 kilo*bit/s* using 60 to 108 kHz group band circuits.

V.36 Covers *modems* for *synchronous data transmission* using 60 to 108 kHz group band circuits.

V.37 Covers *synchronous data transmission* at a data signalling rate higher than 72 *kilobit/s* using 60 to 108 kHz group band circuits.

V.40 Covers *error* indication with electromechanical equipment.

V.41 Covers code independent *error control* systems.

V.50 Covers standards limits for transmission quality of *data transmission*.

V.51 Covers organization of the maintenance of international telephone-type circuits used for *data transmission*.

V.52 Covers characteristics of distortion and *error* rate measuring apparatus for *data transmission*.

V.53 Covers limits for the maintenance of telephone-type circuits used for *data transmission*.

V.54 Covers *loop test* device for *modems*.

V.55 Covers specifications for an impulsive noise measuring instrument for telephone-type circuits.

V.56 Covers comparative tests for *modems* for use over telephone-type circuits.

VSMF Visual search on microfilm (see *microfilm*).

VTAM *Virtual telecommunications access method.*

VTR 1. *Video tape recorder.* 2. Video tape recording.

VT52, VT100, VT200, VT220 Telecommunications *protocols* for connecting *terminals* to a *mainframe* computer. *Microcomputers* may also be fitted with, for example, a VT100 *terminal emulator interface* for the same purpose.

VU 1. *Voice unit.* 2. *Volume unit.* (The two terms are synonymous.)

VU/TEXT A *news database*, run by Knight Ridder in the US.

V2000 A *video cassette recorder* system developed by Philips.

W

W Watt. An *SI* unit of power.

WACK 'Wait before transmitting positive acknowledgement'. A signal sent by a receiving *station* to indicate that it is temporarily not ready to accept a message (see *ACK* and *NACK*).

WADS Wide area data service. A data transmission service which operates on a *network* much like that serving a *WATS* telephone service.

wafer A thin slice of silicon which forms the basis of a *chip*.

waiting time See *latency*.

wait list Synonymous with *queue*.

wait loop A *subroutine* within a program that continually loops until a condition, external to the program, is satisfied.

WAN *Wide area network.*

wand A device, shaped like a stick, which can be used to recognize *optically coded labels*.

Wang US computer manufacturer specializing in *word processing* systems and *office automation* equipment.

WARC *World Administration Radio Conference.*

watermark magnetics A system for encoding information on to a *magnetic stripe*. It is used for magnetic stripes fixed to plastic credit and banking cards. (For their use, see *automatic bank teller machines*.) The watermark's distinctive feature is its performance. The encoded information is not erased, or altered, if the stripe passes through a strong magnetic field.

WATS Wide area telephone service. A service which allows a subscriber to make local calls at a flat monthly rate (ie no charge for individual calls).

waveband See *bandwidth*.

waveform digitization The conversion of a wave into *digital* form by the generation of numbers proportional to the *amplitude* of the waveform at frequent intervals. In particular, waveform digitization is the name given to one technique of *speech synthesis*.

waveguide A metal tube used for the transmission of very high frequency electromagnetic signals. Rectangular waveguides are typically used for the connection between *microwave antennae* (aerials) and associated equipment. They are not normally used for transmission over distances of more than a few hundred metres. Circular waveguides can transmit much higher frequencies than rectangular waveguides (typically 40 to 110 GHz). These would be heavily *attenuated* if transmitted through the atmosphere. A helical waveguide is of a circular cross section, but has copper wire wound round the inside in a helix. This helps attenuate undesired modes of the signal. Circular and helical waveguides are used for transmission over many kilometres. The waveguides must not bend sharply, but can change direction by gradual curvature.

wavelength See *spectrum*.

wavelength multiplexing A technique for transmitting separate signals simultaneously by using a different *wavelength* for each signal. Applies particularly to the transmission of light wavelengths via *optical fibres*.

wayleave Right of way granted for the purpose of laying cables.

WB Weber. An *SI* unit of magnetic flux.

WDC *World Data Centre*. A number of these were established to promote the collection and international exchange of scientific data. There are three main components of WDC: WDC-A in the US, WDC-B in the USSR and WDC-C in several Western European countries, Australia and Japan. The centres collect data covering the earth and space sciences.

WDC-A See *WDC*.

WDC-B See *WDC*.

WDC-C See *WDC*.

web In printing, a method of printing on to a continuous length of paper which moves through the machine.

weighted term See *weighting*.

weighting In *information storage and retrieval*, the practice of assigning weights to *search terms* to indicate their importance. A number of search terms, eg *descriptors*, may be used, each assigned different weights. Only those items are retrieved which carry descriptors whose combined 'weight' is above some specified threshold.

Westar A series of *communications satellites* owned by *Western Union* for communication in the United States.

Western Union Corporation A US *common carrier* offering a variety of voice, video and data transmission services, some of which are based on its *Westar* satellite system.

WESTLAW West Publishing Law System. A US *legal retrieval* system. It enables searches to be made for words and phrases in full legal texts, eg of judicial rulings, US codes.

wheel (printer) A *printer* which has its typeface mounted on the rim of a wheel (see *daisy wheel printer*).

whirley bird Slang for *magnetic disc* equipment.

white noise A signal with equal power over all *frequencies*.

white out Synonymous with *white space skid*.

white space skid A feature of some *facsimile transmission* machines. It allows transmission to be speeded up by the scanner skipping the blank spaces on the document to be transmitted.

wide area data service See *WADS*.

wide area network Covers a much larger geographical area than a *local area network*, and often transmits data at a lower rate.

wide area telephone service See *WATS*.

wideband Refers to a *bandwidth* of the order of 48,000 Hz (contrast *narrowband* and *voice band*).

WIMP Windows, Icons, Mouse, Pointer. Devices used as an alternative to the *keyboard* for entering commands to the computer. The idea behind all these devices is to simplify the entry process and to protect the user from the complexities of an *operating system* (see *window system, icon, mouse, pointer*).

Winchester disc A type of

magnetic disc device in which the *disc pack* and *read/write heads* are sealed in a removable (exchangeable) unit (see *hard disc*).

window   A feature on some *microcomputer* systems which allows more than one application to be viewed *on-screen* at any one time. Any applications (eg *word processing*, *spreadsheet*) and *menus* may be brought on to the screen as though they were separate sheets of paper in a pile; they can be shuffled and re-ordered while the *software* keeps track of what is where. Several windows may be defined on the screen simultaneously and the contents of each handled either independently or together.

window system   *Microcomputer* system (such as that of the Apple Macintosh) which makes use of *on-screen windows* to display a range of applications options. The screen is surrounded by pictures of various possible operations (represented as *icons*) which are chosen by moving a *pointer*. Depending on the operation selected, a further set of icons may be displayed, or a new *menu* may overlay the current one. A number of products are now available which give ordinary microcomputers the same windowing facility as the Macintosh.

wireless terminal   A portable, or hand-held, *terminal* that can communicate with a computer by radio.

WISE   World Information Systems Exchange. An arrangement between several hundred institutions worldwide to encourage collaboration in, and the exchange of data about, *information technology*.

Wiswesser line notation   A widely accepted method of representing the chemical structure of a compound by a *string* of *characters* (see *chemical structure retrieval*).

WLN   *Wiswesser line notation.*

word   A group of *characters* representing a unit of data, and occupying one *storage* location. It is an indication of the number of *bits* that can be handled by the *CPU* of a computer in each computing step. Thus it has become a measure of the size of a computer, eg a computer may be described as a '32-bit word computer'.

word association   See *word/ character frequency techniques.*

word break   A hyphen used to split a word at the end of a line.

word/character frequency techniques   Some *information retrieval techniques* are based on the characteristics of *natural language*. For example, natural language has considerable redundancy, as can be seen from the way garbled messages can often be reconstructed accurately. This provides an opportunity for text compression when putting material into *machine-readable* form. Thus, words do not all occur with the same frequency, nor do letters. In a piece of text, typically a small proportion of the words make up a large proportion of the text, while many words are used very infrequently. It is possible to design codes so that a frequent word or character is represented by a code of very short length, thus making savings in computer storage space. One example is the *Huffman code*. Other methods take whole portions of text which may occur frequently, eg phrases, or ends and beginnings of words, and code them. The frequency of occurrence of words in natural language can also be used as an aid in indexing, classification and retrieval. For example, considerable research has been done on the frequency of co-occurrence of words within documents. Co-occurring words can be used as a method for classifying documents. Word association maps can be drawn, some of which can themselves be categorized, eg 'stars' or 'cliques' or 'clumps', giving rise to different types of classification of associated documents (see diagram). The technique is known as 'statistical word association', and originally derived from early studies on machine-aided translation.

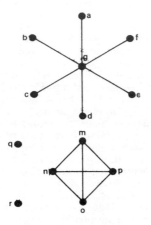

'Star' word (top) association map. The words a to f co-occur strongly with word y, but not with each other.

'Clique' word (bottom) association map. The words m to p co-occur strongly with each other, but not at all with q or r.

word length   The number of *bits*, *bytes* or *characters* in a *word*.

word processing   The term generally used in English to describe the computer handling of text. Although it is applied to a number of different functions, the essential elements are the enhancement of typewriting by the addition of *memory*, electronic *intelligence*, and an automated *printer*. A number of different types of product are now available which provide word processing facilities: electronic typewriters; *dedicated* word processors; *microcomputers* with word processing *software packages*. The origins of word processors are to be found in automated typewriters. These used paper tape, which recorded text as punched holes when the typewriter was operated. The punched tape was then rerun through the typewriter to produce further, identical copies of the text. In 1964, *IBM* introduced a much more useful form of this typewriter employing *magnetic tape* as a recording medium. The magnetic tape could be erased and re-used. More importantly, copy recorded on it could be edited. A major limitation of this system was that a typist could not be sure during the course of operations that amendments were being made correctly. This could only be ensured by scanning the final product. The incorporation of a *display* device overcame this: both text and amendments could be seen before the printout stage. The first 'screen-based' word processors became commercially available in the early 1970s.

All word processors have six elements in common:

a. a *keyboard*. This is usually similar to the *Qwerty keyboard* of a conventional typewriter, but has a number of additional 'control' keys which are used to perform editing and other functions.

b. *internal memory* or *storage*. This is the *work area* of the word processor. Text is entered, either from the keyboard, or from external storage, and is then available for editing or revision. The larger the internal memory, the greater the amount of text that can be manipulated at one time.

c. *external storage*. This refers to the storage of text after its creation, or editing. The most common form today is the *floppy disc* which comes in a range of sizes and storage capacities. It can be removed from the machine and stored separately.

d. *logic*. The logic part of the system provides the editing functions, the means of storing and retrieving text, and, in general, the control of the system. Some of the logic will be in the form of electronic circuits, or *hardware*. But, increasingly, much of the logic is in *software*, or computer *programs*, stored in the internal memory. These programs are brought into action via the keyboard. They drive a *microprocessor* which executes their instructions.

e. a *printer*. Most printers are separate units. The most common types in use today are *daisy wheel* and *dot matrix printers*; a recent development is the use of *laser printers*. The daisy wheel is a *letter quality printer* and provides a clear, dense image, suitable for *camera-ready copy*, but it is slow in operation. It is also impossible to change *founts* or type sizes without physically changing the daisy wheel. Dot matrix printers are faster, and, because they are software-controlled, can handle different founts and type sizes, but the quality of the print they produce is not as high. Laser printers are extremely rapid and quiet in operation; like dot matrix printers they can handle graphics as well as different founts and type sizes; and they produce a clear image suitable for camera-ready copy.

f. a *display*. Most word processing systems use a *VDU* screen which shows a major portion of a standard page of text. The text may be scrolled back and forward for review and possible revision.
Word processing facilities are now available in a number of different forms:

1. Electronic typewriters. Most manufacturers now offer *upgrade* facilities for their electronic typewriters, including full-size screen display and a *disc drive* to increase memory capacity, so that top of the range electronic typewriters offer many of the facilities of dedicated word processors.

2. *Dedicated*. These are self-contained, single keyboard systems, sometimes known as *stand-alone* word processors. They are specialized machines and cannot normally be used for other functions.

3. *Shared-logic* and *distributed-logic* (*shared resource*). With these systems, a number of keyboards can share the processing, storage, printing, or other facilities used in conjunction with a word processor. In a shared-logic system, the individual entry points, or *work stations*, make use of a central processor; whereas, in a distributed-logic system, each has its own *processor* and uses other shared facilities, eg printers, independently. *Time sharing* computer services introduce a further type of system. Here suitable word processors link with a *mainframe* computer to edit copy. Such a computer has the necessary storage capacity for work with very large amounts of text. Large computers, traditionally involved in numerical operations, are increasingly incorporating text-handling capabilities.
A current trend is the incorporation of more logic, or *intelligence*, into each work station of a word processor. This increases their power and the range of their functions. Thus some word processors can be used for limited data processing, *information retrieval* and *telecommunications* purposes. They can also be linked to other *data capture* devices, eg *OCR scanners* for the input of text, or *phototypesetters* to produce high-quality output. (see *text processing*).

4. *Microcomputers*. Most *personal computers* and microcomputers can run word processing software packages. The advantage of using microcomputers for word processing is that they are generally cheaper than dedicated word processors and they can be used for other purposes.

word processor See *word processing* (see diagram).

Word Processor Output Microform A type of Computer Output Microform (*COM*) which produces *microform* from information created by a *word processor* on *floppy disc*.

word proximity A technique used in *online searching* to indicate the sought proximity of two *search* items.

WordStar A *word processing*

software package designed for *microcomputers* by MicroPro.

word time The length of time required to move a *word* from one *storage* location to another.

word-wrap A *word processing* term. It refers to the way in which a partially typed word is moved to a new line if its length proves too much to fit into the existing line.

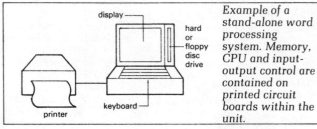

Example of a stand-alone word processing system. Memory, CPU and input-output control are contained on printed circuit boards within the unit.

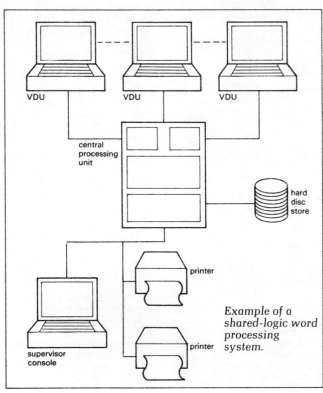

Example of a shared-logic word processing system.

work area Synonymous with *working storage.*

work database A *database* used to hold data prior to *update* of a *master file.*

work file 1. A *file* on *magnetic disc* containing details of the *program* which is currently being run through the computer. 2. A transient file used temporarily for working purposes (eg one of a number of *transfer files* prior to inclusion within a *sort* which produces a *transaction file*).

working memory Synonymous with *working storage.*

working space Synonymous with *working storage.*

working storage Temporary *storage* reserved for *data* which are actually being processed.

work station Sometimes referred to as an *electronic office.* A work station offers access to such facilities as *telephone, telex, facsimile, personal computer, word processor, data transmission terminal, viewdata* and perhaps even *videophone,* from one integrated unit. Often used in a restricted sense to mean a *terminal* with access to one of these facilities (see *station*).

World Administration Radio Conference International meetings held at intervals and mainly concerned with the allocation of frequencies. Meetings throughout the 1970s concentrated on *satellite communications.* Any frequency allocation system agreed at a *WARC* would be run by the *International Telecommunications Union.*

World Aluminium Abstracts A *bibliographic database* produced by the American Society for Metals and covering ore processing, metallurgy and end uses of aluminium. The

database is accessible via *ESA-IRS, Lockheed* and *QL.*

World Patents Index See *WPI.*

World Reporter A *news database,* run by Datasolve, which covers 11 news sources in *full-text* including: *The Financial Times; The Guardian, New Scientist* and the BBC *Summary of World Broadcasts.*

World System teletext A technique used for transmitting *teletext* (broadcast *videotex*) in which the spare capacity of ordinary television channels is used to transmit a limited number of pages. Can be contrasted with the French *Antiope* system which uses full-field broadcasting.

World Textiles A *bibliographic database* covering the science, technology, technical economics, management and trade of textile and related industries. The database is compiled in the UK and made accessible via *Lockheed.*

WORM Stands for Write Once/ Read Many, and refers to storage media which allow the user to write data (ie to record information) only once. The information can be read (ie looked at) as many times as the user requires, but it cannot be erased or altered in any way. Currently, most *optical discs* and *CD-ROMs* are WORM storage media.

wow and flutter A change in *output frequency* of a signal due to variations in *tape* speeds. Wow applies to slow speeds and flutter to high. Flutter has an additional meaning in connection with video tape (see *flutter*).

wp *Word processing.*

WPI World Patents Index. A *database* containing patent information from all the major R&D nations, accessible *online* via *Pergamon-Infoline.*

wpm Words per minute. A measure of speed of transmission in *telegraph* systems.

WPOM *Word Processor Output Microform.*

wrap See *word wrap*.

wrap around A way of displaying data on a *terminal* screen. When the screen has been filled (ie a *character* has been entered in the last vacant position at the bottom right-hand corner of the screen), then following characters are displayed in the first positions on the screen (working from the top left-hand corner), overwriting any characters already present.

write To record *data*, or copy them from one *storage device* to another.

write after read In techniques that restore data in a *storage device* following a *destructive read-out*.

write-enable notch A notch on the jacket of a *floppy disc* which, when uncovered, prevents data being written to the disc.

write head An electromagnetic device used to *write* on a magnetic *storage* medium.

write-inhibit ring See *file protection ring*.

write-once See *WORM*.

write-protect notch A notch on the jacket of a *floppy disc* which, when covered, prevents data being written to the disc.

write-protect ring See *file protection ring*.

write rate The maximum rate at which the phosphor *dot* on a *terminal* screen can produce a satisfactory image.

writing head Synonymous with *write head*.

writing tube A *tube* on which an electron beam *writes*, or scans for information.

WS Abbreviation for *working storage*, or *working space*.

WYSIWYG Stands for 'what you see is what you get', and describes computer *software*, especially *word processing programs*, where what is displayed *on-screen* (text, graphics, etc) will be reproduced exactly as seen when printed out.

X

X 1. An international symbol for *digital* operation. 2. In *micrographics*, refers to the *reduction rate*.

Xenix A computer *operating system* similar to *Unix*.

xenon flash A high intensity short exposure light source used in *phototypesetting*.

xerography Xerography is a technique whereby an electronic image of a document is formed onto a drum. The drum picks up a black powder by electrostatic attraction. The powder is deposited onto blank paper, and fused into the paper by baking to form the final reproduction of the document.

xerox The trade name for a type of document copying machine, based on *xerography*. Owing to the popularity of these machines, photocopying is sometimes referred to as 'xeroxing'.

Xerox 9700 An *intelligent copier* produced by Xerox.

x-height The height of a *lowercase* letter when *ascenders* and *descenders* are excluded.

Xmail A facility of the *Dialcom electronic mail* service which provides a direct connection to *telex* services.

X series of recommendations A series of *CCITT* recommendations covering various areas of *data transmission* over *public data networks*, as specified below:

X.1 Covers international user classes of service in *public data networks*.

X.2 Covers international user facilities in *public data networks*.

X.3 Covers packet assembly/disassembly facilities (*PAD*) in a *public data network*.

X.4 Covers general structure of signals of International Alphabet No 5 code for *data transmission* over *public data networks*.

X.20 Covers *interface* between *data terminal equipment* (DTE) and *data circuit terminating equipment* (DCE) for start/stop transmission services on *public data networks*.

X.20bis Covers V.21-compatible *interface* between *data terminal equipment* (DTE) and *data circuit terminating equipment* (DCE) for start/stop transmission services on *public data networks*.

X.21 Covers the *interface* between *data terminal equipment* (DTE) and *data circuit terminating equipment* (DCE) for synchronous operation on *public data networks*.

X.21bis Covers use on *public data networks* of *data terminal equipment* (DTE) which is designed for interfacing to synchronous V-series modems.

X.22 Covers the Multiplex *DTE/DCE interface* for user classes 3–6.

X.24 Covers definitions of interchange circuits between *data terminal equipment* (DTE) and *data circuit terminating equipment* (DCE) on *public data networks*.

X.25 Covers the *interface* between *data terminal equipment* (DTE) and *data circuit terminating equipment* (DCE) operating in the *packet* mode for terminals on *public data networks*.

X.26 Covers electrical

characteristics for unbalanced double-current interchange circuits for general use with *integrated circuit* equipment in the field of *data communications.*

X.27 Covers electrical characteristics for balanced double-current interchange circuits for general use with *integrated circuit* equipment in the field of *data communications.*

X.28 Covers the *DTE/DCE interface* for start/stop mode *data terminal equipment* accessing the packet assembler/disassembler (*PAD*) on a *public data network* situated in the same country.

X.29 Covers procedures for the exchange of control information and user data between a *packet* mode *DTE* and a packet assembly/disassembly facility (*PAD*).

X.30 Covers standardization of basic mode-page-printing machine in accordance with International Alphabet No 5.

X.31 Covers characteristics at the interchange point between *data terminal equipment* (DTE) and *data circuit terminating equipment* (DCE) when a 200 *baud* start/stop data terminal in accordance with International Alphabet No 5 is used.

X.32 Covers *answerback* units for 200 *baud* start/stop machines in accordance with International Alphabet No 5.

X.33 Covers standardization of an international text for the measurement of the margin of start/stop machines in accordance with International Alphabet No 5.

X.40 Covers standardization of frequency-shift modulated transmission systems for the provision of telegraph and data channels by frequency division of a primary group.

X.50 Covers fundamental *parameters* of a *multiplexing* scheme for the international *interface* between *synchronous* data networks.

X.50bis Covers fundamental *parameters* of a 48 kilobits/s user data signalling rate transmission scheme for the international *interface* between *synchronous* data networks.

X.51 Covers fundamental *parameters* of a *multiplexing* scheme for the international *interface* between *synchronous* data networks using 10-*bit* envelope structures.

X.51bis Covers fundamental *parameters* of a 48 kilobits/s user data signalling rate transmission scheme for the international *interface* between *synchronous* data networks using 10-*bit* envelope structure.

X.52 Covers the method of encoding *anisochronous* signals into a *synchronous* user bearer.

X.53 Covers the numbering of channels on international *multiplex* links at 64 kilobits/s.

X.54 Covers the allocation of channels on international *multiplex* links at 64 kilobits/s.

X. 60 Covers common channel signalling for *synchronous* data applications – data user part.

X.61 Covers the signalling system No 7 – data user part.

X.70 Covers the terminal and transit control signalling system for start/stop services on international circuits between *anisochronous* data networks.

X.71 Covers the decentralized terminal and transit control signalling system on international circuits between *synchronous* data networks.

X.75 Covers the terminal and transit call control procedures and data transfer system on international circuits between *packet switched* data networks.

X.80 Covers interworking of interchange signalling system switched data services.

X.87 Covers principles and procedures for realization of international user facilities and network utilities in *public data networks*.

X.92 Covers hypothetical reference connections for public *synchronous* data networks.

X.93 Covers hypothetical reference connections for *packet switched* data transmission services.

X.95 Covers network *parameters* in *public data networks*.

X.96 Covers call progress signals in *public data networks*.

X.110 Covers *routing* principles for international public data services through switched *public data networks* of the same type.

X.121 Covers the international numbering plan for *public data networks*.

X.130 Covers provisional objectives for call set-up and clear-down times in public *synchronous* data networks (circuit switching).

X.132 Covers provisional objectives for grade of service in international *data communications* over circuit switched *public data networks*.

X.150 Covers *DTE* and *DCE* test loops for *public data networks* in the case of *X.21* and *X.21 bis interface*.

X.180 Covers administration arrangements for international *closed user groups* (CUGs).

X.200 Covers the *OSI Reference Model* for *CCITT* applications.

X.210 Covers the *OSI* Layer Service definition on convention.

X.400 *CCITT* standard for *computer-based messaging systems*.

X Stream The collective name given to digital *data communication* services offered by *British Telecom*: *MegaStream, Packet SwitchStream, SatStream, KiloStream* and *MultiStream*.

x-y plotter Synonymous with a *plotter* also sometimes called a *data plotter*.

Y

yaw Rotation of a satellite about the axis that joins it to the earth's centre (see *satellite communication*).

yoke A group of *read/write heads* fastened together.

Z

zap In computing, to erase, especially from programmable read-only memory (see *ROM* and *PROM*).

zatacode A *code* used to index records in a *data processing* system.

zero access storage *Storage* which gives access in a negligible time (see *rapid access memory*).

zero compression The elimination before storage of non-significant zeros (ie those to the left of all digits in a number). For example, the number 00503.010, after zero compression, would be 503.010.

zero elimination The elimination before storage of non-significant

zeros (see *zero compression*).

zero fill To fill a *storage* space with zeros.

zeroize 1. Synonymous with *zero fill*. 2. To set a mechanical register to zero.

zero suppression Synonymous with *zero elimination*.

zig-zag folding Synonymous with *fan-folding*.

Z.39 An *ANSI* committee working on a standardized *search language* which could be used for *online searching* of *bibliographic databases* (see *common command language*).